The
Good-bye
Door

Anna Marie Hahn, August 1937. Reprinted with permission from the *Columbus Dispatch*.

The Good-bye Door

The Incredible True Story of America's First Female Serial Killer to Die in the Chair

Diana Britt Franklin

THE KENT STATE UNIVERSITY PRESS
KENT, OHIO

© 2006 by The Kent State University Press, Kent, Ohio 44242
ALL RIGHTS RESERVED
Library of Congress Catalog Card Number 2006001254

ISBN-10: 0-87338-874-7
ISBN-13: 978-0-87338-874-0

Manufactured in the United States of America

10 09 08 07 06   5 4 3 2 1

Library of Congress Cataloging-in-Publication Data
Franklin, Diana Britt.
The good-bye door : the incredible true story of America's first
female serial killer to die in the chair / Diana Britt Franklin.
    p.   cm. — (True crime series)
Includes bibliographical references and index.
ISBN-13: 978-0-87338-874-0 (pbk. : alk. paper) ∞
    1. Hahn, Anna Marie, 1906–1938. 2. Murder—Ohio—
    Cincinnati. 3. Women serial murderers—Ohio—Cincin-
    nati—Biography. 4. Trials (Murder)—Ohio—Cincinnati.
    5. Electrocution—Ohio—Cincinnati. I. Title. II. True crime
    series (Kent, Ohio)
HV6534.C5F73   2006
364.152'3092—dc22   2006001254

British Library Cataloging-in-Publication data are available.

In loving memory of Eleanor
1931–2003

Contents

I liken my five years of research into the life of Anna Marie Hahn to assembling a giant jigsaw puzzle that has missing pieces. Sixty-three years after her execution in 1938, I became interested in her story, having seen in a newsletter the briefest of items about her and the electric chair in which she died. I had never heard of Anna Marie Hahn, yet I was drawn to her life—and her death.

Period newspapers on microfilm made clear this was not a simple Cincinnati murder case. It was big, very big, with widespread national and even international interest. Virtually every detail of her arrest, trial, and execution received colorful coverage in daily newspapers. Such detailed reporting comprised the only record of the case. Not a single official document could be found at the Cincinnati police department or at the Hamilton County district attorney's office. Everything had been destroyed long ago, I was told. It was the same story in Columbus, where she sat on death row for a year in the state penitentiary. Even the prison itself had been torn down. Furthermore, all the principals in the case, such as the attorneys, judge, jurors, and witnesses, had passed on. The only document uncovered was a partial transcript in archives at the University of Cincinnati.

The Good-bye Door, therefore, recreates events in Anna Marie Hahn's life largely from the fifteen-hundred-page trial transcript and newspaper accounts, including her twenty-page "confession" published after her death. Where stories seemed to conflict, I chose the most plausible or combined two or more to be as accurate as possible.

While some of the Anna Marie Hahn story went to the grave with her, I believe *The Good-bye Door* to be a historically accurate account of her crimes.

Two newspaper reporters among more than a dozen outstanding ones who covered the Hahn case deserve special recognition. (A complete list of journalists appears in the bibliography.) Joseph Garretson Jr. pounded out the Anna Marie Hahn story for the *Cincinnati Enquirer,* producing up to ten thousand words a day on a manual typewriter. While not quite as prolific, Robert J. Casey, correspondent for the *Chicago Daily News,* was a master craftsman who rarely allowed the facts to stand in the way of a well-turned phrase. His was brilliant, unfettered work, and absolutely delightful to read.

Numerous librarians—God bless 'em—repeatedly came to my aid. Deserving special recognition are: Carol Meyer-Keener, retired librarian, Hamilton County Law Library; Marianne Reynolds and staff, Public Library of Cincinnati and Hamilton County; Kevin Grace, archivist, Archives and Rare Books, Carl Blegan Library, University of Cincinnati; Cleveland Public Library; Special Collections, Cleveland State University Library; and editorial libraries of the *Columbus Dispatch,* the *Cincinnati Post,* and the *Cincinnati Enquirer.*

Also, the many great librarians at the Columbus (Ohio) Metropolitan Library; Ohio Historical Society, Columbus; Upper Arlington (Ohio) Library; the Center for American History at the University of Texas, Austin; San Antonio Central Library; Chicago Public Library; Baltimore County (Maryland) Public Library; Los Angeles Public Library; Jody Jones, special collections, Pikes Peak Library District, Colorado Springs, Colorado; and the University of Illinois Library at Champaign-Urbana, Illinois.

Others who deserve thanks for making my work easier or more accurate include Judge Raymond Shannon, administrator of the Division of Domestic Relations, Hamilton County Court of Common Pleas; Judge Steven E. Martin, Hamilton County Court of Common

Pleas; John Vissman, director of community services at the *Cincinnati Post;* Martha Hildenbrand Perin, Cincinnati; Amy Stodden, Girls and Boys Town, Omaha, Nebraska; Carol Lee (Hahn) Graves, Bremen, Ohio; Patricia Tansey, Vienna, Virginia; Brian Meyer, *Buffalo (New York) Evening News;* Ursula Stolzenburg, New York; David Weltner, Columbus; John Glazer, Cincinnati; Marge Stark, Cincinnati; Eleonore Huber and the Filser family, Fuessen, Germany; Margaret Williams, *Albany (New York) Times-Union;* the family of Ben Hayes and the Ben Hayes Collection, Ohio Historical Society, Columbus; Trisha Brown, Worthington, Ohio; Charles C. Howard, Grove City, Ohio; Jerome Herbort and family, Largo, Florida; Ruth Anne Outcalt, Cincinnati; Ellen Michael, Cincinnati; Mary Hayes, Cincinnati; Bobbie Newbert, Cincinnati; and Elaine Dietrich, Amelia, Ohio.

To America's foremost true-crime author Ann Rule, and former FBI criminal profiler, Robert K. Ressler, my sincere appreciation for their support and encouragement.

The Good-bye Door is dedicated to Eleanor Franklin, who passed away during the writing of this book. Although she was quite ill at the time, she provided invaluable assistance in my research at numerous Ohio libraries, eagerly reading each draft and offering insightful comments and encouragement. I will always cherish her incredible love and support.

A knock on the door of the jury room at 12:06 P.M. summoned the bailiff and electrified the oppressive Cincinnati courtroom. Spectators who had been stretching and chatting quickly took their seats, for the judge had ruled that no spectator would be permitted to stand during the proceedings. For veteran court observers, the summons was the tip-off that the jury had reached a verdict.

Anna Marie Hahn, held in a cell in the women's quarters of the Hamilton County Jail three floors above, was among the first to return to the courtroom, accompanied by Chief Deputy Sheriff George J. Heitzler. She quickly sat down next to her somber defense attorney, Hiram C. Bolsinger Sr., and greeted him with a brief, wry smile. Her ashen face, once cherubic, revealed no emotion and her eyes no sparkle. The short blonde hair framing her soft, rounded features was carefully coifed, every fine hair in its place.

Anna Marie didn't glance at the murmuring visitors crowded into every seat on every bench or at the row of newspaper reporters seated nearby. As she rested her arms on the counsel table, members of the large press corps noted that she clasped a small, twisted, printed handkerchief. She held her knees and feet close together and her back straight, bracing for the worst.

Judge Charles S. Bell, who Anna Marie watched as he mounted the bench, quickly opened the proceedings.

"This court has been informed that the jury has arrived at a verdict," he said, peering over his pince-nez. "There must be no demonstrations. Anyone doing so will be punished for contempt of court."

His statement only heightened the tension in the courtroom, but that was broken briefly when suddenly the judge spotted an overly zealous individual peering in through an open transom over a courtroom door. "Get that man out!" Judge Bell demanded of his bailiffs.

Soon order was restored, and at 12:24 P.M. the jury of eleven women and one man filed in, walking directly past the defendant. Anna Marie looked into their faces, but none looked back at her. Each was somber, but the *Chicago Tribune* reporter observed that the only never-married woman on the panel, blonde, blue-eyed Stella Tragesser, "switched her hips in her customary coy walk as she jumped nimbly into the jury box." Another reporter, sitting close to the jury's entryway, thought he discerned a tear in the eye of jury foreman John Granda, the only man on the "petticoat" panel.

Court clerk Elmer F. Hunsicker, the former Olympic diver, dapper in his new double-breasted pinstriped suit, called the jury roll, and Judge Bell asked the foreman if a verdict had been reached. Granda, who avoided eye contact with the accused as he rose, replied that it had. The previous evening the panel had spent 52 minutes reviewing evidence and electing the foreman. It returned to the Hotel Metropole, home to the sequestered jurors for twenty-three nights, without balloting. This day the jurors took 133 minutes more and two votes to reach their unanimous verdict.

Granda passed the verdict form to Hunsicker. Juror Anna Thompson's double chin quivered and her eyes became watery. Tears were close in the eyes of several of her fellow jurors. The courtroom was silent. Hardly a breath was taken. One or two spectators shifted slightly to get a better view of the small piece of paper the clerk unfolded, as if by doing so the verdict would be visible to them first.

Making the most of his official duty—which he reenacted for news photographers after court adjourned—Hunsicker firmly and loudly intoned, "We, the jury, in the issue joined, find the defendant, Anna Marie Hahn, guilty of first-degree murder as she stands charged in the indictment."

The gallery let out its collective breath and stirred noticeably. An elderly spectator seated in the back row stifled a cry with her white linen handkerchief, and a murmur swelled in the courtroom.

Judge Bell hammered the sounding block with his gavel, and the bailiffs and special deputies jumped into action. "Quiet! Quiet!" they demanded. When the spectators fell silent, the multitudes in the hallway outside the courtroom still could be heard: "Guilty!" "She's guilty!" "Guilty!"

An impassive Anna Marie glanced momentarily at the jurors, then bowed her head and twisted her handkerchief even more tightly. She fought with herself to stop the tears welling up within her.

Bolsinger rose. "Judge, we asked that the jurors be polled." His associate, Chief Defense Counsel Joseph H. Hoodin, was absent, unable emotionally to stand beside his client for the jury's verdict. Philip Hahn, Anna Marie's estranged husband, and Oscar, her son, the twelve-year-old love of her life, were not in the courtroom, either.

"Is this your true verdict?" Hunsicker asked each juror in turn. Granda and ten women each replied, "Yes," but Mrs. Thompson, close to tears, just nodded her affirmation. Anna Marie watched, seemingly without any real interest.

Lost in the drama of the moment was what the jury did not say. It did not recommend mercy. This put Anna Marie directly on the path to "Old Sparky," Ohio's infamous electric chair; without a mercy request, a death sentence was mandatory.

Judge Bell, praised for his firm conduct of the nearly month-long trial, thanked the jurors for their service. "You have measured up to the highest degree of citizenship. You have been patient and attentive throughout a trying ordeal. The court knows that your verdict stands four-square with the dictates of your consciences and your hearts."

When Judge Bell rapped his gavel, ending twenty-seven days of often spellbinding courtroom drama, Anna Marie was among the first to rise. "Get me out. Get me out quick," she quietly but firmly told Bolsinger and Heitzler.

Although the trio moved swiftly to the exit and to the elevator that would take them up to the jail on the sixth floor, reporters and photographers caught up with them and swarmed around them. "Do you have a statement, Mrs. Hahn?" a reporter asked. Her curt, almost inaudible reply was simply, "No." Still journalists pressed her. "Please, gentlemen! Please!" Bolsinger pleaded. "Mrs. Hahn has nothing to say."

Three journalists squeezed into the small elevator with Anna Marie, her attorney, and Heitzler. The two men tried to shield the petite woman from the crush and from the repeated and rapid-fire questions thrown at her by the reporters. Pale and stoic, she uttered not a word. Heitzler felt her tremble and took her arm to steady her.

When all emerged from the elevator, Anna Marie almost ran up the few steps to her cell, which actually was a hospital room in the jail. "Like a frightened rabbit," one reporter said, she dashed inside, slamming the door behind her and falling on her bed, sobbing. Her cries flooded the corridor. A reporter, peering into the detention room through a small grill in the door, called to Anna Marie for comment. "You reporters get outta here!" her cellmate, convicted shoplifter Mabel Hill, yelled back. "Let this poor woman alone!" Hill hung a faded gingham housedress over the grill, thus blocking the view of the woman's suffering.

"I can't understand it! I can't understand it!" Anna Marie cried. "I never did it!"

1 | LITTLE SECRETS

Anna Marie Filser arrived in New York on February 11, 1929, with little baggage and little secrets.

On the deck of the SS *Munchen*, she pulled her cloth coat closely around her, leaned on the shoulder-high port railing, and took a deep breath of the frigid air. As the liner churned slowly through the dark water of the harbor, a cold wind whipped her short blonde hair and her Bavarian patterned scarf. Beyond, in the early dawn, Anna Marie could just make out the Statue of Liberty, its torch burning brightly. Soon New York City's skyline came into view, too. Here, in an America still reveling in the Roaring Twenties, would be a new beginning for her.

As a child, Anna Marie had had a pious start in life. She was born June 7, 1906, the last of a dozen children—nine of them boys—of Georg and Katharina Filser. They raised their family in the idyllic Bavarian community of Fuessen, a few miles north of the snowcapped Alps. Nestled beside the Lech River, which flows north and into the Danube, the little red-roofed resort town sits at the entrance to "the king's nook," so called because of its proximity to the towering, white Neuschwanstein Castle, the last residence of King Ludwig II of Bavaria.

Fuessen also was a center of Catholic learning and craftsmen, some of whom made world-class lutes and violins. Georg Filser, a respected citizen, was a craftsman—a cabinetmaker and a furniture manufacturer.

He and his wife, devout Catholics, raised their family in the church the Filsers in Fuessen had supported for generations.

At the time of Anna Marie's birth, her parents had lost three children, two boys and a girl; all died at an early age. A fourth child, the eldest boy and one of five brothers to serve in the German army during World War I, was killed in action.[1] Anna Marie's brothers liked having a little sister in the comfortable home on Kempter Strasse, but she was closest to her only surviving sister, Katti, and to her mother.

Thoughts of her family and past were on Anna Marie's mind as the small transatlantic liner made the twelve-day crossing from Bremen, Germany, docking at Manhattan's Morton Street Pier shortly after eight that frosty Monday morning in February. Anna Marie was used to having life her way. As the youngest, she often escaped with but a mild rebuke when she strayed from her parents' mark, which was quite often in her teenage years. Sneaking out a window at night to attend teen parties, for example, tested her parents, yet they allowed her liberties not granted her siblings. "Annie" was her mother's favorite.

Still, mother and father saw to it that Anna Marie attended church and a parochial school where nuns prevailed as teachers. A quick if somewhat inattentive student, Anna Marie did well in homemaking skills, such as sewing and cooking. But she never completed her *Hauptschule* (high school) studies, although she would claim to have done so and to have attended "teacher school," as well.

Perhaps for disciplinary purposes, her parents shipped her off to Holland for a short time to be near her wedded sister, now Katti Moergele, and to enroll in a private school. Anna Marie envied Katti, who had a good marriage and was raising a family. She prayed for the same, but it was not to be for her.

On the deck of the *Munchen,* she thought of all that she had left behind, including her son, Oscar. He was born May 31, 1925, the result of a starry-eyed teen's "one gorgeous adventure," Anna Marie would say.[2] Her romantic indiscretion, followed by her pregnancy and the

---

1. During World War I, Anna Marie and her sister, Katti, knitted sweaters, scarves, mittens, and caps for their brothers in service.

2. Oscar's year of birth is uncertain. Mother and son claimed different dates at different times, ranging from 1924 to 1926, but 1925 seems most likely.

birth of her boy, were the reasons she headed for America. Her father and brothers were furious with her, and there had been many heated words spoken at home. Behind closed doors, the community of 2,300 souls "whispered things about my misfortune," the young mother knew. Anna Marie was an embarrassment to her godly parents and to her brothers, all of whom were carving out respected positions in Fuessen. Georg Filser would have abandoned her altogether if it had not been for his wife's pleadings. She thought it best that Anna Marie get out of town, and the United States was about as far as she could go. Frau Filser had one or two relatives in America, whom she hoped would help her daughter. Until Anna Marie could get herself established in America, though, three-year-old Oscar would remain under the care of her mother. Furthermore, in America Anna Marie initially was to keep secret that she had an illegitimate son.

So at twenty-two, Anna Marie was an outcast, traveling alone to an unfamiliar land. After having waited almost two years for a visa, she secured a second-class cabin on the *Munchen,* upgrading from third, thanks to a little money given to her by her mother and a loan from her Uncle Max in Cincinnati.

Max Doeschel wasn't really her uncle; he was a stepbrother to Anna Marie's mother. He had been in the United States since 1881 and hardly knew the present Filser family. It had been twenty-five years or more since he had corresponded with any family in Germany. For many years he worked as a carpenter at the Gambrinus Brewing Company in Cincinnati, then at the Dietz Washing Machine Company. By the time Anna Marie arrived, however, he was seventy-four and living in retirement in two rooms with his wife, Anna. Nevertheless, when Anna Marie wrote to him in 1928, requesting his help to allow her to come to the United States, he loaned $236 to the young woman he had never met. The sum was considerable at the time—it would be equal to $2,686 in 2005 dollars—but he gave it with the understanding that she would repay him as soon as she found employment as a housekeeper.

After an overnight run from New York, the Cincinnati Limited pulled into Cincinnati's old Pennsylvania Railroad station at Pearl and Butler streets at 8:30 A.M., on time. Anna Marie had wired Doeschel the day before, asking that she be met at the Cincinnati terminal.

Ida Pfeffer, Doeschel's daughter, and her brother-in-law, Richard G. Pfeffer, a cousin to Anna Marie, comprised the welcoming party.

Pfeffer, a U.S. Secret Service agent, sized up Anna Marie as "a pretty blonde" with hazel eyes and a good command of English, which she spoke with only a slight accent. The pair warmly greeted the bubbly and charming German visitor, whom they took to the house at 3540 Evanston Avenue that the Pfeffers owned and the Doeschels shared. "As long as you are a good girl and do what is right, you will have a home here," Uncle Max told his step-niece. She kept her silence about having a son.

Before she could find employment, Anna Marie fell ill, perhaps from the strain of the journey. She thought her illness to be scarlet fever, but within three weeks she regained her health and began getting house-work jobs. The Doeschels and the Pfeffers soon noticed, however, that Anna Marie spent far beyond what she earned. Her relationship with them cooled, and they chose to avoid her whenever possible.

Without a word to anyone, Anna Marie suddenly moved out—"ran away," she admitted—securing a furnished room on Walnut Street between Central Parkway and Twelfth Street. For a time, Max Doeschel had no idea where she had gone, and he was concerned. She had not repaid the loan for her passage and gave no indication of doing so. Yet he readily could see by the quantity and quality of what she had bought for herself while living under the same roof that she was doing well—very well, indeed.

Anna Marie maintained that she moved to downtown Cincinnati "to be near Uncle Charlie." Charles "Karl" Osswald, a retired baker who lived six blocks from Anna Marie's rented room, was even more distantly related to her than was Max Doeschel. Osswald's wife, Mary, was Doeschel's sister. She died April 3, 1929, leaving Osswald a lonely widower.[3]

While living downtown, Anna Marie advertised for a position as a housemaid, gave the Doeschels as a reference, and received several inquiries. One well-heeled and elderly gentleman of German heritage

---

3. Some suggested Anna Marie had caused Mrs. Osswald's death. It is not likely, however, and police developed no evidence to support the allegation.

visited Anna Marie in her room, where she "interviewed" for him wearing only a silk kimono. When she told him that her Uncle Max's home "wasn't the proper place" for her, he was somewhat surprised, since she'd named Doeschel as a reference. After visiting Doeschel in his home, the gentleman decided not to hire Anna Marie because he couldn't understand why she had traded such a nice, well-kept brick house for a rather dingy one-room apartment. He made a wise decision.

Anna Marie wasn't in the rented room long, though. The next thing her friends knew, she had moved into one of Osswald's top-floor rooms in a four-story tenement at 304 East Fourteenth Street, above Max Lasky's confectionery at the corner of Sycamore Street. Osswald was seventy-one at the time, and she had just turned twenty-three. Professing to having been a nurse in Germany, she gave him care and companionship, and he gave her stock. In November 1929, she promised to marry him and care for him in his remaining years if he transferred to her ninety-nine shares of Union Gas and Electric, valued at several thousand dollars. He also gave her cash whenever she needed it, which was often.

What few but area bookies knew was that Anna Marie loved the thoroughbreds and wagered heavily and often on them. A friend she met shortly after arriving in Cincinnati introduced her to gambling, and she fell madly for it after winning $260 on a black nag with her first $2 bet at the track in Latonia, Kentucky. She went to area racetracks and gaming casinos in Ohio and across the Ohio River in Newport and Covington, Kentucky. More often than not, however, she took a streetcar to Elmwood Place, a small community bordering Cincinnati, known as a haven for illegal gambling. There Anna Marie became well-known to handbook operators, or bookies, along the village's Vine Avenue, where establishments lured "suckers" to the area through bold newspaper advertising and the mob arrived in bulletproof limousines to rake in the day's take. She set her loss limit at $50 a day (about $710 in 2005), but what she wagered each day grew as she found more sources to fund her fun.

In the spring of 1929, Anna Marie secured a job as a chambermaid at the five-hundred-room Hotel Alms, a turn-of-the-century establishment at the corner of McMillan Street and Victory Parkway. Her wages there were meager, yet she seemed never to want for money. If she needed some, she asked Uncle Charlie for it, and he never refused her. When she told Osswald that she still owed Uncle Max for her transatlantic trip, he gave her the money to repay him. She kept it for herself.

One of Anna Marie's favorite forays was to Coney Island, a grand, 120-acre amusement park about ten miles east of downtown Cincinnati. There were a score of rides for five or ten cents, a huge pool that could accommodate ten thousand swimmers at a time, two roller coasters, the Moonlight Gardens dance hall, and a race track that today is known as River Downs.[4]

While on a boat ride to the amusement park with a date in the summer of 1929, she briefly met Philip J. Hahn, the man she would marry. His physique was a bodybuilder's worst nightmare, slender as a rail and seemingly devoid of muscle. He also was as short as she—a smidgen over five feet—and his small, thin mustache gave him a rather mousy appearance. He noticed that the pretty blonde's date paid little attention to her: "She didn't want any attention," he recalled. He struck up a conversation with her, but it wasn't until they met again some months later at a German dance in the Marie Antoinette Ballroom at the Hotel Alms that they began to date.

Although she had led Osswald to believe she would marry him, Anna Marie chose Philip instead and never whispered a word to Osswald about it. And why would she? In a will created in 1929, he had made her the prime beneficiary of his estate, which at that time totaled some $13,000 ($148,000 in 2005). In the meantime, she was drawing on those funds with constant requests for money.

Philip, twenty-seven, and Anna Marie, twenty-five, wed on May 5, 1930, in Buffalo, New York. "He seemed so good and kind," Anna Marie said of her husband. "He was the way to what I wanted, a home of my own and a home for my son." She told Philip she had a son in Germany but said nothing about the boy's father. Only later did she mention that Dr. Max Matscheki of Vienna, a shadowy figure, wooed her and fathered her boy, even though he was married. "I thought it

4. Coney Island Race Track was closed between 1926 and 1933.

was just one of those things," Philip said of his wife's love affair. "I didn't ask her much about it."

Just as well: It is unlikely he would have received a straight answer. Apparently Matscheki, who Anna Marie said died in 1928, was her own creation. No physician by that name was found to have practiced in Vienna. Her teenage affair was with a man never fully identified.

Upon their return from Buffalo, the couple visited the Doeschels and the Pfeffers and announced they were going to build a home in the College Hill section of Cincinnati. Where the money was to come from, Anna Marie never said. As far as anyone knew, she still was making up beds at the Hotel Alms and Philip was a telegrapher for Western Union downtown, a job he had held for fourteen years. During the visit with her Cincinnati relatives, she mentioned that she would soon return to Germany to see her family. She still said nothing about having a five-year-old son there; that she didn't reveal until she returned from Germany with Oscar.

Tight-fisted Max Doeschel grew concerned anew. He still had not been repaid the money he loaned Anna Marie, and now he saw his $236 sailing away with her. He demanded repayment and mentioned his concern to Osswald. Having given Anna Marie the money to repay the loan, the old baker was shocked. He shelled out the money once again, paying Doeschel directly.

In subsequent years, Doeschel would tell friends that he regretted having sent Anna Marie the money for her trip to America. He died December 27, 1937, a few weeks after she was sentenced to death.

On July 7, 1930, shortly before her departure for Germany, Anna Marie received another twenty-seven shares of Union Gas and Electric from Osswald, which he later denied giving her. She also transferred $700, all his funds in the Eagle Savings and Loan Association, from his account to hers. Then she withdrew it all. Osswald had no idea yet that she had married Philip, or that she had a son, for that matter.

She returned to Bavaria, spent a glorious time with Oscar and a difficult one with her family. Several photographs of her enjoying happy days at the Oberammergau festival—a feather in her Tyrolean hat and a large beer stein in her hand—would appear in newspapers throughout the United States following her arrest. She returned to Cincinnati with

Oscar in late summer and with Philip moved into a modest, newly constructed home at 6332 Savannah Avenue in College Hill.

Fortunately for Anna Marie, her husband worked nights when they were first married. This gave her considerable time to roam, much of which she spent caring for the elderly she met and visiting Elmwood Place handbook establishments, often with little Oscar in tow.

Between January 31 and March 26, 1931, she sold all the stock she had received from Osswald, which might explain how, in the worst of economic times, the Hahns managed to purchase from John Rinck a small bakery and grocery/deli at 3201 Colerain Avenue, on the corner of Bates Avenue in the Cincinnati suburb of Clifton, just north of downtown. At the height of the Great Depression, Philip quit his job with Western Union to join Anna Marie in the business. They struggled mightily, trying to make a go of it, but they did not fare well, even with Anna Marie spreading cream cheese on bagels and taking bets. Fifth District police never caught her at it, although they knew she was running a betting operation from within her establishment.

"We walked in and out of that place so often that we were able to break up the handbook," recalled Detective Fred Stagenhorst.

Less than a year passed before the Hahns sold their business to Aloysius and Harry Franz in 1932. In the same year, the Hahns bought a nearby deli from William O. Laugle, at 3007 Colerain Avenue, but it, too, failed miserably. Anna Marie and Philip sold it three years later. They also lost their home on Savannah Avenue when they couldn't make the mortgage payments.

Anna Marie continued to visit and comfort Uncle Charlie, ignorant still of her marriage, and accept handouts from him. On February 3, 1931, he made out a new will, leaving $5 to a stepdaughter in North Bend, Ohio, and $5 to a stepson in Los Angeles. The remainder was bequeathed to "my beloved niece, Anna Filser Hahn."

In the spring of 1931, when Osswald finally learned the whole story—about the husband, the son, the house, the restaurant and all—he took his dealings with Anna Marie to his attorneys, Bates, Stewart & Skirvin. His suit, filed July 30, 1931, charged her with breach of promise and sought the return of the stock and cash, plus 6 percent interest. "She knew at the time the said representations were made that she was not going to marry plaintiff," the suit stated, "but, on the contrary, intended to marry someone else and did." In the face of the evidence presented, Anna Marie denied everything, and the case went to trial by jury. Before it could be adjudicated, however, there was reconciliation, and the court dismissed the suit on February 21, 1934. Evidently, all was forgiven.

When Osswald died on August 14, 1935, at age seventy-seven, a Deaconess Hospital physician listed the cause as chronic Bright's disease and arteriosclerosis. A week later, Anna Marie received a check for $1,000 as the sole beneficiary of his National Biscuit Company pension death benefit. Osswald changed his beneficiary several times in his final years, each time reflecting the changes in his relationship with Anna Marie. Initially, Anna Filser was listed as the beneficiary, then Mrs. Anna Hahn, then "my estate," and finally, "my great-niece, Mrs. Anna Marie Hahn." His will was not probated "because there were no assets left in the estate," his attorney revealed.

Anna Marie already had every last cent.

From the start, the Hahn marriage was rocky. The couple often argued, mostly over money and men. Philip objected to Anna Marie's flirting with elderly gents and her penchant for betting, sapping what few resources they had. She had little time for him, doting instead on Oscar and on the old men she met. Philip seldom knew where his wife went; she would be gone from the home hours at a time, day or night, taking Oscar with her when he was not in school.

Philip was away from the home, too. He gave up his job as a Western Union telegrapher to run the businesses with her, and when the first one failed in 1932, he drove a taxi for Parkway Cabs on Central Parkway and its subsidiary, the Suburban Cab Company of Norwood.

That the couple was not getting along became clear to Philip's two sisters, Marie West of Cincinnati and Matilda Schaerges of Tobasco, Ohio. While lending a hand in the Camp Washington restaurant, they witnessed a loud argument in which Anna Marie called Philip "a vile name" and shoved him. His mother, Margaret Hahn, was not terribly fond of her daughter-in-law. Maggie, as Mrs. Hahn was known, said that "Anna always laughed at those dumb Americans. She always had high falutin' notions. Nobody was good enough for her. She always felt lots better than the rest of us."

During the argument at the restaurant, Anna Marie kicked her son, Maggie said, but she was not a witness to it. The shoving-kicking incident occurred, she said, at a time when Philip was quite ill, hobbling around the restaurant stiff-legged and on his heels because his joints and feet hurt. A physician might have seen it as what was known as "drop foot," caused by damage to the motor nerve.[1] He was so sick, in fact, that his mother spent $100 to get him into a spa in Dillsboro, Indiana, where he recovered.

Maggie similarly became ill, the family confirmed, after Anna Marie gave her mother-in-law an attractive box of chocolate-covered cherries. At the time nobody suspected the root of the affliction in both mother and son might be poison, but over the years the family came to believe it. Philip would later tell police he thought he might have ingested croton oil, an amber-tinted oil derived from the seeds of croton tiglium, a small tree cultivated in India. Since the turn of the century, the oil had been out of favor with the medical profession, but in Europe in particular it had been prescribed as a powerful cathartic. One-half of a drop, mixed with a liquid, was a sufficient dosage as a laxative. Several drops could kill, and if dropped on the skin it created severe, eruptive sores. Nevertheless, in the mid-1930s a prescription for croton oil was not required, although a bottle of it always bore a poison warning.

Philip's family also expressed concern when they learned that Anna Marie had attempted to insure her husband's life. In December 1935 she applied for a $10,000 double-indemnity life insurance policy on Philip from the Prudential Insurance Company, but because he was unemployed at the time, the application was denied. (Ten thousand dollars was literally a fortune at the height of the Great Depression.) A year later, however, she did secure a $5,000 double-indemnity Prudential life insurance policy on her husband, but for one week in July of 1937 it lapsed because she failed to keep up with the quarterly payments of $17.75.

For Anna Marie, the early thirties were "horrible times," but she proved to be as resourceful as any grifter in Cincinnati. Well before Uncle Charlie Osswald died, she befriended another gentleman, Ernest Kohler, who, she claimed, knew her father. The sixty-two-year-old

1. Also known as footdrop.

teamster's home at 2950 Colerain Avenue in the Camp Washington area of Cincinnati had a bit of history tied to it. The three-story brick house, its colored windows, high ceilings, and hardwood floors resplendent for its day, was built and owned at the turn of the century by Major Charles H. Blackburn, one of Cincinnati's most famous criminal attorneys.

In the fall of 1932, Kohler lived alone on the third floor and rented out rooms he never used. The Hahns rented two rooms and a kitchen on the second floor at the back of the house. Blackburn's son-in-law, Dr. Arthur Vos, who treated Kohler for cancer, had his office on the first floor in front.

Having a doctor in the house who never thought to lock his office afforded Anna Marie unexpected opportunities on two fronts, actually. Until he caught her at it, she used his office telephone to call bookies and place bets with them. Sometimes she would make more than fifty calls in a day. She also found a use for the blank prescription pads she discovered in Vos's rolltop desk. Forging his name on the form, Anna Marie went on a narcotic-buying binge. On April 29, 1933, for example, she had two prescriptions filled, totaling forty-one morphine tablets, each one-quarter grain. Then April 30, forty more tablets; May 1, two prescriptions totaling sixty-one tablets; May 2, twenty tablets; May 3, twenty-one tablets; May 4, twenty-one tablets; and May 5, two prescriptions totaling forty-two tablets.

Anna Marie told the neighborhood druggist, Stanley E. Roth, who had filled prescriptions for Kohler before, that she was nursing Kohler under the direction of Dr. Vos. Even so, the Colerain Avenue druggist became alarmed at the quantity of drugs prescribed. He alerted federal narcotics officers and wrote a letter to Dr. Vos. When he received a written reply from the physician that the prescriptions were correct, the matter was dropped. Little did the druggist, federal agents, or Vos know that Anna Marie had intercepted Roth's letter and forged the reply.

On May 6, 1933, Anna Marie notified authorities that her landlord had died that day, ostensibly due to esophageal cancer. However, an autopsy was conducted after the coroner's office received several anonymous telephone calls, each suggesting that Kohler had been poisoned. When City Chemist Dr. Otto P. Behrer failed to find toxins in the esophagus, Hamilton County coroner Dr. M. Scott Kearns ruled that Kohler had succumbed to throat cancer. He was cremated and his ashes given to Anna Marie, who kept them on the mantel. Oscar delighted in opening the urn and showing Kohler's ashes to his school chums.

The mantel and the entire house on Colerain were now hers. Kohler left his estate "to my friend, Anna Marie Filser Hahn, who has befriended me and taken care of me during my last illness." In addition to the property, valued at $12,000 ($179,631 in 2005) and unencumbered by a mortgage, the bequest included antique furnishings, imported dinnerware and fine silver service, all of which Anna Marie proudly pointed out to visitors as though she had collected and owned them for years. Her inheritance also included $1,167 in a savings account, an old automobile, and a pool table in the basement where Oscar and children of Philip's sisters often played.

The boys and girls who played in the house thought Anna Marie a wonderfully warm and charming mother, who often would feed them generously in the kitchen. Some observed, however, that she was out of the home a lot, taking care of old folk.

Oscar appeared picture-perfect to adults; with wavy blonde hair and the softly carved features of his mother, they accurately described him as "handsome." Another, harsher picture emerged as time went on. He had few friends from school, and it wasn't because he had difficulty speaking English, as he spoke both English and German flawlessly. Rather, many boys shied away from him because he was thought to be "a mean little kid."

On one occasion, a boyhood friend recalled, Oscar tied a boy's hands, hung him from a basement rafter, and then took pleasure shooting him in the buttocks with a BB gun. Neighborhood boys also remembered that Oscar would hang cats on the clothesline in the backyard, then, while the animal struggled to get free, kill them with the BB gun or a slingshot. These were not his only weapons; he also had several knives and a .22-caliber rifle. One day, while showing off to his friends, he fired a shot from the basement through the door to the kitchen.

Police also knew Oscar for having sold at school what were described as "obscene pictures." He also was caught stealing books from a store, a theft that he blamed on a classmate. For that caper he was expelled from school. Of course, once authorities uncovered his mother's murderous exploits, Oscar's participation in her trysts and deadly affairs came to light, too. He seemed to be preoccupied with death, said Philip's mother, Maggie. The pictures the boy constantly drew always were of skulls and crossbones, daggers, guns, and various symbols of death, she said.

That Anna Marie should inherit everything in Kohler's estate drew the ire of his sister and brother in Sindelfingen, Germany, and two other relatives. They contested the will, naming Anna Marie and Charles Rodner, executor of Kohler's estate, as defendants in their suit. Anna Marie professed that she knew nothing about Kohler's intentions until notified by probate court. His will was dated April 22, 1933, just fifteen days before he died. An out-of-court settlement was reached when Anna Marie agreed to pay the Kohler family members a total of $4,000, which she secured after mortgaging the house for $9,000. The remainder helped her pay off some bookies and other creditors.

Anna Marie was not above accepting small sums from the men that she befriended, if she couldn't get large ones. Local restaurateur Walter Walther found the diminutive blonde quite charming when introduced to her by a friend. Conversing in German, she revealed that her restaurant was doing poorly and that she had to have $25 to pay some debts. Her hard-luck story touched his wallet.

"She said that if I would give her a check," he recalled, "she would at once give me another check on her bank," which she did with the understanding it was not to be cashed until the following week. When he tried to do so, the Provident Savings Bank & Trust said it had no account in Mrs. Hahn's name. (The bank had begged Anna Marie to close her account because so many of her checks bounced.) Walther, his wife, and his daughter repeatedly tried to collect from her, to no avail. They even contacted Hiram C. Bolsinger Sr., attorney for the Hahns, which resulted in a check for $5 from Anna Marie. The $25 was "hard-earned money," Walther said, but he never received another nickel.

Railroad worker Joseph Semon had a similar experience. He loaned Anna Marie $100, virtually all of his life's savings. Said she, "the intention was to pay it back," but she never did.

Borrowing money and never paying it back was not the only source of income for Anna Marie. Apparently she found another in fire insurance claims. Shortly before she and Philip sold the deli at 3007 Colerain, there was a "careless smoker" fire and an insurance payment of $300, but that money went to the owner of the building from whom the Hahns rented their space. On June 2, 1935, there was an early morning fire at the Hahn home. That night, a lodger on the third floor, Roger Penny, twenty-eight, barely escaped with his life, dashing to safety through the flames, wrapped in only a bed sheet. Anna Marie collected $2,016 for that blaze. On May 20, 1936, there was yet another fire at the home, this one in a storage room. The insurance reimbursement was but $60. The cause of both home fires was "undetermined," but Cincinnati Fire Chief Barney Houston kept them under investigation because they appeared suspicious.

After Kohler and Osswald passed on, Anna Marie became friendly with bachelor George E. Heis, a sixty-three-year-old coal dealer and agent for the Consolidated Coal Company. Thin and wiry, he had inherited his father's coal business, serving almost exclusively neighborhood German clientele for thirty-three years. He lived at 2922 Colerain Avenue, a block from Anna Marie's home, which was grander than his. Heis was familiar with her home, because he was a friend to Ernest Kohler and had delivered him coal.

He also had known Philip and the Hahn family for more than twenty years. They lived just a block from him in Clifton, a predominantly German immigrant district north of the area known as Over-the-Rhine. The "Rhine" actually was the Miami and Erie Canal that bordered the southern and western edges of the district.

From the late 1800s to the beginning of World War I, Over-the-Rhine was well-known for its infectious gaiety and spirited establishments for merrymaking primarily along Vine Street, described as "the spinal column of the city."[2] It also represented the heart of Over-the-Rhine and its German heritage. In one short stretch, more than one hundred *Biergärten* and saloons—twenty-three on one block alone, it was said— offered free wienerwurst with steins of German or Cincinnati beer.

2. Writer's Program of the Work Projects Administration in the State of Ohio, *Cincinnati: A Guide to the Queen City and Its Neighbors* (Cincinnati: Wiesen-Hart Press, 1943), 105.

"Generous, big-hearted Vine Street cast its spell upon all kinds of people: con men, beggars, prize fighters, trollops, ward heelers, sports, and garden-variety citizens"[3]—and serial killers. In fact, the notorious Chicago serial killer, Herman Webster Mudgett, alias Dr. Henry Howard Holmes, prowled Vine Street in the mid-1890s, but none of his murders occurred there.

By the early 1930s, the area was in serious decline, done in by Prohibition, the Great Depression, the initial flight to the suburbs, and the anti-German sentiment fostered by World War I. German still was the preferred language among the neighborhood's older generation, but it no longer was taught in Cincinnati's schools. Ohio's governor, James M. Cox, made sure of that. In a speech to the state legislature on April 1, 1919, he declared: "I assert without reservation that the teaching of German to our children . . . is not only a distinct menace to Americanism, but is part of a conspiracy formed long ago by the German government in Berlin."[4] The legislature outlawed the teaching of German in 1920.

Still, Over-the-Rhine and neighboring Clifton were communities of modest brick homes and squat tenement buildings hugging the streets. How high a house sat in the hillier north determined in part its place on the district's social ladder. Kohler's large home up on Colerain, one of three similar houses in a row, was near the top rung. On Wednesdays and Saturdays in the warmer months, aproned women with their hair pinned up in neat buns whitewashed the stone doorsteps leading to the three- and four-story brick apartment buildings. They swept the sidewalks every day. As neighbors and friends passed by or paused to rest momentarily, they caught up on the daily comings and goings.

There is little doubt that the Hahns were, on occasion, the subjects of that gossip. Many in the district were aware of Philip Hahn's marriage, the neighborhood delicatessens that he and Anna Marie opened then closed, and Anna Marie's inheritance of the Kohler home. They noted, too, the activity of the attractive and jovial Bavarian blonde,

---

3. Writer's Program, *Cincinnati*, 107.
4. Charles B. Galbreath, *The History of Ohio* (Chicago: American Historical Society, 1925), 2:726.

who always had a friendly smile, a kind word, and a willingness to help the less fortunate. Neighborhood boys described her as "generous," because she often gave them five cents—or as much as a silver dollar for a special chore—for running an errand for her at a time when a penny was the going rate.

Although he owned the large frame house in which he was born, Heis occupied but two first-floor rear rooms, one of which he used for storage. The other served as his living room, dining room, bedroom, and office. He shared a kitchen with Margaret Tweedie, a tenant in the front apartment.

Heis's large desk, crammed with years of paperwork for his coal deliveries, all but overwhelmed the other furniture—a couple of chairs, a bed, a coal stove that also heated the room, and a sink. Between his room and Mrs. Tweedie's was the toilet he also shared with her.

When Anna Marie first visited Heis in June 1936 to inquire about buying some stoker coal, he quickly removed an undervest and shirt from the chair and invited her to stay awhile and enjoy a glass or two of his homebrew. She did, and he was smitten. After Anna Marie bought some coal, which Heis delivered personally, they saw a lot of each other that summer. Heis enjoyed the affection showered on him by an attractive woman more than thirty years his junior, and he began referring to her as "my girl." Her golden tresses, sparkling hazel-green eyes, winning smile, and contagious laugh captivated him. When they drank beer together, either at his house or at hers, she often cooked for him, too. (Under her mother's watchful eye in Fuessen, she had become an accomplished cook at an early age.) She prepared many German specialties, but her excellent *Hügelsheimer Pfannkuchen,* a pancake popular in Bavaria, especially enticed Heis.

Meanwhile, Western Union rehired Philip, but initially not at his old job as a telegrapher. Instead, he worked mostly nights as a messenger and file clerk in the Dixie Terminal Building downtown at Walnut and Fourth streets, scooting from file to file on roller skates and earning about $10 a week. He rarely saw his wife—they grew ever more distant as time went by—but he knew she was seeing Heis. He did nothing about it, though, preferring to stay out of her line of fire, which was both physical and furious. He was, quite frankly, afraid of her.

When Anna Marie told Heis that she had divorced Philip in Buffalo, he believed her. The coal dealer began to talk about marriage. One day Heis saw Philip at the Hahn home, greeted him, and kept eating Anna Marie's marvelous pancakes. When a puzzled Heis asked her what her ex was doing there, Anna Marie explained that Philip only stopped by to pay alimony. Heis not only gulped down her pancakes, he swallowed her lies.

Anna Marie never scotched the idea of marriage. Instead, she milked it. During the course of their yearlong relationship, she repeatedly asked for, and received, money from Heis, who just couldn't refuse her. Sometimes her requests were for amounts of $20 or less, but often they were for $100 or more. By midsummer, her debt totaled more than $2,000, $1,200 of which belonged to the Consolidated Coal Company.

Clarence E. Osborne, credit manager for Consolidated Coal, pressured Heis to come up with its money. Somewhat sheepishly he had to explain that he had loaned it to his paramour, who had given or promised him collateral. This collateral included a wrapped package of Hungarian bonds that he put in his living room office safe for her, a $7,000 trust fund she said she had inherited, and the promise of $14,000 in "gas and electric" stock.

After a couple of weeks, Anna Marie asked Heis to bring the bonds, still wrapped, to her home because the bank president was going to be there to verify them. Heis did so, but after waiting for the banker in vain for more than an hour, he went home, leaving the package with Anna Marie. If he had opened it, he would have discovered that the "bonds" were virtually worthless Hungarian lottery tickets that she acquired from an acquaintance, Julia Kresckay.

As the coal company's collection efforts shifted from Heis to Anna Marie, she busied herself seeking out new friends, this time on the distaff side. Two such women that summer were Mrs. Kresckay, a forty-eight-year-old, out-of-work Hungarian immigrant, and Stina Cable of Greensboro, North Carolina. Cable met Anna Marie the first and only time on July 15, 1936, in the ladies' restroom at the bus station.

On that occasion, Anna Marie was wearing the nurse's uniform that she often donned, even though she never had been a nurse. She invited

Cable to a nearby saloon, where she bought the beer and talked about being a mind reader and a palmist. Only after Cable finished the first beer did she realize something might be amiss.

"She told me a man had died a few days before drinking what I had drank," Cable said. "I was frightened." (Who the male victim may have been, if in fact there was a victim, is not known. Perhaps Anna Marie was thinking of Heis.)

Almost immediately Cable felt numb and unable to control her bodily functions. Anna Marie urged her to stay in Cincinnati to recover, but the woman elected to continue her trip to Los Angeles. Upon arrival there July 18, bus company employees carried her off the bus. The following day she entered Georgia Street Receiving Hospital, where she was treated for poisoning. It took her a year to recover from the illness.

Mrs. Kresckay's eyesight was poor, but she was in robust health when she bumped into Anna Marie at The Blade, a well-known gambling casino at Vine Avenue and Township Street in Elmwood Place. It wasn't long after they met that Anna Marie offered to find her "dearest friend" a government job—for a fee of $100. Thrilled at her good fortune, Mrs. Kresckay gladly paid it, and $100 more a few days later, and then another $100 three or four days after that. A week later, Anna Marie put a note, cosigned by herself and Philip, in front of her friend and convinced her to sign it, thus giving up $200 more. When Anna Marie produced a "receipt" for the money borrowed, Mrs. Kresckay signed that, too. She didn't see that it was really a check for $300, made out to Anna Marie, and written on Mrs. Kresckay's own account at the Eagle Savings and Loan Association.

Anna Marie was again on a roll, but in July 1936 Mrs. Kresckay filed a false-pretenses charge against Anna Marie, seeking the return of the $800. Two Cincinnati detectives, Michael McShane and William Wobbe, urged the complainant to sign a warrant for Anna Marie's arrest, but Mrs. Kresckay refused to do so, telling police that Anna Marie was "my good friend." The investigation was dropped.

Immediately after Mrs. Kresckay filed the charge against her, Anna Marie visited druggist Carroll G. Deming, whose emporium near the corner of Meis and Savannah avenues was less than two blocks from the first Hahn home on Savannah. He knew Anna Marie as a customer from previous visits. This time she requested an ounce of croton oil.

"Madam, that is a strong poison, and I can't sell a bottle to you unless I order it from the wholesaler," said Deming, who remembered the request because croton oil was so rarely sought.

"I know how to use oil of croton," Anna Marie replied reassuringly, allowing how her former husband was a druggist in Germany. "Order me some," she said, which Deming did from a pharmaceutical supply house in New York City through the Cincinnati Economy Drug Company. When she picked up the small bottle of croton oil, she promised to return the next day with the money she owed, but she stiffed Deming.

Anna Marie prepared food for Mrs. Kresckay, who fell seriously ill afterward. She was taken to Good Samaritan Hospital, where doctors noticed that the discharge from her mouth raised large blisters on her skin when she drooled. They suspected croton oil poisoning but said nothing to authorities.

In the same house as Mrs. Kresckay, a male boarder—never identified by name—saw his friend get sicker and sicker each time that Anna Marie fed Mrs. Kresckay food and medicine. When he visited her in the hospital, he learned about all the monies paid to Anna Marie. Indignant that his friend should have been hoodwinked and perhaps even poisoned, the boarder sought out Anna Marie, Philip, and Philip's parents, demanding that the money be repaid, but Anna Marie denied all his allegations. Then he said he was going to the police. Within a few days, Anna Marie paid back the $800. Shortly thereafter Mrs. Kresckay returned permanently to her native Budapest, Hungary, where she once again fell ill, suffering partial paralysis in her legs. Hospitalized in Budapest, she was treated for poisoning.

In October 1936, while still caring for Heis, Anna Marie twice returned to Roth's drugstore, once for an ounce of oxalic acid, a strong poison used as a cleaning agent, and later for twenty-five tablets of bichloride of mercury, a poisonous compound often associated with disinfectants. Roth remembered Anna Marie said she wanted the tablets "for poor Mr. Heis." She also attempted to purchase digitalis, a diuretic and heart stimulant, which Roth refused to sell to her.

Heis felt poorly after eating Anna Marie's cooking; she prepared a variety of dishes for him, including veal chops and spinach that he would wash down with a glass or two of homemade beer. Every time she prepared food for him in the fall of 1936, he became ill with diarrhea and agonizing stomach pains. The first time, he suspected she might have put something in his beer and even told Osborne that he thought Anna Marie had been poisoning him. Three or four days later, she brought Heis some spinach, telling him it would make him feel better. After eating it, he felt worse.

Heis also developed difficulty walking, now a victim of drop foot, with symptoms much the same as Philip's some years earlier. Heis's physician, Dr. George Charles Altemeier, surmised that his patient suffered from arsenic poisoning, but for reasons unknown he kept his concerns to himself. By the middle of October, Heis was bedridden.

When the coal dealer next confronted Anna Marie in his home—she had brought him more spinach—he told her to get out and not ever come back.

That love affair was over.

3 | HIGH-WIRE ACT

The pressure Heis and Osborne put on Anna Marie to pay back the money she had borrowed accelerated "the most gruesome premeditated poison murder plot in crime annals."[1]

Albert J. Palmer, a seventy-two-year-old retired railroad watchman known as "Berty" to family and friends, was the first among Anna Marie's elderly friends to die in 1937. A Parisian by birth, Palmer lived a quiet life in a three-story walk-up at 2416 Central Parkway, just a few blocks south from Heis's home. His sister, Anna, shared the same address.

In the tight little Over-the-Rhine enclave, Heis may well have known Palmer, but it is unlikely that either man knew the other was being romanced and conned by the same woman at the same time. For Anna Marie, it was an extraordinary high-wire act.

One of Palmer's few interests was horseracing. He frequently visited the gambling casinos in Elmwood Place, such as The Blade and the Walk-a-Show on the opposite side of Vine Avenue, a mob-owned casino that also held marathon dances. He first met Anna Marie at The Blade in the waning days of 1936, and their mutual fascination for wagering on the horses established a strong bond between them. Together, and

1. Gerald B. Healy, "School Teacher Faces Trial for Poison of Two Elderly Men," International News Service, Oct. 11, 1937.

sometimes with little Oscar, too, they would take the streetcar to The Blade, her favorite handbook establishment, play the ponies all afternoon, and return to their neighborhood in the early evening. Usually Philip was at work by the time they returned, so Palmer would often stop at Anna Marie's house for a beer and a bite to eat.

Monsoon-like rains and even snow hit Cincinnati in January. It poured barrels, not buckets. The mighty Ohio River rose to record heights; twenty-one feet of water covered the diamond at Crosley Field, home to the Cincinnati Reds and night baseball, and water rushed through the second stories of dozens of commercial buildings and homes. Electricity and clean drinking water were not to be had. To conserve precious energy, residents were ordered to burn but one light in their homes. Many had neither light nor water. When the nineteen-day deluge ended, eight were dead and fifty thousand homeless. Yet, through it all, Anna Marie and Oscar visited Palmer two or three times a week, and the three of them dined on her cooking, which upset Palmer's stomach.

Palmer soon considered Anna Marie to be "his girl," and made no secret about it. He told neighborhood friends, "I am going to the blonde woman's house," and off he would go, with a smile on his lips. He also spoke excitedly about a trip to Florida he and Anna Marie had planned.

When she sought money from him, which was often, she cuddled and cooed until he shelled out. She managed to sweet talk him—he loved it—into giving her $2,000. She, in turn, prepared for him a promissory note, due December 1938, but she kept possession of it. With Palmer's money, she paid Osborne $900 and promised him she would soon pay the remaining $300. She sent Osborne checks now and then, but each bounced—insufficient funds.

She wrote Palmer nearly two dozen perfumed love notes, too—hand-delivered by Oscar—which he carefully saved in a small tin box tied with a blue ribbon. One of the letters began, "My Dear Sweet Dady [sic]," and was signed, "With all my love and a lot of kisses, Your Ann." Another note in her hand said, "Honey, I have to have $100. . . ." Then there was a February 12 Valentine's Day card with a verse that read:

The friends that we cherish
As finest and truest,
Aren't always the oldest
Nor are they the newest.
They're the friends who've stood by
When we need them sincerely,
And that's why I cherish
Our friendship so dearly.

It was signed, "Anna and Oscar."

Nobody ever proved that she had intercourse with Palmer or any of her other elderly chums, but Cincinnati police believed that she did. At the very least, they thought, she provided the gentlemen she befriended with sexual gratification, if not intercourse. There is no question whatsoever that these lonely souls basked in the lavish affections of an attractive woman in full flower. However, for Anna Marie the name of the game was M-O-N-E-Y, not S-E-X.

In late February 1937, Palmer inexplicably came to his senses and demanded Anna Marie repay the money he had loaned her. Perhaps what fostered the turnabout was his hearing from neighborhood gossips about Anna Marie's "affair" with Heis. At the time, however, the once-robust Palmer was feeling poorly. Bouts with stomach cramps, diarrhea, and vomiting invariably followed each dining experience with Anna Marie. Between January and March, his health deteriorated rapidly, according to his sister, Anna, who became alarmed upon seeing her brother in so much distress. Grocer Peter T. Toner, who lived on the second floor of the same apartment house as Palmer, and Anna Horstmeyer, who lived on the first floor, also voiced concerns.

When Heis and Consolidated Coal's Osborne were turning up the heat on Anna Marie, Palmer did so, too, threatening her with legal action. He gave her a choice: Become his girlfriend on a permanent and exclusive basis or repay him. She couldn't, or wouldn't, do either.

Anna Marie became frantic, desperately seeking a way out of her relationship with Palmer. Her egress fortuitously appeared when, on March 26, 1937, he died of an apparent heart attack. The death certificate noted his passing was due to influenza and coronary disease. He died virtually penniless, his personal savings of nearly $5,000 all but depleted.

Three days after Palmer drew his last breath, Anna Marie applied to the Hazel Meyer Employment Bureau for a position as a practical nurse or a companion, stating that she was a "widow with experience." She also noted on her application, "Compensation not important." Although she failed to secure a job through the agency, she had no problem finding more old folks to nurse: she unearthed Jacob Wagner simply by knocking on neighborhood doors.

Wagner, a seventy-eight-year-old widower, immigrated to the United States from Germany about 1885. He settled in Cincinnati and became a gardener to several prominent families in the area, including George R. Balch, president of the Cincinnati Realty Company. For Wagner's years of faithful service, Mrs. Balch presented the gardener with his proudest possession, a gold pocket watch. He was known as a gentle man, who often favored neighborhood children with pennies from his pocket.

In retirement, he lived for eighteen years in a small apartment at 1805 Race Street, a four-story tenement in the Findlay Market area of Over-the-Rhine. His sink was in the hallway, and, because he had been a tenant for so long, he had a key to the community toilet in the hallway so that he could use the facility in private.

His neighbor Elizabeth Colby recalled vividly a visitor to her third-floor apartment, the same floor on which Wagner lived. It was May 13, 1937, and she had just come home from work. She was tired and preparing dinner for herself and her divorced daughter, Josephine Martin, when there came hard, repeated knocks at her door. Not feeling up to visitors, Mrs. Colby first decided to ignore the caller, but changed her mind when the knocking continued. At her door was a well-dressed, well-coiffured stranger, who asked if "any old men lived here." Mrs. Colby immediately felt uneasy because the woman proceeded to walk right into the center of the room for a good look around.

"What do you mean, 'old men'? There are several old men in the building. One lives just down the hall there."

"I knocked on that door, nobody answered," Anna Marie said. That afternoon she also had knocked on the doors of at least three other tenants, including those of Nannie Werks and Ida Martin.

"Mr. Wagner must be out then," Mrs. Colby responded.

"Wagner? That's the name," said Anna Marie. "Wagner." In her German pronunciation, it came out as *vahg-ner*.

Anna Marie identified herself as Wagner's niece, and said she had a letter for him from relatives in Baden-Baden, Germany, concerning a family inheritance. (This all sounded strange to Mrs. Colby, given that the woman professed not to know the name of the person she sought.) She asked Mrs. Colby for a pencil and a piece of paper on which to write a note, which she slipped under Wagner's door. She promised to return another time, which she did several days later, leaving another note for Wagner.

Mrs. Colby told Wagner about the young woman's visit. "Ach, I don't know anyone like that," he said. "*Nein, Nein. Da muss ein Fehler sein.*" ("No, no. There must be some mistake.") Yet, within days he and Anna Marie did meet. He visited her in her home, and she visited him in his apartment, the only woman ever known to do so, neighbors said. He even told a friend, "I have a new girl." Another old man had fallen for Anna Marie's charms, at least for a few days.

Two weeks and two days after Anna Marie knocked on Mrs. Colby's door, Wagner visited Arthur J. Schmitt, assistant vice president at Fifth Third Union Trust Company. He reported that a woman, a *"Lehrerin"* (schoolteacher), had stolen his bankbook when he had briefly left his apartment to fetch a pail of beer to share with Anna Marie. The passbook, which revealed that he had more than $4,000 on deposit, had been hidden under his mattress. He showed Schmitt two passbooks of Anna Marie's, which she had given him: one was foreign with no balance, the other from Security Savings and Loan in Cincinnati. The latter had a bank-generated, machine entry of $3, but also several typewritten entries totaling $15,000 more. Those were forgeries, Schmitt surmised, and he urged Wagner to bring the passbooks back on Tuesday, after the Decoration Day (now Memorial Day) holiday, if he wanted to prosecute.

Anna Marie later explained that Oscar made the typewritten entries while practicing on a new typewriter.

The passbooks were Anna Marie's variation of the bait-and-switch con game. She planned to take Wagner's passbook with $4,831 in it and give him in return, as security, her bankbooks showing a total of more than $15,000 on deposit. Actually, she had no money in the accounts at all. Even the $3, deposited in Oscar's name in 1936, had been withdrawn in May, leaving a zero balance.

On his way home from the bank, Wagner met a friend of thirty years, Joe Elbisser, also seventy-five, a retired shoemaker. "You'll need a cane pretty soon," said Elbisser, teasing his friend. "I have two. You can have one if you need it." Wagner declined, but revealed that he was upset about the "stolen" bankbook.

Upon leaving Elbisser, Wagner joined two other friends, Otto Mackles and Frank Kaessheimer, at Kirsch's, a popular Elder Street watering hole. Recounting the story of the bankbook and what Schmitt had said, Wagner showed them Anna Marie's two bankbooks, slipping them back into his pocket moments before she entered Kirsch's, too. Wagner accosted her and accused her of stealing. "My bankbook is gone," he said, "and nobody else took it but you. You are the only one in my rooms." He told her he had within the hour reported the theft to Schmitt, who suspected her bankbooks were forged. As it had been with Heis and Palmer, Anna Marie suddenly felt trapped by circumstances gone awry.

Embarrassed by Wagner in front of strangers, she became indignant, accusing Wagner of misplacing his bankbook. In her mind, she also sentenced him to death.

"Where are *my* two bankbooks?" she demanded.

"They're gone, too," Wagner lied.

"Come, we will go to your place and look for them," she said. Before they left, Wagner reached under the table and surreptitiously passed to Kaessheimer the two bankbooks in Anna Marie's name. "Keep them until I get back," he whispered.

Within ten minutes the pair returned to the café with Wagner's bankbook—Anna Marie had "found" it—and the old gardener retrieved the pair of bankbooks Kaessheimer had been holding. Anna Marie telephoned Schmitt at the bank to say that Wagner's missing book had been found.

The following day, Mrs. Colby spotted Wagner and Anna Marie together again. Four days after Anna Marie first visited her, Mrs. Colby had moved next door to a third-floor apartment at 1809 Race Street. Now, from her tiny porch, she looked right into Wagner's third-floor apartment, across the alley about ten feet wide. It was a hot day. Wagner's window was wide-open and the curtains pulled back to allow in what little breeze there was in the air. Mrs. Colby spied Anna Marie in Wagner's room. At first Anna Marie was in a rocking chair, then she rose and prepared and poured him several glasses of what appeared to be orange juice. Again Mrs. Colby felt uneasy. She thought it "not right" that a young woman, particularly *that* young woman, should be with Wagner in his apartment. She called her daughter to the window to view the scene. Mrs. Martin, who also watched Anna Marie pass a glass of juice to Wagner, did not share her mother's concern for propriety, however; after all, the woman was Wagner's niece.

Monday, Decoration Day and a holiday, was a special day for Anna Marie's handsome son, Oscar. Together they celebrated his twelfth birthday. Little did either realize it would be the last time they would observe his birthday together. Wagner, on the other hand, did not feel like celebrating anything. He felt just awful.

By Tuesday evening, June 1, Wagner was writhing in agony on his bed. For nearly twenty-four hours he had been vomiting, passing blood, and battling diarrhea. At nine that evening Anna Marie sought a doctor. She first went to the nearby office of Dr. Richard Marnell, but he was not in, so Anna Marie found the portly, ruddy-cheeked neighborhood physician, Dr. James H. Clift, a 1919 graduate of the Eclectic Medical College in Cincinnati. He had a rather freewheeling practice at 28 Findlay Street. He never kept any patient records of any kind, for instance, and conducted what he described as a cash business.

Clift followed Wagner's "niece" to the old gardener's room a block away. Throughout his examination, Anna Marie served as a translator, although Wagner understood English and spoke it, albeit poorly. Dr. Clift never realized that, however. The physician prescribed bismuth-paregoric pills for diarrhea and, although he did not feel Wagner's condition to be critical, suggested that Wagner go to a hospital.

"Is he going to die?" Anna Marie asked.

Dr. Clift said he didn't think so, but advised that he needed care. Anna Marie, who revealed that she had been a nurse in the old country, said she would look after the old man.

Earlier that same Tuesday, Schmitt had expected Wagner to visit the bank with Anna Marie's two bankbooks Schmitt had inspected earlier. Instead, Anna Marie showed up with a note purportedly written by Wagner. Full of grammatical and spelling errors, it read:

> I am very sorry what happent Saturday nith my book I found unter a paper on the self it all was a mistake and I don't want my niece Mrs. Hahn to be acuced of anything. I bin sick since Saturday Evening and leave it up to Mrs. Hahn to straighten this matter out. [*signed*] Jacob Wagner.

Although he actually had been fine on Saturday, Wagner now was very sick, indeed. Tuesday night he had tried to get out of bed and fell, giving himself a nasty gash on his head. Neighborhood gossips later whispered that Anna Marie had done the damage, but head-bashing was not her style. Yet early the next morning, another resident and septuagenarian, Anna Decker, offered to help attend to Wagner and his injury. "No, the room is too dirty," Anna Marie said, blocking the door to Wagner's room. "Mr. Wagner does not want anyone to come in," so Mrs. Decker left Wagner's niece and nurse to deal with it.

Wagner did not like Dr. Clift's bedside manner, or so Anna Marie said, so Wednesday afternoon she visited Dr. Marnell's office twice, urging that he come by, which he did a little after 2 P.M. After his examination, which he conducted without Anna Marie in the room, Dr. Marnell thought that Wagner appeared chronically ill and needed to be hospitalized. She called for an ambulance. When it arrived, Wagner was carried down the three flights of stairs in a chair and placed on a stretcher. Anna Marie rode with him in the ambulance to Good Samaritan Hospital, arriving at 3:30 P.M.

Hospital room admitting clerk Laura Boehm watched as Anna Marie signed Wagner into the hospital. Anna Marie wrote on the admittance form that she was his niece, his nearest relative, and responsible for the hospital's charges. Nothing would be too good for her Uncle Jake, she told Boehm. "Give him the best room in the hospital and the best of care. He has plenty of money." As for herself, Anna Marie told them that she was worn-out from caring for Wagner for the past week.

"You know how it is with relatives," Anna Marie commented to Mrs. Boehm. "They never know you, only when they need you."

Dr. Marnell visited Wagner in Room 190 about 8 P.M. and saw that his condition had worsened considerably. "He was semi-conscious, retching with pain and in a state of shock and dying," the physician said. Elizabeth Morabek, a World War I German army nurse, checked on the patient later in the evening and saw a terrifying image of a man in agony. Tears streamed down his cheeks, and he sweated profusely. His fists were so tightly clenched he could not ring for help. He writhed in pain and begged for water. He barely got out the words, "*Ich könnte ein Fass voll Wasser trinken!*" ("I could drink a barrel of water!") Wagner died just past midnight, Thursday, June 3.

Before Wagner passed on, Anna Marie had returned to his home. "Poor old Uncle Jake," Anna Marie told Ida Martin, his concerned neighbor. "He's awful sick. There are a lot of things in there [in Wagner's quarters] you can use. I will give them to you. He's not coming back."

She was right there. When Anna Marie returned to Good Samaritan at 8 A.M., she learned that Wagner had succumbed. Her "uncle" now became a virtual stranger to her. She refused to sign for an autopsy, professing that she hardly knew the deceased. She only helped other tenants force open the door to Wagner's apartment the previous day, she said, and saw to it that he got to the hospital.

Dr. Marnell had not signed a death certificate because he was unsure of the cause of death, hence the need for an autopsy. Another physician, Dr. Francis M. Forster, explained the situation to Anna Marie, noting that if she didn't authorize an autopsy, Wagner's death would be turned over to the county coroner for investigation. Anna Marie wanted no part of that, so she signed.

Her own funds depleted—she had but $1.10 in the bank—Anna Marie quickly worked to wipe out Wagner's. She left the hospital and headed straight for the Fifth Third Union Trust branch. There she delivered to Schmitt a second note, written in English, and signed "Jack Wagner." It read: "Please give Mrs. Hahn a check 1000 dollars bal. in her name." She had a withdrawal slip for $1,000, but Schmitt refused to honor it because it was written in pencil and incomplete. He gave Anna Marie another withdrawal slip, properly filled out, and suggested that she have Wagner sign it at Deaconess Hospital, which is where Anna Marie told Schmitt Wagner had been taken.

Two hours later, she returned with the receipt signed and a third note from Wagner: "I am giving Mrs. Hahn full power of everything." While she completed paperwork to have the $1,000 transferred to her account, Schmitt called Deaconess Hospital. No patient named Wagner there. When confronted with that information, Anna Marie said she had made a silly mistake. Wagner was a patient at Good Samaritan Hospital, she remembered. Schmitt called there, too, and discovered to his surprise that Wagner had died in the middle of the night. When he challenged the woman, she admitted, with tears in her hazel eyes, that she had signed Wagner's name to the check because he "wanted me to pay his expenses." She pleaded with Schmitt not to turn her in to the authorities for forgery, describing how awful it would be for her, a woman estranged from her husband, if her son didn't have his mother to care for him. Schmitt bought her tearful story, and once again Anna Marie managed to escape the scrutiny of the law.

She came away from the bank empty-handed, but she was not without further resources. At home she carefully penned Wagner's will:

I hereby make my last will and testament and I am under no influence. I have my money in the Fifth Third Bank [sic]. After my funeral expenses and all bills are paid, I want the rest to go to my relative, Anna Hahn. I want Mrs. Hahn to be my executor. I don't want any flowers, and I don't want to be laid out.

Although she had met Wagner only two weeks before, she now possessed a document that awarded her every asset he had.

That afternoon, with the will in hand, she returned to the building where Wagner had lived, where she found Anna Eberhardt and Anna

Decker, both elderly friends of the deceased. Neither Mrs. Eberhardt nor Mrs. Decker read English, yet Anna Marie put before them a hand-written document, in English, which she said required their signatures. The document, Anna Marie explained sweetly in German, was required to admit Olive Louella Koehler to the hospital for treatment. (Hospitalization required no such document.) Anna Marie made no mention that it was Wagner's will the ladies were being asked to witness. The women refused to sign anything, saying that it would be more proper if Koehler's sister, Mary Arnold, signed the paper. Even though all but Mrs. Arnold lived in the same apartment building, Eberhardt and Decker had no idea that Koehler needed to be hospitalized.

Charles Dotzauer, a probate court deputy, considerately greeted the grieving Anna Marie at his office the following morning and agreed to meet her that afternoon at Wagner's apartment to search for a will. Lo and behold, there it was, on the mantel underneath a newspaper. Dotzauer looked at it, saw it was signed and dated January 10, 1936, but not witnessed, which meant it could not be accepted for probate. Charmed by Anna Marie's sweetness and at her urging, Dotzauer took the document with him, nevertheless.

4 | MAKING OLD FOLK COMFY

At Wagner's funeral and burial on Saturday, June 5, at the Baltimore Pike Cemetery, only three mourners were at the graveside service: Mrs. Eberhardt, Mrs. Decker, and a tearful Anna Marie. As she left the cemetery, Anna Marie told the elderly widows, "This is too bad. This is the second uncle I have buried this month." It wasn't the first time the two women thought Anna Marie's comments to be odd. Her revelation a few days earlier about Mrs. Koehler having to go to the hospital also puzzled her two neighbors.

Mrs. Koehler, a seventy-nine-year-old widow, lived in a building at 104 West Elder Street that was connected by a fire escape to the Race Street apartment building where Wagner lived. Anna Marie met her one day in May while on her way to visit Wagner. With Osborne still relentlessly pursuing her to pay up the $300 she still owed Consolidated Coal, Anna Marie was again desperately in need of cash.

Dressed in a quasi-uniform perhaps suitable for a home nurse, she identified herself to Mrs. Koehler as a Salvation Army worker whose job it was to make the elderly and infirm "comfy." The venerable woman loved having company, especially helpful German-speaking company, and she appreciated having such a sweet German lady caring for her, which Anna Marie began to do while still making Wagner comfy, too.

Shortly after Anna Marie began visiting her, Mrs. Koehler missed a small valise of valuables she had hidden under her bed. She suspected the wallpaper hangers who had been in the building had stolen it. Anna Marie offered to get the luggage back, for a fee. Mrs. Koehler wrote her a check for $80 to pay the thief for the return of the contents of the case, which included jewelry, papers, and cash totaling $188. A week later Anna Marie professed failure, even though she knew just where the bag was. It was now under *her* bed, and in her closet was a new rabbit fur coat, bought on sale and paid for in full with cash from the valise.

In a gesture of kindness in the heat of an early summer, Anna Marie twice bought ice cream—on June 22 and June 23—for Mrs. Koehler and her ninety-five-year-old sister, Mrs. Mary Arnold. Each time, after eating the ice cream Anna Marie served, Mrs. Koehler became violently ill with stomach pain, nausea, and diarrhea. Mrs. Arnold, who barely tasted the ice cream the first time and took none the second time, felt uncomfortable for a spell but did not suffer like her sister did.

A Civil War widow on a pension, Mrs. Arnold lived nearby, above a neighborhood grocery and confectionery store at 1812 Race Street where Anna Marie bought the ice cream. Mathilda Propheter, who owned the small shop, disliked the local blonde gadabout right from the start. She called the Salvation Army office in Cincinnati and discovered it had no record of a home health care worker named Mrs. Hahn. When on the evening of June 24 Anna Marie came into the store again, Mrs. Propheter mentioned that Mrs. Koehler was very sick.

"Well, she lived her life," Anna Marie replied. Mrs. Propheter was livid at the woman's callousness. The next day she found Anna Marie back in the neighborhood and upstairs, trying to ingratiate herself to Mrs. Arnold by posing as someone else.

"*Bist du das, Lillian?*" ("Is that you, Lillian?") asked the nearly blind Mrs. Arnold upon Anna Marie's arrival. Lillian Meyer was the old woman's good friend.

"*Ja, sie ist es*" ("Yes, it is"), replied Anna Marie, her face all but hidden by a rather large, broad-brimmed straw hat. She urged the old lady to drink some beer she had brought, but Mrs. Arnold refused it. So Anna Marie busied herself with tidying up Mrs. Arnold's one room, all the while searching it. When she raised the corner of the mattress and saw $200 "hidden" there, she could not resist. The money fit easily into her pocket.

"Lillian" volunteered to do some clothes shopping for Mrs. Arnold, but just as the old woman was signing a blank check for that purpose, Mrs. Propheter arrived, realized what was going on, and confronted the visitor.

"Why are you deceiving these old people?"

"She was so happy to think it was Lillian visiting her."

"But what is your interest in these old people?" Mrs. Propheter demanded.

"Oh, I love them," Anna Marie replied.

"Well, we don't like you around here. To us, you look like a mess."

Now it was Anna Marie's turn to be angry. "I have a good reputation," she insisted, her face flushed. "I run a big hospital on Colerain Avenue."

Mrs. Propheter demanded a phone number from Anna Marie to check on her story, which she did the next day. When she called the number, she discovered she was talking not with a hospital administrator but with nineteen-year-old Olive Winter, a secretary in Dr. Vos's office in Anna Marie's home. After hearing Mrs. Propheter's story, Winter suggested that she notify the authorities. The next day the police received a call from Mrs. Propheter, but they took little note of what they considered to be a domestic squabble among neighbors.

On July 10 Mrs. Koehler entered Longview State Hospital for the insane. Her sister shakily signed the lunacy warrant, and a friend and neighbor, Blanche Mullikins, signed the commitment papers.

Four days earlier, on the morning of July 6, neighbor August Schultz had discovered the body of sixty-seven-year-old George G. Gsellman in his $5-a-week, fourth-floor attic room at 1717 Elm Street where he had lived for a year. Mrs. Koehler's home was three short blocks away. Gsellman, a German-speaking Hungarian immigrant who enjoyed smoking his carved meerschaum, once owned a farm in Symmes Township, Hamilton County. However, shortly after his divorce in 1920 from his Hungarian-born wife, Elizabeth, he moved to Cincinnati's Over-the-Rhine district.

Gsellman was not wealthy, although he appeared otherwise. He had worked in Cincinnati as a railroad crossing gateman and lived on the $25-a-month income a small annuity produced. He prided himself on being a natty dresser and "quite a ladies man," who enjoyed the nightlife, according to neighbors. In his closet, for instance, he had six suits and thirty white dress shirts, all hung uniformly on hangers. Each shirt had a gold button inserted in the front and back buttonholes at the neck to which a starched collar could be affixed. Yet, when he was found dead on the bed of his small, one-room tenement home, he was nude save for a pair of slippers on his feet. A pair of neatly creased pants with thirty-six cents in the pocket hung over the back of a chair.

Today Gsellman might be described as "a health nut." In writing his life's story, recorded in a manuscript found in his room, he penned his "Fifteen Rules of Health." Rule Number 12 was "Do not allow poisons to enter your body." Neighbors and then police noticed that on July 5 the small table where he ate his meals alone, night after night, had been set for two. Two pots were on the stove, one containing meat and the other gravy. City chemist Dr. Otto P. Behrer later determined for the police that together the meat and the gravy were laced with almost eighteen grains of arsenic trioxide, enough to kill two dozen men.

Earlier that summer Gsellman's marriage proposal to an unidentified woman had been rejected. When he next ran into her, he told her, "You wouldn't marry me, and now I went and got a young blonde German schoolteacher." He told friends that he was going to marry "a blonde woman and move to California." He even had a wedding day in mind—July 6.

The blonde was, of course, Anna Marie. She knew Gsellman slightly, and perhaps because he always appeared so dapper and prosperous, she believed he had money to burn. Two weeks before he died Anna Marie came knocking on his door and pursued the relationship in earnest. After years of loneliness, Gsellman was swept off his feet by Anna Marie's charm and affections. On July 1, when she asked for $100, he willingly withdrew it from his bank, although his banker could not recall Gsellman ever withdrawing such a large amount. Nevertheless, Anna Marie was on a roll again and able to send Osborne $50. He kept up the pressure for $250 more.

When she appeared at Gsellman's hillside tenement house on the morning of July 6, Schultz accosted her. He recognized her as the visitor who had been with Gsellman the night before. Both Schultz and his wife had seen Anna Marie several times during that evening, helping Gsellman down the stairs to the second-floor bathroom and back up to his fourth-floor garret.

"No use going upstairs," Schultz told Anna Marie upon her arrival. "Gsellman is dead."

"Oh, my goodness," Anna Marie replied, acting stunned by the news. It seemed to Schultz that she would faint, but she quickly composed herself and went up to the room anyway. After a few minutes there, she left the building.

The day after Gsellman's body was discovered, Detective William Sweeney arrested Anna Marie, but not for murder. He brought her into police headquarters on a $10 bounced check charge, which she resolved immediately, paying her debt to the Alms & Doepke Department Store with cash Gsellman had given her.

And so she continued her deadly ministrations to the elderly, undetected.

5 | ONE FOR THE ROAD

The first trip of any distance Johan Georg Obendoerfer took in more than forty years was also his last.

A cobbler of German descent, Obendoerfer and his wife, Gretchen, arrived in Cincinnati from Russia in 1892. Before she died twenty years later, they raised a son and two daughters while he worked for a number of local shoe companies. After twenty-five years at the Duttonhoefer Shoe Company, he retired and operated a small cobbler shop in his home part-time, keeping busy helping neighbors and making shoes for his eleven grandchildren. Shortly after he turned sixty-seven in early 1937, he sold his modest frame house at 2150 Clifton Avenue for $2,600 because he could no longer afford the taxes or the upkeep. He remained a resident there, though, securing a five-year lease on two rooms in the attic. His little shoe shop was on the steeply slanted street, tucked underneath the front porch of the house.

It was a warm June day when Anna Marie arrived at Obendoerfer's shop for the first time. A friend, she said, had directed her to him because while out shopping she had broken the heel on her shoe. Obendoerfer did little repairs like that and immediately the very pleasant *Hausfrau* in his home was his friend. He invited her to sit a spell, and in German they talked the afternoon away.

Over the next few weeks and into July, the couple spent considerable time together, or so it seemed to family, neighbors, and friends.

In fact, when talking about Anna Marie, Obendoerfer allowed words like *Verlobung* (engagement), *Hochzeit* (marriage), and *Hochzeitsreise* (honeymoon) to creep in. To appear younger, he shaved off the full and flowing mustache that he had cultivated and combed for years. His daughter, Louise Nau of Cincinnati, was surprised how infatuated her father had become with this woman less than half his age, but she did not admonish him. Good daughters did not do that, but neighbors told her that her father "was talking like a young man, talking of a honeymoon" with Anna Marie.

For the Bavarian woman July was another busy month. After all, she had a husband with whom she had been fighting; a son she usually took on assignations; a hospitalized Mrs. Koehler; Gsellman anxiously waiting to take her hand; and now Obendoerfer, whose home was within a half-dozen blocks of Gsellman's in the Over-the-Rhine neighborhood. Somehow she was able to keep all her affairs sorted out and out of sight.

Anna Marie delighted Obendoerfer to no end when she said she and Oscar had planned a train trip to the mountains of Colorado and invited the shoemaker to come along. He accepted and told friends—Henry Fuhs for one—that his *Liebchen* (sweetheart) owned an $18,000 home on a Colorado cattle ranch, and if they found the setting to their liking, they would spend the rest of their lives in Colorado. Fuhs said his friend was in love.

After her last visit to Gsellman on the evening of July 5, Anna Marie devoted all her energies to Obendoerfer and the trip. The "honeymooners" put their Colorado travel plans in motion on July 16 when they visited Obendoerfer's bank. He withdrew $350, which he gave her to buy his train ticket and sundries for the trip. Two hundred and fifty dollars went into her bank account, perhaps to cover a final check to Osborne, but she never paid her remaining debt to Consolidated Coal. When questioned later about the $250 deposit, she would vehemently deny that the money had been from Obendoerfer, insisting that she had won it betting on the horses that day.

On Tuesday afternoon, July 20, a happy, healthy Obendoerfer packed a small, rather dilapidated wicker satchel, stopped for a beer at the Albert H. Schell Restaurant at 1732 Elm Street, and then, with a spring in his step, jauntily walked to Anna Marie's home where he spent the night. She prepared a special dinner for him, so special that by 11 o'clock Wednesday morning he needed help to get into Otto Walke's Yellow Cab. Obendoerfer leaned on Anna Marie's arm as she led him to the taxi, which Oscar had directed to the back of the house, out of sight from the street. Oscar carried Obendoerfer's bag to the taxi.

"Depot." That simple directive was the only word spoken by Anna Marie on the ride to the Union Terminal. Once there, she paid Walke 50 cents, bought some sandwiches and coffee for her son and the shoemaker, then left them in the station's large, domed rotunda while she returned home. She told Obendoerfer and Oscar, however, that she had an errand to run downtown before the train left for Chicago at 4:40 P.M.

Before she left the house, Anna Marie had put a note on the kitchen table for her husband, telling him that she was going to Colorado for a few days. They had not seen each other since they argued violently on July 1, which arose after Oscar found a small bottle, marked "Croton Oil—Poison X," in the cushions of an easy chair and showed it to Philip. When Philip asked Anna Marie about the bottle and its contents, she hurled abuse at him, demanding that he give it to her. Despite her screaming, which was loud enough to be heard by a neighbor, Philip refused to hand over the bottle. He left the house with it and didn't come back.

On July 21, Anna Marie, Oscar, and Obendoerfer arrived in Chicago. She registered Obendoerfer at a 25-cents-a-night flophouse near the train station while she and Oscar secured a room for $8 a night at what was for many years the world's largest hotel, the Stevens on Michigan Avenue. When she helped the elderly Obendoerfer check out of his hotel the next morning, she failed to notice that she had left her camera in his dingy room.

The day-and-a-half trip west was uneventful, save for Obendoerfer's growing discomfort. He complained of being "dry," so Oscar kept getting him glasses of ice water.

On July 23 their train arrived at Denver's Union Station. From there the trio walked one block to the venerable, five-story Oxford Hotel on busy Seventeenth Street. Built in 1891, it recently had been remodeled into an art deco showcase. Anna Marie and Oscar secured a room for $1.50 a night; Obendoerfer's nearby single room cost $1 a night.

The following day a hotel porter saw Obendoerfer's door slightly ajar and peeked in. Obendoerfer was writhing on his bed. "He appeared awfully sick and was in agony," the young man said.

Anna Marie didn't like anyone nosy like that, so on July 25 she checked out and moved, with Obendoerfer, to the much smaller Midland Hotel at Arapahoe and Seventeenth streets, five blocks away. There, too, the staff could not help but notice Obendoerfer's poor condition and commented on it to the proprietor, Louis Straub, who also was a Denver city councilman.

When Midland Hotel chief clerk George Mathews asked Anna Marie about her elderly companion, she assured him, "He'll be all right in a few days. I just gave him a good dose of croton oil." She also fed him watermelon, which was, at the time, a well-known agent for feeding arsenic to rats. With little apparent concern for his mother's friend, Oscar watched blindly as Obendoerfer repeatedly vomited after eating the watermelon.

In the Mile High City, Anna Marie penned a letter on Oxford Hotel letterhead to Harry H. Becker, director of the Clifton Heights Savings and Loan in Cincinnati. In hindsight, it revealed her scheme to secure money from Obendoerfer's savings account and abandon him in Colorado, dead or alive. Her inadequacies with the English language are evident:

Dear Mr. Becker, inclosed you find Mr. Obendorfer pass book. I adviced him to the Denver Nat. Bank, they will take care of him. I am leaving for Newcastle tomorrow to take care of my own business matters, then I will return to Cinc by Saturday or Sunday. Mr. Obendorfer is going to stay in Colo. With his sister-in-law or whatever relative she is to him. He also has quite a number of friends here from the old country and he'll enjoy life more than he ever did before. He was thinking of buying a little chicken farm, he has one in mind if he can get the right price for it he'll take. Mr. Obendorfer wants the Building and Loan to send him a check for $1,000 and sent to the Denver Natl. Bank where he is going to deposit the money; he would like to have it as soon as possible in case he would find a nice place so he could take it right away; as soon as I return to Cinc. I'll stop in and see you about some property.

Anna Marie signed it, "Respectfully, A. Felser," using a form of her maiden name, Filser. The letter was dated July 24, the day after her arrival in Denver. That Saturday she also visited the Denver National Bank, posing as Mrs. Obendoerfer. She asked Edward J. Weckbach, assistant vice president, to transfer $1,000 from Obendoerfer's account at the Clifton Heights Building and Loan so she and her "husband" could "buy a little farm" in Colorado. Weckbach asked that Obendoerfer himself show up to complete the necessary paperwork, since it was his account, not Anna Marie's. She explained that at the moment, he was visiting family out of the city and unable to come to the bank. Actually, Obendoerfer was writhing on his bed at the Midland, less than three blocks away. She returned to the bank the following Tuesday, Wednesday, and Thursday, becoming more agitated each day when the funds did not arrive. She exhibited little concern for Obendoerfer, who by now was unable to control his bodily functions.

By July 29 the stench in Obendoerfer's room at the Midland had become so bad that housekeeping refused to enter it. Straub asked Anna Marie about the condition of the old man and the room when she and Oscar returned from the bank.

"Are you traveling with that old gentleman?" he asked.

"I met him on the train," she said. "I don't know who he is, but he is very sick, and I was taking care of him. He's not as bad as he was." She said if Straub provided her with clean linens, she would clean up Obendoerfer's room herself.

The following day, when Anna Marie and Oscar were out again, Straub visited the old cobbler's room to see for himself. He immediately saw the watermelon on the table, then Obendoerfer. He was alone, sitting in a large chair in a fetal-like position, and in agony. The chair, the bed, the floor—all were fouled with excrement and vomit. Straub covered his nose and mouth with his handkerchief, thinking it couldn't have been much worse.

Upon her return, Straub confronted Anna Marie again.

"This man has to have a doctor," he said. "He is going to die."

"Oh, I don't think it is *that* serious, is it?"

"From the looks of him, yes. He has to go to the hospital, or see a doctor," Straub insisted. When she said Obendoerfer had no money, he offered to use the weight of his city position to get the distressed man into a local charity hospital.

"I promised his people in Cincinnati I would see him to Colorado Springs," Anna Marie said, not realizing she had contradicted her story that she had only just met Obendoerfer on the train.

Another nosy person was getting too close for Anna Marie's comfort, so she immediately went upstairs, packed the bags and called a taxi to take the three of them to the train station. Anna Marie and the cab driver almost had to carry the wobbly Obendoerfer to the taxi. The three travelers barely made the 4:40 P.M. train to Colorado Springs.

Had she had the patience to wait, Anna Marie might have had $1,000 in her pocket. The money from Obendoerfer's account in Cincinnati arrived at the Denver National Bank that day, but Weckbach was suspicious and decided not to send the funds on to a bank in Colorado Springs, as Anna Marie had requested.

On the train Obendoerfer again asked for water, a lot of it, which Oscar got for him. After arriving in Colorado Springs about 7 P.M., the threesome walked across the street from the Denver & Rio Grande Western Railroad depot to the Park Hotel, run by Rosie Turner and her husband, Pell. Anna Marie again registered "Gg. Obendoerfer, Chicago, Illinois." She secured two rooms at $1.50 and $1.00 per night, and she, Oscar, and Pell Turner helped the feeble Obendoerfer upstairs and into bed. Then mother and son went for dinner in downtown Colorado Springs.

During what was a brief stay in the western city, Anna Marie sent a postcard to her brother, Hans, in Fuessen. She said she and her husband were on vacation and "all was well by us." The next morning she scored again when she noticed the door to the Turners' private rooms was ajar. Anna Marie walked in, looked around, swiftly pocketed two diamond rings she spotted on a dresser, and was leaving when confronted by Mrs. Turner.

"These are our private quarters," Mrs. Turner said, testily. "What are you doing here?

"Oh, it's very nice. I was just curious, that's all." Mrs. Turner did not notice her rings were missing, but when she did, her discovery would turn Anna Marie's life upside down. No other single act—not the lies, the forgeries, the previous thefts, or the murders—contributed more to her date with the electric chair than the theft of those two rings.

Although the Turners expressed concern for Obendoerfer's health, Anna Marie and her son left him alone and in agony again most of the day Saturday while they went sightseeing. Upon their return, however, his miserable state caused Anna Marie to call a cab to take the doubled-over Obendoerfer to the nearby Beth-El Hospital.

While she escorted him inside, Oscar remained in the taxi and launched into a long conversation with the driver, Charles Mundy. "I don't understand why mama did not get rid of Mr. Obendoerfer, as he was sick and took much trouble and had a very bad odor about him," Oscar said, wrinkling up his nose. The loquacious lad also revealed that Obendoerfer had "a lot of money" in Cincinnati and that he had planned to buy a Colorado chicken ranch with it. Actually, Obendoerfer at the time possessed no money or papers. Anna Marie had picked him clean of both before checking him into the hospital as an indigent.

At 6:30 P.M. Sunday, August 1, Obendoerfer died. In Cincinnati that same day, authorities authorized the exhumation of Jacob Wagner's body, buried at the Baltimore Hill Cemetery.

A simple death notice placed in the *Colorado Springs Gazette* on August 2, 1937, by the Law Mortuary, noted, "Mr. George Obendoerfer passed away at a local hospital Sunday evening. Funeral announcement later." The announcement was terse because the mortuary knew nothing more about the deceased. When the hospital reached Anna Marie at the hotel to inform her of Obendoerfer's passing, she responded, "Why notify me? I don't know him. I met him on the train between Denver and Colorado Springs, and I got to talking with him because he was Swiss, and I am Swiss, and we both were from Cincinnati."

About 7:30 that evening, Pell Turner saw Anna Marie in the lobby of his hotel. Two Colorado Springs police detectives had visited him earlier, making inquiries about Obendoerfer and his traveling companion.

"Did you hear that Mr. Obendoerfer was dead?" he asked his guest. Once again Anna Marie professed no interest, stating that the old man was just someone she met by chance on the train.

Anxious now to get out of town, she checked out of the Park Hotel early the next morning and, holding Oscar tightly by the hand, walked to the railroad station across the street and boarded the train to Denver. Just before doing so, however, she checked Obendoerfer's wicker grip at the depot. Inside were a few items of clothing, a pipe, and two salt shakers, one empty and the other containing eighty-two percent arsenic trioxide that she had hidden inside. She certainly never expected local police to recover the bag two weeks later.

When she and Oscar arrived in Denver on the afternoon of August 2, she returned to the Midland Hotel. "How's Mr. Obendoerfer doing?" Straub inquired as she registered.

"Oh, he's getting along nicely," she replied with a smile, knowing full well that Obendoerfer was lying in a mortuary, dead for more than twenty-four hours.

The following morning Oscar and his mother visited the Curtis Jewelry Company, a Denver pawn shop, where she received $7.50 for Mrs. Turner's two diamond rings. She pawned them under the name of "Marie Fisher, Steffens Hotel, Chicago," misspelling the name of the Windy City hotel where she and Oscar stayed thirteen days earlier.

"If anyone ever asks you where we got those rings," Anna Marie told her son, "you say you found them in the street." Oscar nodded.

The pair headed back east, traveling to Chicago on the sleek Burlington Zephyr, and arrived in Cincinnati Monday, August 9. Since she failed to reap a financial bonanza from Obendoerfer, Anna Marie immediately sought new opportunities. The following day she spotted a classified ad in the "Female Help Wanted" columns of the *Cincinnati Times-Star* that called for a white woman, about thirty, to care for an elderly gentleman for $10 a week, but she didn't have time to apply for the position. In the early afternoon there was a knock on her door.

It was the police.

incinnati's acting chief of detectives, Captain Patrick H. Hayes, poked his head into the smoke-filled pressroom at police headquarters, where a few reporters were lounging, waiting for some news of substance.

"Hey, you guys, come on," the burly Hayes said. "I've got a hot one for you."

Three or four journalists assembled around Hayes's desk, hoping for some news to break the boredom of the afternoon. Until then, the day's biggest story for them had been the death of a twenty-three-year-old man who fell asleep at the wheel of his car and crashed into a utility pole. Not much to write about there.

"Here's a real story for you," began Hayes. With obvious excitement, he proceeded to unfold what little he had learned up to that point in what was an exploding investigation of "the Blonde Borgia," a description the press repeatedly would use to describe Anna Marie in the months ahead.[1] His impromptu press conference sent the reporters scrambling for their typewriters and telephones.

From that moment forward, Anna Marie was *the* major news story in Cincinnati for weeks on end, fed by a publicity-hungry police force,

---

1. The name Lucrezia Borgia, an early-sixteenth-century Italian dutchess, became synonymous with female poisoners. Historians have discounted the story, however.

an ambitious district attorney's office, and a highly competitive press corps. Reporters and photographers from across the land tumbled into the Queen City for what one reporter described as "one of the most amazing police cases in the history of the city."

The next nineteen days became the most frantic ever in the annals of Cincinnati homicide investigations. The inquiry began innocently and quietly, then layer after layer was slowly peeled back, like leaves on a cabbage, to reveal a case of multiple murders.

TUESDAY, AUGUST 10

Colorado Springs Detective Inspector Irvin B. Bruce, a dedicated, twenty-five-year law-enforcement veteran, dispatched a routine telegram to Cincinnati police, requesting that Mrs. Anna Hahn be held for questioning in a matter of grand larceny. Mrs. Turner, coproprietor of the Park Hotel, told police that she had found Anna Marie in her private quarters at the hotel and had chased her out. After Anna Marie had checked out, Mrs. Turner noticed that her two diamond rings, valued at $305, were missing from her dresser. Suspecting that her guest had departed with them, she called Colorado Springs police.

Bruce also wanted to question Anna Marie concerning Obendoerfer. His identity initially baffled the local officers; all they had was a body that had been "dropped off" in their city, ostensibly by the same Mrs. Hahn. The man was not from Chicago, they discovered, although he had been registered at the Park Hotel as such. So they telephoned Cincinnati tailor Frank J. Van Alstine, whose clothing label was in the dead man's coat. Yes, he remembered the coat and the customer. It was Obendoerfer.

In Colorado Springs, El Paso County Coroner Dr. J. Thomas Coghlan performed a routine autopsy on Obendoerfer after the Law Mortuary had embalmed the body, draining the stomach in the process. Coghlan wasn't asked to look for poison, so he found no traces of it.

In Cincinnati two neighborhood boys, playing on the roof of the Hahns' one-car garage, watched with fascination as detectives William Sweeney, John Bugganer, and Frank Kammer took Anna Marie into custody shortly after 1 P.M. Incensed, confused, and upset, she called Philip and asked him to return home to be with Oscar when he arrived home from school. What nobody knew then, not even the police, was that Anna Marie had but 484 days to live, every one of them behind bars.

Waiting at headquarters to question this German woman was Captain Hayes, a formidable six-foot-two-inch, 265-pound son of an Irishman, known as an officer whose meaty fists would bloody a nose on occasion. An officer for nearly thirty years, Hayes was of the old school, believing that the end justified the means, even if somebody was roughed up along the way.

When Hayes first laid eyes on Anna Marie, he found her "voluptuous and appealing. . . . I could see how her light-blue eyes seemed so friendly to Wagner and Heis." During a later encounter, he described her face as "cruel [with] a dumb look in her green eyes." Anna Marie had hazel eyes, which might account for the varying color descriptions. In any event, Hayes sized her up as an easy mark for his brand of intimidating questioning. He was wrong.

Several other detectives stood around the boss's desk, providing a gallery of sorts and waiting for the show to begin on the hot, humid afternoon. Hayes pulled his chair closer to the seated Anna Marie and quizzed her about her trip to Colorado. At the time he really knew very little about her and her travels, but experience told him he had hooked a big fish.

Immediately Anna Marie breathed fire, becoming combative, righteously angry and threatening to sue the city for false arrest. It took some minutes for the gentle side of Hayes to calm her down. When he did, he started anew in a softer tone.

"You went to Colorado Springs?"

"Yes."

"Why?"

"Just to have a good time."

"Who did you go with?"

"Nobody. Only my son."

"You're sure about that?"

"Of course!" It didn't take much to fire her up again.

"Do you know this man?" Hayes asked, handing her a "mug shot" of a dead Obendoerfer that had been supplied by Colorado Springs Police Chief Hugh D. Harper.

"Yes. That's Georg Obendoerfer."

"Did you go out West with him?"

"No."

However, she suddenly remembered that she had run into him "accidentally" at the Chicago train station, learned that he was going to Denver, too, and sat with him on the next leg of the journey. "I felt very sorry for him," Anna Marie told Hayes. "He was old and all alone."

Upon arrival in Denver, Anna Marie said she had checked the three of them into the hotel there. When she and Oscar traveled on to Colorado Springs, Obendoerfer went along with them once again. He was to meet relatives there, but they didn't show up. They all checked into a hotel, but Obendoerfer was very sick. "I felt sorry for him," she repeated. "I'm kindhearted that way."

"Did you give him anything that made him sick?" the detective asked.

"Do I look like a woman who would do a thing like that?" she responded indignantly. Hayes thought to himself, no, she didn't, but in his years on the force he had dealt with many deadly criminals who appeared saintly.

"It was just my kindness that got me into all this trouble," Anna Marie insisted. "If you think anything strange happened, tell them to examine Mr. Obendoerfer. They won't find anything."

During the questioning, Homicide's Lieutenant George W. Schattle happened by, saw the attractive woman sitting with Hayes, and asked who she was. The name, Hahn, rang a bell with him, because she, he had learned, had befriended Wagner, whose death two of Schattle's detectives, William Rathman and Frank Kammer, had been investigating since early June.

"I assigned two men to the case," Schattle explained, "but we didn't do anything about it because we didn't have enough information."

Schattle's team did learn from Wagner's neighbors, however, that on June 6, the day after Wagner's burial, Anna Marie vacationed in the Dix Dam region of Kentucky. Also along were Oscar and Anna Marie's new paramour, identified only as Ray, who drove them to Kentucky in his small house trailer. He was a gambler and hazard dealer, who befriended Anna Marie at a Kentucky gambling spot. They took a lakefront cabin at Herrington Lake, Chenault Bridge, Kentucky. While there, she wrote two postcards to Olive Winter, secretary to Dr. Vos. "Having a wonderful time, fishing and swimming. . . . Say hello to the doctor. Love, Mrs. Hahn and Oscar."

Schattle dispatched Detective Walter T. Hart to Kentucky to investigate her movements. Hart learned that a retired automobile dealer, James Theodore Woolridge, had died rather mysteriously at Chenault Bridge while Anna Marie vacationed there. After she had returned to Cincinnati, his body was found in Herrington Lake, twenty feet from her cabin. A boat chain around his neck was fastened to a box containing thirty pounds of rocks. The thought that Anna Marie might have had a hand in Woolridge's death heightened the interest of Schattle's team, but when the local coroner ruled the death a suicide, Cincinnati police ended their probe. However, the few days of pleasure Anna Marie enjoyed with her son and the man called Ray would come back to embarass her at her trial.

While Anna Marie was "fishing and swimming" in Kentucky, Rathman and Kammer were looking into Wagner's death, at the insistence of a few friends, among them Mrs. Propheter and Fritz Grafmeyer. Wagner, a frequent customer at Grafmeyer's popular restaurant at Pleasant and Elder streets, told Grafmeyer that he had been seeing "the blonde," but he denied that Anna Marie was his niece. Because Wagner's illness came on so suddenly and he died so quickly, the restaurateur was convinced Anna Marie had done in his friend. He called the police four times and even turned up at the police station, demanding action. Finally, he got the ear of neighborhood Patrolman John Carroll. He took Grafmeyer back to the police station and introduced him to detectives Richard Crampton and Elmer Zwissler. Believing that the man's story had a ring of truth to it, they passed the case on to Homicide's Schattle for a further look. After a preliminary examination, Rathman told Schattle that "something looked funny."

Schattle then learned that the Hamilton County prosecutor was looking into Wagner's death, too, having received the same citizen's complaint from Grafmeyer. Early in August, Schattle's team had tried to find Anna Marie for questioning, but learned that she was out of town.

Armed now with Schattle's suspicions, too, "the case was breaking in all directions," said Hayes. Police found it difficult to sort the truth from the lies she spun. Anna Marie said she was the widow of a Viennese physician. Not true. She said she had been a schoolteacher. Not true. She claimed to have inherited the Colerain Avenue house from Ernst Kohler. That was true. She admitted to knowing Wagner, Heis, and Obendoerfer. That was true, also, but she denied ever having taken care of them, which was not true.

"My conscience is clear. I never did anything wrong!"

During the questioning about Wagner's death, police found in her white, crocheted purse a crumpled note, in English, that she said Wagner had written. It read, "Feel sorry for Mrs. Hahn. She is not to blame." Only later did the investigators learn that Wagner wrote only in German, not in English. Only later did they learn that the purse they confiscated as a matter of routine when she was jailed would be the single most important piece of evidence at her trial.

After nearly three hours of intense interrogation by Hayes, Anna Marie was locked up for the night in the women's quarters of the county jail, known as the Place of Detention at police headquarters in city hall. Now the police department was high on the excitement of the chase. Hayes assigned as many detectives as he could spare to verify aspects of her story and to follow the many new leads in Colorado and in Cincinnati. After dinner, Hayes himself and Detective Stanley Grause returned to Anna Marie's home for another look around and to talk to Oscar. It already had been decided that the boy would stay with Philip's parents for as long as Anna Marie was in custody.

The police also had citizens come to the police headquarters to identify Anna Marie. Among the early arrivals was Obendoerfer's daughter, Mrs. Nau, who had met Anna Marie briefly. Mrs. Nau arrived at headquarters "uninvited" to express her concerns about her father's death in Colorado Springs. Subsequently, she was joined by her sister, Rose Davis of Carthage, Ohio, and her brother, George Obendorfer, a compositor from St. Louis who had slightly altered the spelling of the family name. Two elderly neighbors of Obendoerfer's also came to Central Station. They said they saw the same woman and a young boy visit the friendly shoemaker on several occasions.

Late in that first day, Cincinnati Police Chief Eugene T. Weatherly sent a telegram to Inspector Bruce in Colorado Springs, confirming that Anna Marie knew Obendoerfer well. "We have Anna Hahn solidly with the George [*sic*] Obendoerfer case if you can find any trace of these poisons [arsenic and dysenteric oil] in his body. She admits feeding him in hotel opposite depot and after eating he became very sick."

Armed with this new information, Bruce immediately asked coroner Coghlan for an "exhaustive" chemical analysis of Obendoerfer's organs to determine whether he had been poisoned. Lacking burial instructions from a family member, Obendoerfer rested still at the mortuary.

WEDNESDAY, AUGUST 11

Anna Marie was in custody for but a few hours when Heis learned of her arrest. He called police Tuesday afternoon and unfolded his story of the love-hate relationship he had with her. The following day police sent three officers in a squad car to pick up the man who became known throughout Cincinnati as "the living victim." When they arrived at police headquarters, Heis was unshaven, gaunt, and so feeble that he remained in the back seat of the police car while shakily signing a warrant for the arrest of his former sweetheart, charging her with grand larceny. He said she stole from him $140 in cash and a $75 diamond ring.

Hamilton County District Attorney Dudley Miller Outcalt and his staff questioned Anna Marie in the morning while Detectives Hart and William B. Burks went to the home of Philip's parents to bring in Oscar for questioning. Philip, on his way to work, was initially questioned at home. He told the officers he knew nothing about his wife's trip to Colorado until he came home and found her note on the kitchen table. He then admitted that he and Anna Marie had fought over the bottle of poison that Oscar found. Phillip told police he had secreted the bottle in a cigar box in his locker at Western Union. Hayes demanded the bottle.

"I intended to turn it over to the police," Philip insisted, "in case anything happened." At that point, he said nothing about his suspicions that his wife had poisoned him with croton oil several years before. Hayes and Sergeant Harry Tobertge accompanied Philip to

Western Union's office at Fourth and Walnut streets, where they took possession of the bottle.

The discovery of that bottle of croton oil added yet another twist to an already complex investigation. "If it turns out that croton oil has been the cause of these deaths and illnesses," a fired-up Outcalt told the press, "we will know that the person administering it was one of the cleverest we ever have had to deal with. Croton oil is the one poison that is not included in the standard lists for autopsy. Its presence would be entirely overlooked in ordinary autopsies."

Oscar's questioning went well for police but not for his mother. The boy lied a lot, but several times Hayes caught him at it. For instance, Oscar denied knowing anything about stolen rings.

"Now look here, son," Hayes said. "There's no use lying to us about this. We already know that your mother took you to a pawnshop, didn't she?"

"Yes, but she didn't steal them. We were walking along, and I found a ring on the sidewalk and gave it to her."

Oscar told Hayes that he and his mother had met Obendoerfer in Chicago. "We rode on different coaches to Chicago. We were not together." Hayes called the boy's bluff.

"Sonny, you are too young to start lying. We know all about that, too. Your mother bought the tickets for all three of you right here in Cincinnati, didn't she?"

"That's right," Oscar replied, but then tried to salvage something by stating that he and his mother rode to Chicago in a separate coach from Obendoerfer. On the way to Colorado, the old man ate some sandwiches with them and drank a lot of water, Oscar said.

Oscar's responses were taken to the prosecutor's office, where Anna Marie then admitted to having left Cincinnati with Obendoerfer and to finding two rings in the street.

In the afternoon Detectives Hayes, Burks, and Hart and *Cincinnati Post* reporter Charles Rentrop accompanied Anna Marie to her home. During the short ride in the police car, there was casual conversation until Hart popped an unexpected question.

"Did you kill these old men by screwing them?"

Rentrop sucked air. Burks and Hart smiled. Hayes laughed. Anna Marie flushed in anger. "Don't talk to me like that!" she said, then muttered under her breath, "*Schwein!*" (pig).

When they arrived at Anna Marie's home, Hayes told the reporter to remain outside while, with Anna Marie's permission, the three detectives searched her rooms in the rear of the house. As Hayes headed for the basement door, Anna Marie "became visibly excited," he recalled.

"What do you want down there?" she asked. "There's nothing down there."

Anna Marie remained at the head of the cellar steps, watching intently, nervously, as Hayes rummaged through the basement, his flashlight peering into the darkest corners. He searched the rafters, too, and discovered, "tucked away," a four-ounce bottle missing its cork stopper and containing about one-quarter inch of "a white powdery substance."

"What do you want that thing for?" she demanded, shaking visibly, her face flushed. "That's probably just an old bottle my son brought in from somewhere. Give it to me!"

Hayes could not help but notice Anna Marie's mounting anger. When he refused her repeated demands for the bottle, "Why, she almost went into a dance," he recalled. Hayes knew he had touched a nerve and enjoyed Anna Marie's discomfort. He held on to the bottle and later handed it to Burks to hold as evidence.

Upon her return to jail, she underwent more questioning. For more than three hours, Schattle, Hart, and Burks probed for truthful answers from Anna Marie, who often skirted the facts. She remained stoic, maintaining her innocence. "I love old people. I would not be the cause of any harm to them," she said. "It is strange that when I am trying to help them these things should happen. It's what I get for trying to be helpful."

Immigration and Naturalization Service agents also took a few minutes to question the suspect. Fresh in many minds was the name Bruno Richard Hauptmann, the German illegal immigrant executed in 1936 for the 1932 kidnapping and death of Charles A. Lindbergh's infant son. Within days, though, the INS determined that Anna Marie had entered the country legally.

Detectives Kammer and Bugganer visited the Clifton Heights Loan and Building Company and recovered the letter Anna Marie wrote from Denver to Harry H. Becker, director of the bank. Also, acting on a tip from Hayes, Sergeant Robert Wraith of the Colorado Springs police recovered at a Denver pawnshop Mrs. Turner's two diamond rings that he said had been pawned by Anna Marie for $7.50. (She had tried to pawn them before leaving Colorado Springs, but she wasn't offered enough money for them.)

At the request of Colorado Springs police, fugitive warrants—charging larceny and murder—were filed against Anna Marie late Wednesday by Detective Hart. Given the developments in the investigation in Cincinnati, there appeared little chance that she ever would be returned to Colorado for prosecution, but the warrants ensured that she would remain in custody while the investigation continued.

Sensing that Anna Marie—and perhaps he, too—was in a pack of trouble, Philip retained the Cincinnati law firm of Bolsinger & Hoodin. Hiram C. Bolsinger Sr., the senior member of the small firm in the downtown Fountain Square Building, had been the Hahns' attorney for several years, handling civil matters for the family. In 1935, he took Joseph H. Hoodin, then twenty-six, into Bolsinger, Hoodin & Freiden, which became Bolsinger & Hoodin about a year later. Neither attorney had ever handled a serious criminal case, much less one that would evolve into capital murder.

THURSDAY, AUGUST 12

The name of another elderly German widower surfaced in the investigation, that of George Gsellman. The body had been in the mortuary since July 6, waiting for family to claim it. When nobody did, the Anatomical Society of the School of Medicine in Cincinnati picked it up August 3 because, as Hamilton County Coroner Dr. Frank M. Coppock Jr. said, the morgue was "packed full." The was returned, untouched, a week later and finally, this day, taken to the Baltimore Hill Cemetery and buried within a hundred feet of the open grave where Wagner's body had been exhumed twelve days earlier.

Gsellman's burial coincided almost to the hour with a visit to police headquarters of Richard C. Uible, attorney for the Gsellman estate. He had learned, he said, that his client had known Anna Marie, whose name now was on the front page of every Cincinnati newspaper every day.

Outcalt could not believe what he was hearing. Another death associated with Anna Marie? He immediately ordered Gsellman exhumed, an easy task for Ferdinand Reinhardt, cemetery sexton, and his assistant, Joseph Yates, inasmuch as the grave had been only partially filled in hours before the exhumation order arrived.

Investigators returned once again to the Over-the-Rhine neighborhood and found Gsellman's friend and neighbor August Schultz. He was brought in to identify the suspect. When he saw Anna Marie in Hayes's office, he pointed his finger at her and cried out, "You are the woman! I know you by your looks and your voice!"

"I am not!" Anna Marie shouted back. "You lie! I never knew the man!"

Schultz told police about having seen Anna Marie take a sick Gsellman to a hallway bathroom several times on the night of July 5. Schattle later questioned Anna Marie in her cell, but again she denied knowing Gsellman.

"Can you tell me, Anna, how many old men and women you knew who have died suddenly?"

"Yes. There was Wagner, Palmer, Kohler, Obendoerfer, and my uncle, Osswald, and Mrs. Koehler." At the time, Mrs. Koehler was still in Longview State Hospital in critical condition. Schattle missed the discrepancy or chose to overlook it. In Anna Marie's mind, though, Mrs. Koehler was toast.

"Didn't you know Mr. Gsellman, too?"

"I did not, and if that man [Schultz] said he saw me at his home, he lied. I never knew the man. Why don't they say I killed *all* the old men who died in Cincinnati? Can't you believe me?"

The unspoken answer was no.

Hayes questioned her anew about the purchase of poison. Once again Anna Marie was combative. She now hated Hayes for not giving her the bottle he found in her basement, for laughing at Hart's vile remark the day before, and for making the last two days the most miserable she had ever spent on earth.

Hayes pressed forward. "Where did you buy the bottle of croton oil?"

"I don't know. I won't tell you. I don't know anything about it. If you know so much, why don't you tell me?"

"We have the bottle."

"Keep on trying. You'll find out where it came from."

"We are going to keep you here until we do find out."

"Me? You can keep me here five months, and I won't tell you I did things I didn't do."

"You are pretty smart, aren't you?"

"I've got a brain as big as this room," she said smugly, spreading her arms wide. Hayes decided to wait another day. As Eugene Segal of the *Cincinnati Post* reported, by now the police knew "they were dealing with either one of the most appalling cases of murder-for-profit in criminal annals or a remarkable instance of coincidental deaths."

FRIDAY, AUGUST 13

"Friday the thirteenth. Thirteen is my lucky number," Anna Marie commented to a reporter.

It certainly was an unusual day at police headquarters. The investigators and the press took turns questioning Anna Marie and occasionally interrogated her at the same time. She also gave her first exclusive, one-on-one interview to Alfred Segal of the *Post*.[2] "Once she must have been very good looking and even today she seems not unattractive," Segal wrote.[3] He described her as "baffling. The police don't know what to make of her. She disarms inquisitors with smiles."

"Were these old gentleman interested in you?" the journalist inquired, as delicately as possible.

"She laughed," he wrote in the newspaper the next day. "'They tell me that Mr. Obendoerfer is supposed to have said that I was a new woman of his. That is to laugh. I should be interested in a man like him! He was such a stupid old man.'"

---

2. Alfred and Eugene Segal, reporters for the *Cincinnati Post*, were brothers.

3. Alfred Segal, "Kindness Brought Her Trouble, Blond Tells Writer," *Cincinnati Post*, Aug. 13, 1937, 1.

She told Segal it was her "duty" to see that some of her acquaintances—namely Wagner, Kohler, and Osswald—received decent burials. "'It's the least you can do for people, isn't it?'"

While Anna Marie was with Segal, Outcalt questioned Philip, who said he knew only Kohler, whose home Anna Marie inherited, and the "living victim," Heis. "I liked them as well as she did," the nervous husband said. "If you knew her as I know her—gentle, generous, and motherly—you would understand how impossible it would be for her to murder anybody."

With Bolsinger standing at her side and here and there directing her not to respond to a question, Anna Marie calmly endured another grilling from press and police alike. There were questions about her upbringing in Germany; her secret marriage to a Viennese physician; and about Obendoerfer, who, she said, "insisted" on going to Colorado. "I didn't want him along," Anna Marie asserted.

Why, Sergeant Tobertge wanted to know, did she deny knowing the old man or where he was from?

"I had so much trouble with him on the trip," the prisoner replied. "I didn't want to be bothered [with him]."

"You knew he was from Cincinnati. Why didn't you give the hospital the address?"

"I thought he had no relatives, so I didn't bother."

"Please believe me," she pleaded. "I have done nothing wrong. . . . I have nothing to fear. If I am in trouble it is because of my goodness to old people. I am so bighearted."

"Mrs. Hahn, you want us to believe everything you say, but you won't explain the presence of that bottle in your home."

"That bottle! That's for you to find out. You found the bottle. Now you find out about it."

Later in the day, Hayes got another shot at his personal punching bag, hoping to determine the origin of the bottle of croton oil. With a light tan fedora—"me hat me father wore," he would say in a thick brogue—pushed back on his head and black suspenders holding up pants that looked slept in, the jacketless detective sat down beside her in her cell. Once again Bolsinger stood nearby.

Incredible as it sounds today, Hayes lulled Anna Marie into admitting that she bought the poison by softly crooning an old Irish ditty about a mother's love for a child.

> Oft times in dreams I wander to that cot again,
> I can feel her arms a-hugging as when she held me then.
> I can hear her voice a-humming to me as in days of yore,
> 'Twas then she rocked me fast asleep outside the cabin door.

The "iron maiden" turned to mush. The song truly touched a cold heart, perhaps flooding Anna Marie's head with thoughts of her mother in Germany or of her son. After conferring briefly with Bolsinger, she finally gave her first explanation of "the bottle."

"I tell you, captain," she began, tears welling up in her eyes. "I bought it. I bought it in either June or July of last year. I got it from Mr. Deming in North College Hill. I remember I had been out in Elmwood. I had won some money. I went over to College Hill. I gave the druggist a dollar bill for the bottle, and he gave me some change."

Tobertge immediately paid a visit to Deming, who confirmed that Anna Marie had acquired croton oil there, although he could not recall the date accurately. No matter. Both Anna Marie and investigators confirmed that it was July 1936.

In a surprise move, Bolsinger and Hoodin filed a writ of habeas corpus, hoping to get their client released from custody, but Judge Louis J. Schneider denied the writ. Joining him on the bench for the Court of Common Pleas hearing was Judge Charles Steele Bell, who would conduct the Hahn trial. Cincinnati police countered the defense swiftly with a warrant charging her with the murder of Gsellman after Cincinnati City Chemist Dr. Otto P. Behrer discovered in the deceased a "metallic substance," probably arsenic, and traces of yet a second poison, perhaps croton oil. Five days later, though, Behrer determined that no croton oil was present in Gsellman's body.

"This makes our case," declared Outcalt, but a confident, smiling, beautifully coifed Anna Marie had a different view. For the first time she posed for the news cameramen as she sat in the office of Sheriff George J. Lutz, waiting for the writ hearing to begin.

"Come on, boys. Take all the photographs you want," she said cheerfully. "This is one case I am going to win, I'll tell you that. I am not guilty. I can face anything there is to come."

After the hearing, as she returned to her cell in the custody of Chief Deputy Sheriff George J. Heitzler and Deputy Sheriff Raymond B. Kies, the photographers asked Philip to pose with his wife. He was willing, but Hoodin wouldn't allow it. Already the rocky state of the Hahn marriage was becoming obvious.

SATURDAY, AUGUST 14

After four days, police and investigators for the prosecutor's office were exhausted. What began as a simple case of grand larceny in Colorado now had multiple leads, sapping the strength of the investigators. "It's hard to tell where this thing will stop," said Outcalt, who claimed to already have on his hands "one of the biggest mass murders in the country." He sent out a public appeal for help, asking citizens "anywhere having knowledge of mysterious deaths to communicate with me."

Lieutenant Schattle, who had enjoyed very little sleep since the case broke, believed the police faced "the biggest fortune-hunting case ever to develop in Cincinnati and possibly in the United States." At the time, it was thought Anna Marie had acquired as much as $70,000 ($946,000 in 2005) from her victims, but the total proved to be somewhat less.

Hayes questioned Anna Marie about Gsellman yet again. Once more she denied she knew the man.

"Isn't it peculiar that all the old people you were friendly with died of dysentery a short time later?" Hayes asked.

"I know it looks bad for me," she admitted, "but I didn't do anything."

As each hour passed, her situation looked more grave. She was arraigned before Municipal Judge Clarence E. Spraul on a charge of murder in connection with Gsellman's death and on the charge of larceny that Heis had filed. After the arraignment, her custodians allowed Anna Marie to spend a few moments with Oscar. The pair cried as they kissed and hugged each other. "Son, don't you believe all those things about me," she said, holding her son's face in her hands and looking deep into his eyes. He shook his head. "I won't."

Assistant Prosecutor Gordon H. Scherer departed for Washington and the Federal Bureau of Investigation with samples of Anna Marie's handwriting for analysis. Police sent photographs and fingerprints to authorities in Bavaria.

SUNDAY, AUGUST 15

The day began with Anna Marie attending the nondenominational jailhouse service. She requested the hymn, "I'll Go Where You Want Me to Go," written by Homer Rodeheaver, the organist for evangelist Billy Sunday. Her request was not fulfilled.

Associated Press reporter Paul Mason won permission to interview the prisoner in jail while she reluctantly ate a breakfast of eggs and potatoes. She did so with the only utensil allowed, a spoon, which she complained was dirty. It was rewashed. Sheriff Heitzler sat at her side, listening, as Anna Marie spoke freely of her dreams and ambitions.

One ambition of hers was "to have enough money to take care of the poor and the children. . . . One thing: It took me a long, long time to find out that it is wrong to be good to people—that it doesn't pay to be good to them. This doesn't mean I am going to be hateful from now on, because that is against my nature.

"Down in my heart and in my mind, I know I am innocent of this terrible crime. There may be more people on the outside who are guilty of crimes like I am accused of than there is are in here. Why don't they go out and find the real criminals?

"They can take a human's body, but they can't take their soul, because that will go where there is justice.

"All of this [jail] is kind of hard to take, even though it's nice in here and the matrons treat you wonderfully, but it doesn't take much to throw someone innocent into the gutter. It seems when one is in trouble, everybody is against them."

Hayes kept his name in the newspapers, too, by reporting his every move to journalists. This day he teased them by displaying a small, cardboard box labeled "Poison," but revealed nothing about its importance to the investigation other than it contained pills. The police captain did say that he had evidence that Anna Marie had bought "enough poison to kill half the town" and that she had sent Oscar to a drug store for a poison. The pharmacist refused to sell it to the boy, Hayes said, because Oscar was underage.

Later Hayes referred to the death of Ernest Kohler, who died May 3, 1933, shortly after taking up with Anna Marie. "Mrs. Hahn administered enough morphine to Kohler to kill a dozen persons, all within a few days," Hayes told reporters.

MONDAY, AUGUST 16

Fifteen members of the Hamilton County grand jury listened to Outcalt describe Anna Marie again as "the biggest mass murderer in history." After hearing evidence for less than an hour, the panel returned two indictments against her for the "malicious and premeditated" murders of Wagner and Gsellman. Arraignment was set for Wednesday morning in Judge Bell's court.

At 10:30 A.M. the tall and handsome Sheriff Lutz served Anna Marie the grand jury papers in her county jail cell. Everyone, including Hoodin and Bolsinger, reenacted the service for photographers while standing outside her cell. Anna Marie's fetching smile was missing in the published photographs.

A couple of hours later, more trouble for Anna Marie. Lieutenant Schattle and Assistant Prosecutor Frank M. Gusweiler Jr. revealed that through an unnamed neighbor and friend they had linked her to the illness of another old woman, Mrs. Julia Kresckay, now in Budapest, Hungary.

The Hahn case already had captured the attention of newspapers from New York to California. Now interest was spreading overseas. In the evening Hayes received a radio-telephone call from Gilbert Carter, a reporter for the *London Daily Herald.* He wanted to know if Anna Marie had confessed, and he sought an accounting of the investigation to date. The detective was only too happy to provide all the details of the case, which was, Carter said, "such a big thing" in England.

Such attention did not sit well with everyone. A citizen identified only as "E.G.T." complained to *Cincinnati Post* columnist Alfred Segal (known as "Cincinnatus") that the Hahn case overshadowed current world news, such as the Japanese bombing of Shanghai and the slaughter of thousands there during the Chinese-Japanese War that was raging at the time.

Segal wrote, "'And yet, to the newspapers of Cincinnati what was the most important news?' asks E.G.T. 'Oh,' he snorts, 'Mrs. Hahn had the big headlines; Shanghai was one of the day's lesser incidents. In our newspapers the alleged doings of Mrs. Hahn were of more significance than a world event.

"'Even if Mrs. Hahn had put croton oil in the soup of a dozen old men, would it have been bigger news than bombs thrown on the heads of innocents in Shanghai?' inquires E.G.T."[4]

The Hahn case attracted all kinds. Among them were the trial watchers, who intended to be in the courtroom when and if Anna Marie was prosecuted. Charles Jacobs, bailiff to Judge Bell, took a call from a woman who requested that she be assigned "a good seat" during the entire trial.

"I told her she would have to take her chances, like any other citizen," Jacobs said. "However, she was insistent. She told me that if I would make the arrangements, she would 'make it all right' with me. I hung up."

With the demand for seats building, even for the preliminary hearings on the case, Judge Bell arranged to use the courtroom of fellow judge Nelson Schwab. It was the largest courtroom in the county and almost twice as large as Judge Bell's.

Telegrams and calls also came into the offices of Cincinnati authorities from "experts," who offered a variety of services, such as handwriting analysis. One wire came from Arthur P. Myers of Baltimore, Maryland, who was one of the handwriting experts the prosecution employed in the Bruno Richard Hauptmann trial.

Few noted that the old cobbler, Obendoerfer, was buried in Evergreen Cemetery in Colorado Springs this day, far from home. The family spoke of transferring the body to Cincinnati, but it was never done. He rests for eternity in a place he never knew.

4. Segal, "Cincinnatus," *Cincinnati Post*, Aug. 17, 1937, 8.

TUESDAY, AUGUST 17

Anna Marie received even more bad news from police. Another one of her "patients" died. Mrs. Koehler succumbed the night before at the Longview State Hospital, where she had been since July 10. The press reported her death as the twelfth linked to Anna Marie, but how they arrived at a deadly dozen never was spelled out by name or dates. Investigators admitted they were looking into eleven deaths, but the names of victims were being withheld "for purposes of the investigation," Schattle said.

As soon as she learned of her sister's death, Mrs. Arnold, accompanied by Mrs. Propheter, headed for the police station, dressed in a house frock, slippers, rolled-down hose, and a crocheted shawl. She couldn't wait to tell her story to police. "I believe my sister was poisoned by Mrs. Hahn," she told them in a frail, wispy voice.

Assistant Prosecutor Scherer returned from his trip to the FBI offices in Washington and told the press that three different and independent FBI examinations of the documents submitted, including Wagner's will, determined that it was Anna Marie's handwriting on each of them.

George Elliston, whose first name often fooled readers of the *Cincinnati Times-Star* into believing she was a male reporter, was in on a jail-cell interview, one that Anna Marie at first refused to give. Then she relented, offering her "life's story," except for details of her love affair with a Viennese physician that led to the birth of her son, Oscar. "I wanted to forget everything of that but my son," the accused told Elliston.

Anna Marie proudly said she "knitted pretty good" before she became a teenager, making things for her five brothers—George, Hans, Max, Fritz, and Franz—who served in the German army during World War I. She also denied a newspaper report that her mother had died.

"In all this trouble, my thoughts are mostly with her," she told Elliston and other reporters. "She will not believe these terrible charges against me. She cannot believe them, knowing me. I am more worried about her than about myself. If anything happens to her . . . it will kill me."

The interview came to an abrupt end when one reporter said Anna Marie had imparted very little information.

"Well! I will not talk any more. . . . I won't say any more, and I won't stand for having my picture taken again!"

Two days later Anna Marie sent her mother a cable. "Don't worry about me," she said. "I am innocent. That is all that counts. Pray for me."

WEDNESDAY, AUGUST 18

By 9 A.M. the courtroom was absolutely packed for Anna Marie's arraignment before Judge Bell on the Wagner and Gsellman indictments. One estimate had 250 in attendance, which would be pushing out the walls. Even the jury box was filled with spectators, who stormed into the courthouse when it opened at 6:45 A.M. In the courtroom, onlooking women outnumbered the men ten to one, and their chattering created a constant buzz that reached a crescendo when the defendant entered, led to the defense table by Sheriff Heitzler and Criminal Court Bailiff Charles Stagnaro.

"Did you sleep well?" Heitzler asked, just to pass the time of day.

"No," she replied. "It was too hot."

"Well, compose yourself," he said.

"I am all right. I have nothing to fear."

When she took her seat, the chair all but swallowed her. Just her head topped the back of the chair, which is all most spectators saw of her. As she sat down, she straightened her navy blue, lace-trimmed dress with its wide, pink piqué collar and gazed neither to the right nor the left. She had worn the same dress and a large white gold crucifix—a 1936 Christmas gift from Philip—around her neck every day since her arrest eight days earlier. Hoodin soon arranged through Philip to get her a fresh frock or two.

Oscar and Philip entered the courtroom through the side door, and once again the boy ran into his mother's arms. As flashbulbs popped, they hugged and kissed and tears came to her eyes, as they did for a number of the mothers watching the touching scene. A portly lady seated in the front row of benches sobbed louder than the rest. A few women near the rear of the room stood on the bench seats to get a better view, but Stagnaro quickly ordered them down. When Judge Bell entered and took the bench, he gaveled everyone into silence.

"Quiet must be kept in this courtroom, or I'll have it cleared," he said sternly.

Bolsinger, Hoodin, and Anna Marie rose and stood before the judge. She cast her eyes downward and steadied herself by placing her well-manicured hands on the brass rail that ran in front of the bench. Judge Bell, who never allowed trial attorneys, defendants, or plaintiffs to touch the bar, chose this day to ignore Anna Marie's indiscretion. When it came time, Hoodin entered her plea of "not guilty" to the two murder charges.

Hoodin said his client would seek a change of venue, especially in view of the prosecution's effort to try its case in the newspapers. He also charged the state's attorney with hiding the facts from the defense.

"I don't know what counsel is talking about," replied Assistant County Prosecutor Simon Leis. Judge Bell told Hoodin to file written motions concerning such matters, which would be heard Friday. Leis announced the state was ready for trial.

The press interviewed a number of spectators after the proceedings. "I am German and I couldn't believe a German woman could do the things she stands accused of," said one woman from Westwood. Another spectator described Anna Marie as "pretty, downright pretty," but a third said, "She doesn't look like much." A fourth, seeing Anna Marie in the flesh for the first time, believed "she could never have done all the things they claim she did." Anna Marie certainly had the sympathy of most of the female spectators, Elliston thought.

THURSDAY, AUGUST 19
For days Anna Marie repeatedly denied that she ever knew Gsellman. But investigators knew and Anna Marie didn't what was found in Gsellman's room the evening of August 13. The police already had been through the room, but reporter Charles Ludwig and photographer Peter Koch, both of the *Cincinnati Times-Star*, visited the room with Richard C. Uible, attorney for the Gsellman estate.

While pouring over a disorderly pile of personal papers, Ludwig came across a plain envelope, inside of which was a College Hill streetcar pass dated July 5, 1937, the day before Gsellman died. On the back was written, "Go home. I'll be there." There was no signature. The evidence was turned over to the district attorney's office with the understanding that it would be kept under wraps until more evidence could be gathered.

Anna Marie said she first met Gsellman at her "Uncle Charlie" Osswald's funeral in August 1935. At that time, according to Anna Marie, Gsellman promised he would pay her $314 he had borrowed from Osswald.

Captain Hayes revealed that he had recovered in Anna Marie's home a small-caliber automatic pistol. As it turned out, the "weapon" was but Oscar's toy cap gun.

From Washington, FBI director J. Edgar Hoover declared the Hahn case "purely a local matter." His comment came in response to a suggestion by Colorado Springs District Attorney Clyde L. Starrett that the case could be pursued on the federal level under the provisions of the 1932 Lindbergh kidnapping law inasmuch as Anna Marie had brought Obendoerfer to Colorado.

FRIDAY, AUGUST 20

Judge Bell was not happy. Not only was it hot and stuffy in the large courtroom, but at the morning hearing, on a variety of defense motions, the prosecution and the defense engaged in acrimonious argument that tried the judge's patience. Hoodin was most vociferous, charging Outcalt's staff with blocking defense access to witnesses and withholding evidence. He even took the witness stand to give specifics of his charge, stating that Outcalt had told him that he would receive the records "when he got damn well and ready." Assistant Prosecutor Leis denied all of Hoodin's allegations.

"If the prosecutor is guilty of hampering the defendant, on trial for her life, it is a very serious [charge] and the court could not lightly lay it aside," the jurist said. "On the other hand, if such a charge is being made without evidence, then the prosecutor is being done a serious injury."

Each side claimed that the other was attempting to try the case in the press. Judge Bell gave the attorneys fair warning: "When this case comes to trial, I can assure you, if it is necessary, that the case will *not* be tried in the newspapers."

Anna Marie—neatly attired in a dress of brown net over brown silk and trimmed in white on the collar, cuffs, and pockets—sat through it all with seeming indifference, cooling herself with a small fan given to her by Philip, who sat just behind her. Later Anna Marie expressed disgust with a few of the spectators, who clapped whenever the prosecution won a legal point.

"It seemed strange to be there," she said of the court session. "I wondered if this were me, but the people were real enough. The judge in his white suit and blue tie. Faces and faces and faces peering at me, like I am some ogre. Mr. Hoodin making a plea that my boy be kept out of this, that was the finest thing of all the morning."

During the day, Cincinnati police chief Weatherly received an official report from Colorado Springs that Denver toxicologist Dr. Frances McConnell had detected arsenic in Obendoerfer's kidneys and liver. Weatherly added the report to the mounting evidence against Anna Marie.

SATURDAY, AUGUST 21

The investigation into Anna Marie's activities and Obendoerfer's death continued. Carson T. Hoy, an assistant prosecutor in Outcalt's office, began an odyssey by air that retraced Anna Marie's train trip to Colorado. His first stop was Chicago. Before he left, he told the press that the state would demand the death penalty in the Cincinnati case.

While Hoy was on the road, Anna Marie and her defense counsel made another appearance in municipal court, this day for a routine request for a speedy arraignment on the minor grand larceny charges filed by Mrs. Turner and Heis. Actually, Hoodin expressed hope that both charges would be dismissed, given that his client had been arraigned on the more serious charges of murder, but Judge A. L. Luebbers refused to take any action, much to the satisfaction of Assistant Prosecutor Loyal S. Martin. Luebbers continued the grand larceny cases indefinitely.

After only a few minutes in court, Anna Marie, looking tired and wan, was returned to the county jail in a patrol wagon. For the first time, she appeared truly depressed. She would become even more depressed upon learning what her brothers in Fuessen were saying about her.

The Filser family received Anna Marie's telegram but kept it from her sixty-nine-year-old mother, who still had not been told that her youngest had been charged with murder. "If she knew, it would kill her," said one of the five brothers. "Annie was mother's pet." He told an Associated Press reporter that no member of the family would travel to Cincinnati, because a trip to America "cost too much." Then he added: "We are uninterested."

"I can't believe my brothers made such a statement!" Anna Marie said from jail. "They always have been kind and loving, and my sister and I have always loved each other with more than the usual love of sisters."

SUNDAY, AUGUST 22

The body of Mrs. Olive Koehler, who had died three days earlier, was cremated. The results of an examination of her viscera for poison revealed "no lethal quantity" of arsenic, Dr. Behrer reported, but the finding was not unexpected. Mrs. Koehler had been ill for two months prior to her death, and any poison she may have ingested would have dissipated in that time.

While Mrs. Koehler's remains were being turned into ashes, Anna Marie was singing. She participated in the Sunday service held in the jail by its jail chaplain, Reverend Alexander Patterson. At her request, he added to the service the hymn "Mother's Prayers Have Followed Me."

> I'm coming home, I'm coming home,
> To live my wasted life anew.
> For my mother's prayers have followed me
> The whole world through.

The service, which was broadcast on the radio, drew an unusually large number of worshippers. Suspecting that they were there to commune with Anna Marie rather than the Lord, jail officials refused to admit them. By the same token, virtually every visitor to the jail made a point of stopping by Anna Marie's cell, a practice her jailers had to restrict.

MONDAY, AUGUST 23

Women once again jammed Judge Bell's courtroom to observe Anna Marie facing justice. Two ladies anxious to get a seat in the first row began the line outside the courtroom door at 6:30 A.M. and waited there nearly eight hours before being admitted for the afternoon hearing.

What they heard was a lot of legal wrangling over whether the prosecution had hampered the defense in its attempt to obtain statements and other documents, causing Anna Marie's attorneys "as much inconvenience as possible," Hoodin charged. However, after listening to the arguments all afternoon, Judge Bell sided with the prosecution. "From the evidence submitted, the court must conclude that neither the prosecuting attorney nor any of his assistants has in any way hampered the administration of justice in this case."

Anna Marie, wearing the same brown dress she had worn the day before, sat quietly throughout the afternoon session. At times she even looked bored.

Hoy, retracing the accused's trip, arrived in Denver and met with Denver toxicologist McConnell, among others. She told him she had found lethal quantities of arsenic in Obendoerfer's brain, kidney, and liver. Hoy told the local press, "If we fail to win the death penalty in this case, we are prepared to turn Mrs. Hahn over to Colorado," where the investigation began. Upon hearing of his arrival, Anna Marie responded to a reporter's question.

"They've gone out west now to see what they can learn," she said, fingering the cross hanging from her neck. "I have my faith. I have told the truth. There is nothing greater than the truth. They'll never get a confession out of me, because I can't confess to something I never did. But I suppose the death of anyone past sixty anywhere in the country now will be laid to me."

TUESDAY, AUGUST 24

Sergeant Tobertge filed the formal homicide report, charging Anna Marie with having administered arsenic to Wagner and causing the old gardener's death June 3. Detective Hart left Cincinnati on his second trip to Harrodsburg, Kentucky, armed this time with photographs of Anna Marie. The district attorney's office wanted positive identification from those she came into contact with there.

It also was the day her steadfast denial of knowing Gsellman unraveled completely, much to the amusement of Cincinnati police.

"Of course she knew [Gsellman]," Hoodin told the press, "and she never told anybody otherwise." It was damage control at its finest. "If Captain Hayes said she denied being acquainted with Mr. Gsellman, he was placing his own interpretation on irrelevant statements she might have made after hours of questioning."

What triggered the turnaround by the defense was an FBI report that confirmed that Anna Marie's handwriting matched that of the person who wrote, "Go home. I'll be there" on the streetcar transfer found in Gsellman's room after his death.

That night Anna Marie heard on the radio in her cell that she was "breaking down." "I certainly am not breaking down," she said, stamping her foot.

WEDNESDAY, AUGUST 25

Assistant Prosecutor Scherer left on a second trip to FBI headquarters in Washington to confer with handwriting experts there. He took with him Wagner's will and other documents bearing Anna Marie's handwriting. The will had special importance to the prosecution: if the defendant forged it, as the prosecution believed, a motive would be established in the Wagner case.

THURSDAY, AUGUST 26

Armed with investigative reports from Chicago, Denver, and Colorado Springs, Hoy returned to Cincinnati to prepare for trial. Anna Marie never would be charged with Obendoerfer's death, but the peripatetic case would play an important role in her trial.

Leaving no stone unturned, the police examined list after list of those who died in and around Cincinnati during May and June. They sought the names of anyone who may have come into contact with Anna Marie.

FRIDAY, AUGUST 27

"Mrs. Hahn wants this case heard as soon as possible," Hoodin told Judge Bell. The state had intended to proceed with the Gsellman case first, but the court allowed the prosecution to reverse the order. Outcalt believed that having Wagner's forged will made a stronger case, because it provided a solid motive for the crime. Also, Assistant Prosecutor Leis said the state possessed "new evidence" in the Wagner case.

"We, too, have some newly discovered evidence," Hoodin countered.

Both sides wrangled for days over the validity of the chemical analysis of Wagner's viscera, so Judge Bell appointed Frank C. Broeman & Company, consulting chemists, to make an independent analysis of internal organs previously examined by Cincinnati's chemist, Dr. Behrer. "You are to report to the court personally," the judge told Broeman. "This report is not to be sent or shown to anyone else."

SATURDAY, AUGUST 28

Following a brief hearing on final motions, Judge Bell established the date for the beginning of the trial and ordered that the names of seventy-five veniremen be drawn from the criminal court jury wheel. Forty-one of them were women.

"The defendant in this case is indicted for the most serious offense under the law," he said. "This is a rather unusual case, with my very slight knowledge of it, inasmuch as the indictment charges the administration of poison. Unless some good reason is shown, I am setting the trial date for October 11."

"I don't care if [the trial] starts tomorrow," a defiant Anna Marie told the court bailiff as she was led back to the jail.

7 | TRIALS AND TRIBULATIONS

A fter nearly fifteen years of service in the office of the district attorney, Dudley Miller Outcalt had earned plaudits from courthouse
veterans as one of the ablest of Hamilton County prosecutors.

Tough, commanding, and forceful, he loved the chase and the
victory. That was reflected in his avid, lifelong interest in flying and
automobile racing. During World War I, he had been a fighter pilot
in the famed 94th Aero Squadron commanded by the celebrated Ace
of Aces, Eddie Rickenbacker of Columbus, Ohio. Outcalt returned to
Cincinnati after the war to study at the University of Cincinnati and
its law school. After a short stint in private practice, he became an assistant county prosecutor in 1923 under District Attorney Charles S.
Bell. Subsequently, Outcalt served under two other Hamilton County
prosecutors, Nelson Schwab and Louis J. Schneider, both of whom also
became judges. In 1936 Outcalt succeeded Schneider as prosecutor.

Rickenbacker and Outcalt remained friends after the war, sharing
a passion for speed. Rickenbacker turned to auto racing, driving at
the Indianapolis Speedway, which he subsequently bought. When the
renowned Indianapolis 500 race came around, Outcalt invariably found
a job working in the pits. He also took Rickenbacker-owned race cars
out for a spin on the track and, on occasion, rode as copilot.

Outcalt shared the prosecutorial duties with three of his most trusted
assistant district attorneys: Carson T. Hoy took the Obendoerfer case,

Simon Leis was assigned to the Palmer and Heis cases, and Loyal S. Martin took charge of the Gsellman case. Outcalt would handle the prosecution on the indictment, namely the death of Wagner. It was a formidable team.

The team for the defense, Hoodin, thirty, and Bolsinger, fifty-eight, appeared to be at a disadvantage. Both were civil attorneys who now had on their hands their first capital murder case, and an extremely high-profile one at that. Assisting the pair in preparing for the trial were Sidney Brant, Sidney Kahn, and Hiram C. Bolsinger Jr.

Anna Marie's trial would be held in what was known as "The Big Courtroom" on the third floor of the Hamilton County Courthouse. As the presiding criminal judge at the time, Nelson Schwab occupied what was the largest courtroom in the county, but recognizing the frenzy of interest in the Hahn case, he loaned his bench to Judge Bell.

The courthouse was designed to suggest to all who entered the weight and majesty of the law. Built in the Greek Ionic style, in six floors it housed the courts, county offices, and the county jail. Cincinnati's favorite son, William Howard Taft, laid the cornerstone in 1915, two years after he had left the White House. The massive structure was completed in 1918 at a cost of $2.5 million.

Indiana limestone decorated the exterior, and inside, twenty-five different varieties of marble dominated the décor. Halls and stairways were of Vermont marble, but each courtroom had marble from a different Midwest quarry. The building also boasted an innovative ventilating system that worked much like air-conditioning today. A large fan in the basement drew in outside air that then passed through a water bath to clean the air of soot and contaminants and to cool it. The air was then forced throughout the building and out through vents in the courtroom. Five oversized windows directly behind the jury box let in light and air.

Brass and bronze hardware was used throughout, and the Seal of Hamilton County appeared on every doorknob. A pair of polished brass lamps and shades, twenty-four inches high, graced each side of the bench.

The G. Henshaw & Son's furniture company of Cincinnati made all the courtroom furniture of Honduras mahogany. Four rows of wooden benches on each side of the center aisle began at the rear of the courtroom. Devoid of upholstery, the benches were most uncomfortable, yet spectators "lucky" enough to gain admittance to the trial sat there hours on end.[1]

The court added sixty folding chairs for the trial due to the tremendous interest in the Hahn case. The large press corps sat at tables directly behind the tables for the prosecution and for the defense. A highly polished brass railing, or "bar," enclosed the bench, the cramped witness stand that faced the jury, and the court reporter's desk. When Judge Bell was on the bench, attorneys were allowed to approach the bar, but they were not permitted to touch it.

Judge Bell disappointed the press corps initially, particularly the large contingent representing out-of-town newspapers. They had petitioned for telegraphic services in the courtroom during the trial. He ruled against that—a wire room was established elsewhere in the courthouse—and further ruled that there would be no photographs permitted while court was in session. The cameramen had a field day before and after court and during recesses, however, posing the defendant, attorneys, bailiffs, and even the jury, as needed.

Fifteen deputy sheriffs, an unusually large number, were summoned to ensure order in the court during the trial.

On the sixth floor of the courthouse, Anna Marie held celebrity status while in the county jail, where a higher-than-usual number of visitors stopped by just for the chance to walk by her cell and see her. On the first weekend, she strolled the hall, greeting passersby warmly. Newspapers began referring to her as the jail's "prima donna," reigning over her fellow prisoners. Each day she was to appear in court, two other prisoners attended to her every need, curling her hair, straightening her dress, and manicuring her nails. A third brought her cigarettes or coffee.

"I have my faith and the knowledge that I have told the truth," she said as she sat in a straight chair, having her hair done. "They will never get a confession out of me, because I can't confess to something I never did."

---

1. Today the courtroom, now designated Courtroom 340, remains virtually the way it was in 1937. A 1938 bar association photo montage on the wall includes Bell, Outcalt, Hoodin, and both Bolsingers, father and son.

Jail matron Mary King revealed that Anna Marie became upset each time a reference was made to her jail cell. "It's not a 'cell,'" she insisted. "It's a room!" Mrs. King had to agree, inasmuch as the women's quarters also served as hospital rooms on occasion. Each room contained a dresser, a chair, and a cot. Curtains appliquéd with tulips graced the windows.

After two weeks of questioning and preliminary trial proceedings, it was clear to Mrs. King that Anna Marie was tired. The accused tried to keep busy, though, particularly with her sewing, embroidering, and knitting. She instituted informal sewing classes for the other female inmates, classes that became a regular part of the jail's rehabilitation program after Anna Marie had departed.

A month before the trial, George Elliston of the *Times-Star* obtained an exclusive jailhouse interview with Anna Marie. Elliston was the newspaper's "sob sister" but as hard-nosed covering crime as any of her male counterparts. Anna Marie told Elliston, somewhat bitterly, that she had never "cheated" anyone out of money. What she owed was "largely to tradespeople whom I didn't get a chance to pay when I was locked up here."

The accused went on at length about her trials and tribulations.

"If I were guilty of one-half or one-fourth of the things they accuse me of, I would be a monster. I pick up the paper every day, wondering what new charge they will hunt up. I read that I am supposed to have murdered or stolen or defrauded someone or other. Half the time it is some person I never even have heard of.

"My comfort is that no one can be judged guilty of any crime until it is proven he has done the deed. I am innocent of murder, arson, and theft and of everything they have charged to me. I can and will prove it. . . . The only thing that worries me is the lies they tell. But even that doesn't make a great deal of difference, because I am innocent."[2]

Anna Marie hoped her sister, Katti, would be able to come to Cincinnati for the trial. "It would be a comfort to me to have some member of my family with me," she said. Because Katharina Filser, Anna Marie's mother in Fuessen, was sixty-nine and not in good health, her sons

2. George Elliston, "Mrs. Hahn Trying to Bring Sister to Cincinnati for Trial," *Cincinnati Times-Star*, Sept. 7, 1937, 1.

and daughter withheld from her the news of her youngest child's arrest and pending trial. Anna Marie had sent her family a cablegram: "Please don't worry about me. I am innocent. That's all what counts. Just pray for me. Lovingly, Annie."

Nobody from her family came for the trial. In fact, nobody from her family ever saw her again.

8 | PETTICOATS PREVAIL

The jury trial for "the greatest mass murder in the history of the country" began at 10 A.M. Monday, October 11.

Gloomy skies that morning didn't deter Cincinnati from turning out early and in large numbers to see the Blonde Borgia, the German housemaid, the Poison Angel, the Angel of Mercy—all names used by the newspapers to describe the woman on trial for her life. Four hours before the court opened, would-be spectators lined up four abreast in the corridor. Women, wearing Sunday-best hats and coats trimmed in fur, dominated the crowd once again. Some thought ahead and brought packed lunches. The aged, a few so elderly that they had to be helped to their seats, waited like everyone else for the little white admission ticket issued by the court for each session. Members of the press were issued their own credentials.

"Lollypop Joe," a courthouse fixture, hawked peanuts, chewing gum, and candy in the hallways while others worked the crowds with sandwiches and coffee. An estimated 150 spectators—only six were men, it was reported—finally gained admittance to the courtroom and stuffed themselves onto the hard benches and the added chairs. Those left outside fumed and fussed for having waited so long for naught. Still, a sizeable number chose to remain in the hallway, hoping to gain access at a later session.

From the outset Judge Bell had made it clear that observers would not be permitted to stand. The three rows of folding chairs added for special visitors, such as members of the bar, were a rare sight in any Cincinnati court, but especially Bell's. Everyone realized this would be a trial unlike any other in Cincinnati's history.

"The courts are yours by reason of your being part of the public," Judge Bell told the visitors, "but I want it distinctly understood that this trial will not be a performance. It is a serious trial in a court of justice. So long as the public confines itself to listening to the evidence, as many as can be seated will be admitted. But at no time will this court tolerate any interference or disturbances."

Among Cincinnati jurists, none stuck closer to proper court procedure than Judge Bell. Off the bench, the fifty-seven-year-old jurist was said to be "friendly, considerate, and obliging," but in his court he was stern and demanding.

As a young man in his hometown of Cincinnati, he worked on the railroad before turning to law. He passed the bar in 1908, after having attended evening law classes at the YMCA's McDonald Educational Institute, one of the earliest part-time evening law schools in the United States. Cincinnati voters elected Bell Hamilton County prosecutor in 1922, and, after two terms in that post, he won a seat on the Court of Common Pleas in 1926. Since then he had tried more than eight thousand cases and had been reversed only four times, a testimony to his astute and strict interpretation of the law.

Chicago Daily News reporter Robert J. Casey was not alone in thinking that the selection of a jury panel, to begin this day, could be difficult. "There seems to be no one in the Cincinnati area who has not formed an opinion, one way or another," he wrote. He was convinced that a large portion of the population had put Anna Marie in the same class with "the great typhoid epidemic of the '80s—not quite so omnipresent, perhaps, but more deadly."

The defense had its reservations, also, and hinted that it would seek a change of venue, but three days before the start of trial, and after much soul-searching with their client, Hoodin and Bolsinger issued a statement: "Mrs. Hahn feels that a jury can be drawn in Hamilton

County which will judge her case honestly and fairly." The game was afoot in Cincinnati.

In the beer halls throughout the Over-the-Rhine district the talk centered on the Blonde Borgia now capturing headlines every day. According to one neighborhood lyrist:

A bunch of the guys were whooping it up
in Bill Durbin's Butchertown bar.
The night was fine, the beer was good,
but Annie wasn't thar.

Many a man fondly remembered an encounter they had with Anna Marie, such as when she smiled at them, sang *Lieder* (songs) with them, or sat on their laps. "She called me darling," recalled an infatuated customer in Bill Durbin's Inn. "Gosh, she was a pretty woman." said Durbin, himself an Anna Marie admirer. "She was awfully popular around here. She was so kind to old people. She always looked after them."[1]

In the next breath, though, most thanked their lucky stars that they had not become attached to her—or worse, eaten a meal prepared by her. Others wondered how, with all her charms, she had been able to ingratiate herself to her victims so quickly.

At this point, the discussion invariably turned to sex. It was stated as fact that Anna Marie had spread arsenic on her ample breasts, which her male victims sucked. They ingested the poison and died happy. This scurrilous story arose after the prosecution, in pretrial hearings, declared that the state believed poison was administered orally by Anna Marie, but suckling was not what it had in mind.

In the Elmwood Place casinos where Anna Marie once hung out, bookies talked of the markers she had stuck them with. As one bookmaker put it, "Anna Marie's is a name more famous around here than Man o' War," the greatest thoroughbred of the 1920s.

Prior to the trial, Judge Bell received a letter from Joseph Sudbeck of St. Louis, asking that it be forwarded to Anna Marie's attorneys. It

1. Robert J. Casey, "'Blonde Angel' Still a Pal to Men She Didn't Poison," *Chicago Daily News*, Oct. 13, 1937, 3.

read: "Gentlemen: If Mrs. Anna Hahn is in need of financial assistance, please let me know. My holdings consists [sic] of oil bonds and industrial bonds valued at $7,000,000 [$98 million in 2005]. Any financial assistance that I may give must be understood that it is a charitable donation, not a loan. I would like to hear from Mrs. Hahn attys [sic], also from Mrs. Hahn, stating that she will accept financial assistance to carry on her fight."

Sudbeck, whose occupation was listed as a salesman, subsequently was arrested and charged with using the mail to defraud. He was all but penniless.

Oscar showed up with Philip for the first day of court, wearing his first pair of long pants. His mother, so proud, hugged and kissed him as photographers popped flashbulbs all around them. Philip leaned over and told his wife, "Regardless of our marital difficulties in the last few years, I absolutely believe in your innocence and will stick by you." Anna Marie gave him a smile, but no kiss.

The defendant looked her best. She wore a black crepe dress trimmed with white silk braid, her hair coifed, a slight touch of rouge, and immaculately manicured fingernails. Around her neck was the gold crucifix she would wear until the day she died. A wedding ring and a diamond engagement ring adorned her left hand. After the photographers left the courtroom each day, she put on a pair of rimless eyeglasses.

Cincinnati Post columnist Alfred Segal, writing in his "Cincinnatus" column, was of the opinion that "what Mrs. Hahn wears at the trial is not in the least relevant since this isn't a matinee. Nor is the fact that Mrs. Hahn was seen kissing her son a cause for photographs. After all, mothers have been kissing sons since Eve's time."[2]

Oscar, with Philip's arm around him, sat behind his mother for a part of the morning session, then at the recess he was taken from the courtroom by Philip after Judge Bell ruled that "a murder trial is no place for children." He barred from the courtroom everyone under the age of seventeen.

Ohio Supreme Court Associate Justice Robert N. Gorman, the first of several judges who would attend the proceedings over the next

2. Cincinnatus, "At a Trial," *Cincinnati Post*, Oct. 12, 1937, 8.

month, joined Judge Bell on the bench as an observer as jury selection began. Hoodin's biggest opportunity in his young career to shine in Cincinnati's biggest murder trial got off to a sickly start. He felt terrible, due to a heavy cold, and he had to leave much of the opening work to Bolsinger.

Outcalt questioned every talesman as to whether they accepted the death penalty and whether their verdict would be influenced by the fact that the defendant was a woman. The defense focused on determining whether potential jurors were biased against their client—for example, for being German, betting on horses, or having a bastard son. "Would it prejudice you either way if it should be brought out in the evidence that the defendant is the mother of a twelve-year-old boy born out of wedlock?" Hoodin asked.

At one point during his questioning, Hoodin invoked the ire of Judge Bell by asking Magdalene Mitchell, "Would you vote for acquittal if it were shown that numerous other persons were implicated in the [Wagner] murder—if it was murder?"

"You can't ask that!" said the judge.

If the defense wanted to plant the seed that a killer other than Anna Marie was responsible for Wagner's death, Hoodin succeeded in doing so, but during the trial the suggestion that "numerous other persons" might be involved never surfaced again.

The first to be seated on the jury was Emma Cassidy, a housewife and the spouse of a "dramatic artist." When asked if she believed that women are equally responsible for their crimes as are men, she replied, "More so." Mary Arnold,[3] on the other hand, did not believe that to be true and thus was rejected as a juror. Mary Garland also was excused because she was first cousin to Outcalt. Seven men were passed over when each said they could not accept a verdict of death for a woman.

One who told her "inside" story as a talesman to the *Cincinnati Enquirer* was Stella Tragesser, a spinster living with her mother.[4] She was number thirty-seven out of forty-six to be examined. At first she was nervous, but by the time she was called, at 9 P.M. Wednesday

3. No relation to Olive Koehler.
4. Stella Tragesser, "Hahn Trial to be Vivid Memory!" *Cincinnati Enquirer,* Nov. 19, 1937, 12.

at Judge Bell's first night session, she recalled, "I wasn't the least bit nervous or excited and went strutting into the courtroom as though I might have been Myrna Loy."[5]

Yet, when she realized she might be on the jury, she said she "actually prayed that they would call my name [to be excused] because even the mere thought of being a part of the tragedy ahead of me scared me beyond words." She was the second to be seated, and she felt "doomed."

After a day of adjournment Tuesday to observe Columbus Day, jury selection resumed. The photographers were again out in force prior to the opening of court. A smiling, amiable Anna Marie asked the group if there were any pictures of her in Monday's out-of-town newspapers. When told that there were, she asked that clippings be sent to her.

For a time Philip also enjoyed the attention of the press. While on a break from his job at Western Union, he visited a newsstand to buy copies of the New York newspaper with his photograph in it.

Before the trial, the only attention Philip received was when a customer asked about sending a Western Union telegram. "Now everybody in Cincinnati knows him," Casey told his Chicago readers. "When he steps into a night club or the old neighborhood saloon, he is 'that husband of that Mrs. Hahn.' People ask him if his wife poisoned anybody—and he says she didn't."[6]

Philip was "there" for his wife, yet he wasn't. He offered his support, gave her a fan to use in the courtroom, and sent her a basket of fruit every Thursday while she was in the jail. He even posed for photographs with her on occasion, but she preferred that he not do so. She blamed him for her predicament inasmuch as he had turned over to police that bottle of croton oil. She never would forgive him for that, and yet, as her husband, he made an effort to do right by her.

"If you knew Anna as I know her—gentle, generous, motherly and always fearing to hurt someone's feelings—you would understand how physically impossible murder in any form would be to her," Philip told the press before the trial. Of course, he felt it necessary to lie a little. He knew well her temper, remembered their many arguments, and mulled over her many assignations.

5. Myrna Loy was a popular Hollywood actress at the time.
6. Casey, "'Blonde Angel,'" 3.

"I would have been worse than a sap to live with Anna all these years and have no suspicion that something was wrong."

Nevertheless, he professed her innocence and vowed not to be "such a heel" as to abandon her in her time of trouble. "Oscar and I are sticking with her to the bitter end," he said, and he did, until she received the death sentence. Then, although he tried to visit her, she almost always rejected his requests. As time went by, he stopped asking.

The jury panel, said to be death-qualified inasmuch as each member accepted the ultimate penalty, was completed shortly before noon Thursday with the seating of Florence E. Bartlett, wife of the president of Cincinnati Discount Company. John Granda, a machinist with the Cincinnati Milling Machine Company, was the lone male, although Frederick Juergens, a mechanical engineer with Crosley Radio Corporation, would serve as alternate. Granda would be named jury foreman.

Veteran court observers could not remember an Ohio jury in a murder trial so laden with women. It also was a rarity in the history of American jurisprudence, they said. The press promptly labeled the panel the "petticoat jury."

Seated in the back row of the jury box were Mrs. Cassidy; Miss Tragesser; Mr. Granda; Mrs. Jennie Greenwald, widow; Mrs. Bartlett; and Mrs. Marjorie Bishop, wife of a tailor at Storrs-Schaeffer Company, where she worked, too.

In the front row were Edna Clark, wife of a retired Traction Company worker; Ella L. Black, widow; Frances G. Sullivan, widow; Georgia McDonald, a twenty-two-year-old divorcee and laundress, the panel's youngest member; Anna Thompson, wife of a farm produce sales manager; and Alice Peters, widow. Alternate Juergens sat to one side of the jury box.

Immediately after the jurors were sworn in, several journalists bolted from the courtroom to get to telephones and call their newspapers. Not pleased that the decorum of his court had been violated, Judge Bell made it clear he would not tolerate such behavior again. But it did occur again: as soon as Judge Bell declared the noon recess and left the bench, press photographers seeking pictures of the panel stormed the courtroom, "literally taking possession of the place," said

Tragesser. "Some were on chairs, tables, every place, and in whatever direction we looked we were staring into the face of a camera. I was terribly frightened and wanted to be home more than I ever wanted to be in all of the twenty-eight years of my life."[7]

Much of the press attention focused on Granda, a handsome, dark-haired man with dimples when he smiled and a cleft in his chin. Resplendent in a well-tailored green suit, he appeared as though "he stepped out of a bandbox," said bailiff Ann Roberts. *Ohio State Journal* reporter Sarah L. Dush dubbed him the "Adonis of the jury." Anna Marie gazed intently at every juror seated, but she seemed to take a particular interest in Granda.

Criminal Court Bailiff Charles Stagnaro, assisted by special bailiffs Nettie Douglas and Mrs. Roberts, had the responsibility for the care and feeding of the thirteen jurors impanelled. Each had come to court Thursday with extra clothes, enough to last several weeks of sequestering at the Hotel Metropole, on Walnut Street, two blocks from the courthouse. A modest hotel, its four hundred first-class rooms began at $1.75 a night.

During the week, Judge Bell said, court would be in session each day from 10 A.M. to 4:30 P.M. with one hour and a half for lunch. On Saturdays, there would be a two-hour morning session, and on Mondays, Wednesdays, and Fridays the judge, despite Hoodin's objection, called for evening sessions of about two hours.

Thursday night the jurors had their first dinner together in the dining room of the Metropole and became acquainted with one another. Among the most animated in her conversation was the tall and stately Mrs. Peters, described as "the most socially prominent member of the jury." Her attire and demeanor were "faultless," said the *Chicago Daily Tribune,* which also described Mrs. Bartlett as "one of the town's more prominent matrons."

After dinner, jurors and bailiffs retired to the large dayroom on the ninth floor that was exclusively for their use. "We had an awfully good time," said bailiff Roberts, playing cards and games such as bingo and Monopoly. A few immediately wrote letters home, though

7. Tragesser, "Hahn Trial," 12.

all correspondence to or from the jury was censored to eliminate any mention of the trial itself. Family visits were permitted, but only in the presence of a bailiff.

That night the bailiffs locked the jurors in their rooms on the ninth floor, a procedure that initially unnerved a few on the panel. In the morning, promptly at 10 A.M., the state would begin to unfold one of the most bizarre, cold-blooded murder cases in the nation's history.

9 | CLEVER SCHEMES—AND GREED

A ccording to the State of Ohio, Anna Marie Hahn "unlawfully, purposely and by means of poison killed one Jacob Wagner," and in doing so violated "the peace and dignity of the State of Ohio."

With his reading of the indictment against her, Outcalt launched his devastating opening statement to the jury Friday, October 15, in a courtroom overflowing with spectators, journalists, and lawyers. As before, many more patiently stood in the hallways, hoping against hope they would be admitted, too.

After the victim's body was "brought up from the ground," Outcalt said, an autopsy "disclosed that Jacob Wagner died from the adminis-tration of a poison commonly used for rats!" He forcefully hammered the last word home while staring at the expressionless defendant.

Anna Marie went through the building where the seventy-eight-year-old gardener had lived for many years, the prosecutor said, and identi-fied herself to tenants as Wagner's niece. Hers was a "plan, scheme and design to enrich herself by the acquisition of Jacob Wagner's life savings," Outcalt said, "and as you will see when I talk to you a little later about the cases of other old men, you will see, ladies and gentlemen. . . ."

The entire team of defense attorneys jumped out of their seats to object. Hoodin took the vociferous lead, protesting strenuously the mention of "other old men . . . for the purpose of inflaming the minds of the jury."

For the first of many times, the jury was excused while the defense and prosecution argued at length whether other alleged crimes should be mentioned. At one point, Outcalt told the court that he would show Anna Marie had "killed so many men that there is not another person like her on the face of the earth." He convinced Judge Bell that the prosecution had the right to mention in opening argument other acts of the defendant. A distraught Hoodin asked that the jury be dismissed and that he be allowed time to prepare a defense beyond the Wagner case as charged in the indictment. His motion was denied.

When the jury returned some minutes later, Judge Bell carefully explained to the panel that opening statements were not evidence and that in their deliberations, only evidence could be considered in reaching a verdict.

Outcalt continued, describing the defendant's "very clever schemes" to enrich herself, "to satisfy her greed." She dealt Wagner "a terrific dose of arsenic" and "he was in agony" before he passed away on June 3. Afterward, she forged Wagner's will, "which purported to give her every cent that he had."

The prosecutor also detailed the deaths "in utter agony" of Obendoerfer, Gsellman, and Palmer and then the poisoning of the state's "living witness," Heis.

"We will show you, ladies and gentlemen . . . that if arsenic is followed by the administration of croton oil—which in itself is a deadly poison, the croton oil being a violent purgative—[the croton oil] will wash out most of the arsenic from the stomach. The arsenic will remain in the other organs, but if the stomach alone is examined, we will show you, ladies and gentlemen, that there is a greatly increased possibility of evading detection."

In conclusion, Outcalt said he intended to show "the guilt of this defendant beyond any reasonable doubt, beyond any possible doubt," demanding that "the supreme penalty be imposed."

Anna Marie sat stone-faced throughout the prosecutor's forceful presentation, apparently unimpressed by it. Outcalt's oratory captivated others. One member of the press from Chicago described Outcalt's performance as the "greatest opening statement in Ohio court history." Another painted it as "brilliant oratory [that] charged the courtroom with electric tension."

In a raspy voice from the cold that still gripped him, Hoodin took his best shot in his opening statement on behalf of Anna Marie. "Our defense is pure and simple," he said at the outset. "She did not administer poison to Jacob Wagner . . . a very nice person, well versed in reference to flowers." At no time, defense counsel told the jury, did his client "administer poison to anyone." She was in court because she sought vindication, he said.

As expected, Hoodin attacked anew "the great Captain Hayes . . . who supposes himself to be another Sherlock Holmes, another great detective who is attempting in this case, I believe the evidence will indicate, to cover himself with glory as having been the person who in this case uncovered this crime."

Hoodin, who correctly noted that he was not as capable an orator as Outcalt, told the jury that one of its biggest jobs during the trial would be "to watch the witnesses, their attitude and demeanor on the stand. You are to judge whether they are telling the truth [and] whether Mrs. Hahn tells you the truth. All we ask of you . . . is a fair and impartial verdict."

Casey told his *Chicago Daily News* readers that the prosecution turned out the whole neighborhood "to tell of [Anna Marie's] volunteer mercies to old men who seldom lived long enough to express their gratitude." In backyards and on fire escapes, he reported, the neighborhood "jury" gossiped about local indiscretions, "and some day the whole business will come back to you—when you are receiving the Florence Nightingale medal or sitting on trial for your life—as, indeed, it came back to Mrs. Hahn last night."

The state opened its case by calling to the stand Wagner's neighbors, most of whom testified with German accents. The first was Nannie Werks, who lived on the fourth floor of the apartment building where Wagner lived. She recalled that Anna Marie came to her door, and said, "'I am looking for an old gentleman, a bachelor that lives alone,' and she had a letter in her hand, and she says, 'I just received a letter from my mother in Germany, and she gave me this address to hunt him up. He fell heir to a lot of property.'"

Mrs. Werks asked Anna Marie for the name of the relative.

"She says, 'I don't know. I would know him if I would see him.' . . . She never mentioned Mr. Wagner's name."

Other neighbors, like Elizabeth Colby and her daughter, Josephine Martin, recounted having a similar visit from Anna Marie. She asked if "any old men were living here," Mrs. Colby recalled. "I was waiting for her to say a name, and she wouldn't say a name." Mrs. Colby identified Wagner as one of her elderly neighbors.

It was at Mrs. Colby's kitchen table than Anna Marie wrote a note that she placed under Wagner's door. Two weeks later, on "a really hot day," Mrs. Colby and her daughter saw the defendant in Wagner's room from across a small alley. Anna Marie "got up and walked to a table, and there was a glass there, and she poured something in a glass and walked to the other side of the room, handing somebody some liquid stuff," the witness said. In cross-examination by Hoodin, Mrs. Colby admitted that she didn't know what was poured into the glass.

Ida Martin, Josephine's ex-mother-in-law and also a Wagner neighbor, remembered Anna Marie telling her that "I sent the old man to the hospital." Then, the day before he died, Mrs. Martin said Anna Marie told her that there were things of Wagner's left in his room. "She said . . . 'I will give them to you. He's not coming back.'"

The portly Dr. James A. Clift, uncomfortable in the tight witness chair, told the jury that the defendant summoned him to Wagner's apartment at about 9:30 P.M. He recalled that she identified herself as a nurse from "the old country," and that her husband there, in Germany, was a doctor.

"I asked her—see, he talks German; I don't, you see—I asked Mrs. Hahn, I says, 'How long has this man been sick?' She says over a week . . . She said, 'He has [been] running off of the bowels.' I says, 'Ask Mr. Wagner how many times his bowels run off.' So she asked him in German and then she told me 'fifteen to seventeen times.'"

In his cross-examination, Hoodin tried to pin Wagner's poisoning on the physician by intimating the tablets Dr. Clift prescribed for dysentery contained arsenic. Not true, said the doctor.

Judge Bell adjourned the court after what had been an exhausting, long first day for all. In the evening, the jury was taken to see Joan Crawford and her real-life husband, Franchot Tone, in *The Bride Wore Red*. It was the first of several movie outings the jury would have during the trial.

SATURDAY, OCTOBER 16

Assistant Prosecutor Martin called to the stand the second neighborhood physician to visit Wagner, Dr. Richard Marnell. His examination of Wagner was more thorough than Clift's, and his testimony more precise about Wagner's condition.

"Will you tell us just what your examination of Jacob Wagner showed?"

"His general complaint was vomiting and pain in the stomach. . . . The patient stated that the vomitus was bloody in color. . . . Eating did not relieve the pain. The patient had been taking some type of liquid medicine. The patient likewise stated that he had disurine and hemaurine. Disurine is painful urination, and hemaurine is blood in urine. The patient stated that he had been drinking large quantities of beer in the past few weeks. The patient also stated that he had fallen and struck his head two days ago. There was an abrasion on the scalp and forehead on the right side. The patient did not lose consciousness at the time of the fall."

"Those were the statements, doctor, that Jacob Wagner made to you, is that correct?"

"That's right."

"Where was Anna Hahn at that time?"

"In the start of my history Mrs. Hahn was in the room, and during the course of obtaining my history she left the room."

Marnell testified that to him, Wagner appeared "chronically ill. . . . The patient was advised to enter the hospital, to which he gave his consent."

"And doctor, did you recommend a hospital?"

The physician said Anna Marie had approached him about a hospital "before I had even seen the patient."

"Mrs. Hahn had approached you about a hospital?"

"She did."

Marnell confirmed that he had seen Wagner twice on June 2, once in the early afternoon and again about 8 P.M., after Wagner had been taken to Good Samaritan Hospital. Martin asked the doctor to describe Wagner's condition at the hospital.

"Mr. Wagner was in a semi-reclining position, in bed, semi-comatose;

I mean by that semi-conscious, retching with pain, in a state of shock and dying."

The somber trial was not without some humor. John Decker, another neighbor and friend of Wagner's, brought smiles while he responded to questions posed by Martin.

"Now, Mr. Decker, do you remember when Jacob Wagner died?"

"Listen. I tell you. I explain. I seen him on Sunday morning about six o'clock, meet him in the hall."

"That is the Sunday morning before he died?"

"I tell him, 'What's the matter?' in German. 'What's the matter, Jake?'"

"You talked to him in German?"

"Yes. 'Oh,' he tells me . . ."

Hoodin objected to the response.

Judge Bell reminded Decker that "you are not permitted here to tell what you said to him or he to you. You just listen to Mr. Martin's questions and answer what he asks you and don't add anything. Just answer his questions." Decker nodded affirmation.

"Mr. Decker," Martin resumed, "when you saw Jacob Wagner on that Sunday morning, just tell us how he looked."

"On Sunday morning, six o'clock, I tell him, 'What's the matter, Jake?' 'I am awful sick; awful sick . . . '"

This time Bolsinger rose for the defense. "Now, if the court pleases . . ."

An exasperated Judge Bell, peering over his pince-nez at the witness seated immediately in front of him, addressed Decker once again.

"Mr. Decker, I just said you are not to tell what he said to you. I have said three times you are not to tell that. The prosecutor will ask you the questions and you just answer them. He [Martin] asked you how Mr. Wagner looked."

"Well, he had a towel around his neck and, 'My stomach' is all he told me," Decker responded, totally ignoring the court and once again bringing an objection from the defense.

Martin asked if Decker noticed what Wagner was doing with his hands the morning he went to the hospital.

"Yes. He answered me, 'Awful sick.'" Hoodin rolled his eyes, but did not object. Judge Bell smiled in frustration.

"What did you see about his hands was the question," Martin continued.

"I can't understand you," Decker replied.

"I'll withdraw the question," said Martin, done in by his witness, who was excused.

Elizabeth Morabek, the nurse on duty when Wagner was brought in to Good Samaritan Hospital, described the "terrifying" picture of the patient who begged for water. She said she spoke to Anna Marie the day after Wagner died. "She said she didn't know the man," Morabek said. Yet the hospital registrar, Laura Boehm, testified next that the defendant told her that she had been "taking care" of Wagner but she "was worn out," so she brought him to the hospital "because she needed a rest."

Dr. Francis M. Forster, one year out of University of Cincinnati Medical College, attended to Wagner at the hospital. Outcalt questioned him about Wagner's condition early in the evening of June 2.

"He was definitely in a state of what we speak of as shock, which means death is imminent unless something is done for the patient."

"Did you do anything for him at that time, doctor?"

"Yes. I consulted with Dr. Marnell and under his orders gave the customary drugs used in such a condition, which were glucose and strychnine and caffeine."

"In how many hours did he die?"

"He died at approximately midnight."

Forster then related how later the following morning he had sought out Anna Marie.

"I requested permission for an autopsy, which is customary, and stated that we were particularly anxious—Dr. Marnell and I were both anxious—to obtain permission because we were not certain of the cause of death of the particular patient."

"What did she say?" Outcalt asked.

"Mrs. Hahn refused."

"Then what did you say to her?"

"I told her that since Mr. Wagner had died within the twenty-four-hour limit [for the signing of the death certificate], which is set by the state, it would then become a coroner's case. If we performed an autopsy at the Good Samaritan by our own men, the report would be furnished to the coroner's office, but if not, I would have to notify him, and it would be within his discretion for the autopsy."

"What did she say to that?"

"She said she would like to think it over."

"Did you see her again that morning?"

"No, I did not see her anymore."

"Do you know whether or not, as a matter of fact, she did subsequently consent?"

"She did."

Salesman Frank Kaessheimer drank beer with Wagner, his neighbor, at Kirsch's restaurant. It was there, on May 29, that Wagner reported that his bankbook had been stolen. He suspected Anna Marie. During the course of their conversation, she arrived at Kirsch's, too.

"What happened when she came in?" Outcalt asked his witness, "and tell us what conversation there was after she was there."

"She said, 'Mr. Wagner, I was looking for you all over. I left a note saying I was coming down this morning. Where was you?' Mr. Wagner was sitting there with his hands on the table. He said, 'Yes, my bankbook is gone and nobody else took it but you.' She said, 'Your bankbook isn't gone. Nobody can do nothing with that bankbook, you ought to know that.' He said, 'It is gone.'

"Mrs. Hahn said, 'Where are *my* two bankbooks?' He said, 'They are gone, too.'"

"What did she say when he said, 'They are gone, too'?" Outcalt asked.

"Mrs. Hahn said, 'Let's get up and go to your room and see if we can find it.'" In about ten minutes, the pair returned with Wagner's "lost" bankbook.

The conversation then took a strange twist, one that clearly demonstrated Anna Marie's disregard of the facts. She asked Kaessheimer to guess her age. He said he didn't know. "I am much older than you," Anna Marie told the thirty-nine-year-old salesman. "I am forty-eight-years-old. You are not *that* old." Kaessheimer agreed he was not, but then, neither was she. Why Anna Marie, then thirty, would want to add eighteen years to her age is unknown, but perhaps she wished to appear closer to Wagner's seventy-eight years.

Kaessheimer also testified that she told him, "'I was married in

Germany already to a doctor, but he died. When I came to the United States I married again.'"

Arthur J. Schmitt, assistant vice president at Fifth Third Union Trust, Wagner's bank, delivered some of the most damaging early testimony. He recalled for the court a visit Anna Marie paid him June 1, two days before Wagner died. She reported that Wagner's passbook "had been found in the cupboard at her uncle's [Wagner] home in the same place where he always kept it [and that] she intended to take her uncle to her home to care for him. She also inquired of me how her uncle might procure some of his funds in the event he could not get down to the bank."

The chances were, of course, that Wagner would not make it to his bank ever again. Anna Marie already had begun to poison him.

Shortly before 10 A.M. on June 3, Anna Marie appeared at Schmitt's desk again.

"Did she present anything to you at that time?" asked Outcalt.

"Yes, sir."

"What did she present?"

"She presented a withdrawal receipt, Mr. Wagner's passbook and another note from Mr. Wagner," which the prosecutor introduced as evidence.

Schmitt said he telephoned Deaconess Hospital, where Anna Marie said Wagner was a patient, only to be informed that Jacob Wagner was not there. "She said she was slightly confused," the banker said, and said Good Samaritan Hospital was correct. He called there, too.

"What did you say to her then?" Outcalt asked.

"I told her that the Good Samaritan Hospital had informed me that Mr. Wagner had died at 12:15 A.M. that same morning. I also asked her who signed that withdrawal order, and she admitted she had signed it."

Schmitt said he told Anna Marie that forgery was a criminal offense.

"What did she say about that?" Outcalt asked.

"She got rather excited and begged me not to institute any proceedings against her on account of her son, eleven years old." She also told Schmitt that she was estranged from her husband, he testified.

The trial adjourned at noon.

SUNDAY, OCTOBER 17

Sunday was a day of rest. Some jurors were escorted to morning church services, while others read books or wrote letters and cards, which the bailiffs scanned for content. After the midday meal, the panel took a bus ride through Cincinnati's northern suburbs. In the evening, both Granda and alternate juror Juergens were visited by members of their families.

Anna Marie spent part of the day knitting in her cell and wandering the corridors of the jail in a plain housedress, chatting with prisoners, guards, and visitors. Asked if she would have preferred an all-male jury, she shrugged and said, "I had nothing to say about it. Anyway, I have nothing to fear."

"She seems to have her old pep back," observed Deputy Sheriff Heitzler.

10 | NEVER AN UNKIND WORD

O n Monday, October 18, Captain Patrick H. Hayes, all 265 beefy pounds of him, squeezed into the witness chair. His work on the case had been praised by the prosecution, but the defense was armed to shoot holes in it—and in Hayes himself, if possible.

Loyal S. Martin began by leading the officer through the key points of the police department's investigation, including the August 11 visit to Anna Marie's home when he found the bottle of arsenic in her basement rafters.

"Now, Mr. Hayes, will you just tell the jury where you found that bottle?"

"As you go down the steps, when you get about the third [step] from the bottom, in the rafters there were some boards there, those beaded ceiling boards, and they were—a couple of them—were missing, and back in there, about one foot from the entranceway, that bottle was standing in there."

Martin asked the officer to describe the condition of the bottle.

"It was a clear glass bottle, small bottle, square, and was clean, and no dust or nothing on it. The bottle was clean."

"I will show you this bottle here, captain, and ask you to tell the jury whether or not that is the bottle which you took from up in the rafters of the cellar of Anna Hahn's home."

Before handing it to Hayes, Martin held the bottle high, making sure the jury—already leaning forward in their seats to see the first real evidence introduced—got a good look at it. The witness identified the container.

Hayes went on to describe the bottle further. "The bottle had no cork in it. There was no cork in here, and there were streaks of white all over the sides of the bottle. There was about a quarter of an inch of white substance in the bottom of the bottle."

"Now, at the time that you found that bottle, Captain Hayes, will you tell the jury what Anna Hahn said and what she did?" the assistant prosecutor inquired.

"She was on the steps right in back of me, and Detective Hart was [in] back of her, and when I took it out she asked me for it, and I refused to give it to her, and she asked me several times for the bottle, and I still refused to give her the bottle."

"Now, at the time you started down to the cellar to search down there, will you describe what Anna Hahn told you at that time?"

"When I first started down, she said, 'Now what are you looking for?' and I said, 'I came here to make the search and want to finish it.' She asked me over and over again what I was looking for here and what I was looking for there, and when I took this bottle out she wanted the bottle, and I refused to give it to her."

After Hoodin registered an objection to the repetitious testimony, Martin asked Hayes to describe the defendant's "appearance" when he found the bottle.

"I object to the question, if the court pleases," Hoodin said.

"What is the objection?" asked Judge Bell.

"As to the question what her appearance was. I don't know what he means—how she was dressed, or her facial appearance or what."

"Objection overruled."

"Note our exception."

Hayes completed the reply. "Her face became flushed, and she was very excited."

Again Hoodin objected but was overruled.

"And you gave that bottle to Detective Burks, is that correct?" Martin asked.

"I did."

In his cross-examination, a fired-up Hoodin, itching to discredit Hayes and paint him as a rogue cop, sought additional responses concerning the police search and the bottle. In a voice so loud that it could be heard in the hallway outside the courtroom, Hoodin asked, "Do you remember, captain, that you talked to Mr. Bolsinger and that you gave him your word that you would not . . . take her anywhere unless he was with you?"

"No."

Outcalt quickly rose to challenge the manner in which opposing counsel was proceeding. "I don't think there is any necessity for shouting that way," he told the court. Judge Bell, in a calming manner, said he did not find the questioning objectionable. "The court appreciates that counsel on both sides in a case of this kind have tremendous responsibilities, and at times, raise their voices. I don't think that makes it objectionable, but I want to hear from Mr. Hoodin on the proposition, assuming that Mr. Hayes said what you say he said, Mr. Hoodin, how that could bind the State of Ohio. This is not Mr. Hayes's case, but the State of Ohio's case."

"I think I have the right to show by the great Captain Hayes's testimony his conduct in this case, his attitude in this case, just the type of person he is. I think I have a right to show that to the jury."

"You have a perfect right to show any interest, any bias or prejudice of this or any other witness who may appear to testify," Judge Bell said. "There is no question about that, [but] you are asking now about a conversation with someone else. What you are attempting to do is bind the State of Ohio by a conversation you claim this officer had, and the state cannot be bound by it."

Hoodin persisted but lost the argument. Judge Bell sustained the prosecution's objection because the defense was not prepared to bring into court a witness to testify that Hayes had been untruthful.

Hoodin switched his attack to the witness's first visit to Anna Marie's home with her.

"On the way out, did you make any statements to Mrs. Hahn?"

"I did."

You made certain statements which you would not like to repeat here, would you, Captain Hayes?"

"No. I would repeat anything I have ever said."

"You would?" Hoodin asked snidely.

"Yes, sir."

As for the search of Anna Marie's quarters, Hoodin made an issue out of Hayes finding Oscar's toy chemical set in the basement.

"Captain Hayes, didn't you pour water out of those faucets at the laundry trays, didn't you pour it on that chemical set?"

"I did not."

"And didn't you continue to do that for three or four minutes?"

"I did not."

"And isn't it a fact that Mrs. Hahn came to the head of those stairs and told you not to do it?"

"No, she didn't. She . . . came down the stairs several times after me, and I sent her back up, and she asked me, continued to ask me, 'What are you looking for?' . . . She never mentioned the chemical set."

"And she was sore at you for that reason?"

"No, she was not sore at me, because I handled that woman with the greatest care."

"You did?"

"Yes, sir."

"At all times?"

"At all times, yes, sir."

"What do you mean by 'with the greatest of care' Captain Hayes?"

"Well, I showed her every courtesy I could possibly show her."

"And respect, too?"

"Yes, and respect, too."

"Didn't make any statements you would not make to any other woman, did you?"

"I never made an out-of-the-way statement to her in one way or the other."

"You never did?"

"Not myself, no."

"What do you mean? Did any others make them?"

"If they did, I didn't hear them," Hayes avowed.

After spending a few minutes on other issues, Hoodin returned once again, like a bulldog to a bone, to what Hayes had said to his client.

"Now, captain, did you have a conversation with Mrs. Hahn on the way back [to police headquarters]?"

"I did not, no."

"Did anybody else have any conversation with her?"

"Yes, they did."

"Who?"

"I heard them talking in the machine [squad car], but I didn't pay any attention to that. That was some of the other boys in the machine, but I paid no attention to what they were saying or what was going on."

"You know that a vile remark was made to her, don't you?"

"No."

"And you know what she said, that she told you and the rest of the detectives that she did not . . . like to hear those kinds of words from you. Do you remember that?"

"She was talking to them fellows in the machine there, but what was said I can't tell you because I paid no attention to what was going on. I was doing the driving." Burks was in the front seat with Hayes; Rentrop, Anna Marie, and Hart sat in the rear.

Today it seems incredible that a veteran police officer, driving with an unrestrained, suspected killer in a police car, would not be attuned to everything that was going on, but Hoodin did not pursue that matter. Instead, he turned to what Hayes purportedly said to Oscar during his interrogation at home and at the police station.

"Did you make any remarks to that little twelve-year-old boy which were vile in character?"

"I did not. Not one word out-of-the-way to the boy."

Hoodin asked if Oscar was questioned while Anna Marie was present, but he wasn't.

Almost shouting again, the defense counsel asked Hayes if he remembered "that you called that little boy—and I don't like to say this—a son-of-a-bitch?"

"No. That's what you called me," Hayes snapped, "but I never called the boy that."

"When did I call you that?" Hoodin demanded, shouting once again.

Outcalt objected, and Judge Bell halted the acrimony. "Mr. Hoodin, you must certainly appreciate that that is not a proper question."

"I think I have a right to demand an explanation from him, whenever I called him that," the bruised defense attorney said.

"What light will that throw on the issue in this case?" the judge asked.

"I think he is casting some remark against me, and I know I never, never have done such a thing."

Nobody apologized and the trial moved on, only for Hoodin to return a few minutes later to the bottle and the language police used in talking to his client.

"You asked Mrs. Hahn whether that bottle belonged to her, didn't you?" he asked.

"Yes."

"And she told you 'no,' didn't she?"

"She didn't say 'yes' or 'no.' She said it might have been brought in out of the yard or it might have rolled in out of Dr. Vos's office."

"But she told you it didn't belong to her, is that right?"

"In a way she did, yes, but not direct."

"Now, Captain, do I understand from you that at no time during your conversations with Mrs. Hahn did you use vile language towards her."

Martin's objection was sustained, but Hoodin pursued the same line of questioning, nevertheless.

"Do you remember the time, Captain Hayes, in our office when you and Mrs. Hahn were alone and that you said to her, using vile language, 'I ought to knock you clear across the room'?"

"I never used an unkind word to that woman as long as she was with me, not once."

When Hoodin began questioning Hayes about his authorship of a magazine article, Outcalt jumped to his feet to object, strenuously. Judge Bell sent the jury out, heard arguments from both sides, and then overruled the objection. "Either side has the right to attempt to show that any witness is biased or prejudiced," the jurist said.

Hayes, who had no schooling beyond eighth grade in the little Clermont County community of Glen Este, Ohio, admitted giving an interview to a reporter for *Official Detective* magazine. The lengthy article detailing Hayes's investigation was told to J. Porter Henry Jr., who crafted the piece for the magazine.

At the dinner break, Anna Marie gave another jailhouse interview, this time to Karin Walsh of the *Chicago Daily Times,* who referred to the defendant as "Iceberg Anna." Dressed in her simple prison blue and gray apron, she stood at the door to the double-room "cell" that she shared with Mabel Hill, the shoplifter serving a short-term sentence. "I like it here," Anna Marie said happily. "There are worse places. The girls are all nice to me."

After each session in court, the other incarcerated women crowded around her as she recalled details of the trial. The basket of fruit she received from Philip every Thursday she shared with all.

For the first time, Anna Marie admitted that she had agreed to take the stand in her own defense. Would she be convincing? Walsh asked. "Anyone who tells the truth is convincing, so of course I will be," replied Anna Marie. "I am ready to face anything. I am not afraid."

Standing nearby was jail matron Maude Burkhardt, who described Anna Marie as "a model prisoner" who worked in the sewing room and helped with the jailhouse wash. Anna Marie put her arm around Mrs. Burkhardt's shoulders and said, "She's my pal."

The Monday night session was raucous, instigated by the testimony of Wagner's neighbor, Mattie Monroe. What she had to say caused the defense team to explode and to call for a mistrial. While visiting Wagner's bathroom following his death, the fifty-eight-year-old witness told the court that she found "a small bottle containing arsenic and one containing strychnine and a doctor's needle."

Immediately Hoodin leaped out of his chair to object, declaring in a voice bordering on hoarse that by her testimony the witness was "taking the life of Mrs. Hahn and throwing it away." At his request, the judge ordered the jury from the courtroom.

"If the court please, at this time, I make a motion that the entire panel of this jury be dismissed," Hoodin said. "I make that motion with full knowledge of all the hardships it is causing and will cause to the county as far as funds are concerned. But whenever you have a witness on the witness stand making a bald statement that she found a bottle in the toilet containing arsenic and strychnine, I don't care what you tell that jury on the question of regarding or disregarding that, that has sunk into their minds and nothing that your honor can say or do . . . will ever undo that this woman in one or two words has said and done. . . . I move that this entire panel be dismissed."

Judge Bell denied the motion, but he instructed the jury to disregard Monroe's mention of the specific contents of the bottles. Later, however, Monroe was allowed to describe what she saw in them. "They was white," she said. "It was dry. It looked like baking powder or soda. It was very fine."

TUESDAY, OCTOBER 19

Anna Marie's pretty brown dress, adorned with gold birds in flight, brightened the courtroom as her trial resumed. But the scene soon became ugly, as the testimony of Dr. Behrer, city chemist for nineteen years, began. When he related how he found traces of arsenic in Wagner's exhumed corpse, Hoodin vigorously objected, stating that the poison could have come from any number of sources and circumstances. The defense argument bordered on the incredible.

"Who are we to say . . . that somebody might not have, in the dead of night, opened that grave, opened that casket and placed arsenic in that body?" Hoodin asked in utter seriousness. "Expert toxicologists will testify that that can be done, and further, that when it is done, it [the poison] seeps into the parts of the body, namely the rectus muscle, kidney, liver, brain, in the same manner and in the same way that it might seep into the body if any person took that poison."

Judge Bell interrupted defense counsel from his grasping at straws. "I think the court has heard all I care to hear on this matter. Objection overruled."

Behrer continued, droning on about removing organs and measuring them and taking samples to test for metallic poison. Hoodin was beside himself, tenaciously objecting to the prosecution's every question and the doctor's every response. The courtroom "took on the aspects of a schoolroom of horror conceived by a concocter of blood-curdling thrillers," Sarah L. Dush wrote for readers of the *Ohio State Journal*.

"In the liver, how many grains per kilogram did you find of arsenic trioxide?" Outcalt asked Beher.

"I object," said Hoodin.

"Overruled."

"Exception."

"I found one point five eight."

"And in the spleen, how many grains per kilogram of weight did you find?

"I object."

"Overruled."

"Exception."

"One point three six."

"In the kidney, how many grains per kilogram of weight did you find?"

"Objection."

"Overruled."

"Exception."

"Two point one nine," Behrer replied. At each answer, Outcalt wrote the number on a large blackboard.

And so it went, for the stomach, rectus muscle, bowel, and the hair. Finally, Outcalt wrote in chalk "7.8 grains," the total amount found by the chemist, and underlined it. When Outcalt asked, "Do you know, doctor, what is the fatal dose of arsenic trioxide in grains?" Hoodin objected yet again, requesting that his argument be heard without the jury present. This time he disputed Behrer's qualifications as a toxicologist, but in the end, the doctor was allowed to answer the prosecution's question.

"The fatal dose is given as anywhere from two to three grains," Behrer said. Finally, despite Hoodin's many protestations, Outcalt got to the crux of the matter with his witness.

"Doctor, I wish you would state your opinion . . . as to whether Jacob Wagner had a lethal dose of arsenic?"

"I have an opinion."

"And, in your opinion, doctor, I wish you would state to the jury, did Jacob Wagner receive a lethal dose of arsenic trioxide?"

"From my analysis of the vital organs, I would say he received a lethal dose."

In his cross-examination, Hoodin asked once arsenic is placed in the body, "how long does it preserve the body?"

"It might preserve it for years," Dr. Behrer replied.

"And you could detect the arsenic?"

"Yes. The arsenic isn't destroyed, even though the body may be decomposed," the witness replied.

When she returned to her cell, Anna Marie received from a matron an article in the previous day's *Chicago Herald and Examiner.* It was one of many she read during her incarceration, but this one was one of the more bizarre. It was written by C. A. Bonniwell, "noted psychologist and personality analyst." Using a method known as the Bertillon System that was developed by French criminologist Alphonse Bertillon, Bonniwell examined two photographs of Anna Marie, discovered eighteen "revealing" features in her face—each one diagrammed for the reader—and concluded that she was a "feminine enigma."

His gobbledygook analysis included such revelations as: "The relatively flat eyebrow ridges would indicate that her thinking would be in the sphere of the theoretical. . . . The medium weight and the color of the eyebrows goes with a rather fearless disposition. . . . The position of the eyelids in relation to the eyes shows the ability to hide or conceal one's thoughts. . . . The width of the jaw is remarkable in a woman and shows that she can and would crush any obstacle arising in her path."[1]

Anna Marie found the article amusing.

WEDNESDAY, OCTOBER 20

Dr. Frank C. Broeman, the court-appointed chemist, testified that he used "the official A.A.C.S. [American Agricultural Chemical Society] method" to test the samples of organs he received from Behrer. "It is the recognized method on all food products for determining arsenic," he said. "It is commonly known as the Gudzeit method . . . the most accurate method known." Under Outcalt's prodding and over numerous objections from Hoodin, he confirmed all of Behrer's findings, including that Wagner had died from a lethal dose of arsenic. He also testified that the substance in the bottle Detective Hayes found in Anna Marie's home was determined to be arsenic.

1. C. A. Bonniwell, "Mrs. Hahn Found Enigma in Study of Her Features," *Chicago Herald and Examiner,* Oct. 18, 1937.

Dr. Frank M. Coppock Jr. had the distinction of fielding the trial's longest hypothetical question from Outcalt. The 231-word twister, detailing Wagner's symptoms, death, and autopsy, ended with the prosecutor asking, "Now, doctor, are you able to state an opinion as to the cause of death of that subject?" Coppock was, and did: death by arsenical poisoning.

"Isn't it possible, doctor," Hoodin asked in his cross, "that this person could have died of a heart condition?" Wagner's death certificate on June 7 cited heart failure as the cause of death, but that was long before the autopsy that revealed arsenic.

Coppock said that arteriosclerosis failed to appear in the postmortem examination.

Everyone familiar with the case tensed up when Mrs. Helen Smith took the stand at the evening session. They knew she was a neighbor to Obendoerfer and her testimony surely would open the door to a new phase in the prosecution's case, namely those other men and women Anna Marie allegedly did in. But Mrs. Smith no sooner spoke her name and address than Hoodin, red in the face, objected strenuously. Judge Bell sustained the objection, ruling that witnesses would not be permitted to testify about any other deaths the prosecution linked to Anna Marie until the state showed that the hardening compound used to embalm Wagner did not contain arsenic. The judge wanted to make sure the state completed its Wagner case before proceeding further.

He adjourned the trial until morning. Several reporters staked out Wagner's grave all night in the mistaken belief that Outcalt would have the body exhumed again.

The jury's evening was considerably more pleasant. It was the guest of Roger Prior and his Orchestra at the Hotel Gibson.

THURSDAY, OCTOBER 21

For those who packed the courtroom and the hallway outside—some estimated nearly a thousand turned up once again—it was a day of disappointment, if not outright boredom.

The only testimony came from Frank Moeller, who embalmed Wagner at the Busse & Borgmann Funeral Home, and from A. O. Spriggs, the chief chemist at the Champion Chemical Company of Springfield, Ohio, which made hardener for the embalming fluid. Both witnesses confirmed that the Champion product contained no arsenic. The prosecution again called Mrs. Smith to the witness stand, but her testimony was not heard.

After hearing the two witnesses, the jury panel was excused and returned to the Hotel Metropole for the day. In its absence, the court heard arguments by the prosecution and defense on whether related acts, not contained in the indictment, should be admitted. Anna Marie, who had shown heretofore a noticeable lack of interest in the trial, perked up, reading the citations in the stack of several dozen law books on the defense table and hanging on every word Hoodin delivered.

When she returned to the jail for the evening, there was a change in the norm for her. For almost two months, Philip had been sending the fruit basket to his wife every Thursday, but today Sheriff Lutz put a stop to the deliveries. So many gifts—clothing, candy, and flowers—were arriving at the jail from "well-wishers" who hoped to see Anna Marie personally that Lutz halted the practice for her own safety.

While incarcerated, Anna Marie occupied herself with more than fruit and bonbons. She read *Gone with the Wind* twice, amused herself with true confession magazines, and knit. She knit an infant's sweater for the wife of the cocounsel for the defense, Dorothy S. Hoodin, who recently had become a mother. Mrs. Hoodin ended her thank-you note optimistically: "Please believe that I wish you the best of luck, and that I have faith in the fact that you will prove your innocence."

FRIDAY, OCTOBER 22

Judge Bell's written decision was that the defense would be permitted to introduce evidence of related acts. It was a stunning victory for the prosecution, which now could spread before the jury five cases of poison instead of just the one for which Anna Marie was being tried.

So, for the third time, Mrs. Smith took the witness stand and opened wide the prosecution's Pandora's Box containing the names of Obendoerfer, Palmer, Gsellman, and Heis. Mrs. Smith said she had known Obendoerfer for about two years and last saw him, grip in hand, at the restaurant where she worked as a waitress on the night before he left for Colorado. In chatting with him that evening, she thought he appeared in good spirits and in good health.

Outcalt next put Cincinnati Yellow Cab driver Otto Walke on the stand. When he arrived at the Hahn home on July 21, Oscar jumped into the back seat, Walke said, and instructed him to drive around to the rear of the garage.

"What was the next thing that happened?"

"The boy got out and went in through the garage and in a minute came out with an old man and a woman."

Outcalt picked up state exhibit twenty-three, a photograph of Obendoerfer, and asked Walke to identify it as the man that came out of the Hahn home.

"I object," said Hoodin.

"Overruled," replied the judge, to which the defense registered yet another exception.

"That is the gentleman," Walke said.

"I will ask you if you will look at the defendant Mrs. Hahn, and state whether or not she is the lady that came out of the house."

Walke took a quick look at Anna Marie and said, "Yes, that was the lady." She affirmed him with a smile.

"And what did you do then?"

"They entered the cab and the lady said, 'Depot,' and that is all the words that were spoken, and I took them to the Union Terminal and discharged them, and the lady paid the bill, which was fifty cents."

Denver innkeeper Louis Straub, the first of several witnesses from Colorado, recalled for Assistant Prosecutor Hoy that he had asked Anna Marie to come to his office at the Midland Hotel because of his concern for Obendoerfer's health.

"I said to her, 'Are you traveling with that old gentleman?' and she said, 'I met him on the train. I don't know who he is, but he was very sick, and I was taking care of him.' 'Well,' I said, 'he is pretty sick, isn't he?' and she said, 'Yes, but not as bad as he was.' That was on the twenty-ninth [of July]."

"Is that all you can recall at this time?"

"Well, I asked as to whether he [Obendoerfer] had any money, and she said, 'No, he's broke. All the money he had was $4.85.'" Straub also recalled that he spoke to Anna Marie about the deplorable condition of Obendoerfer's room. "I told her the help refused to go in there."

The following day, when he went to see the room for himself, Straub said he saw Obendoerfer sitting in a big chair, "all drawn up . . . he was barefooted and had his pants and undershirt on, that is all."

"Before you describe his condition as you saw him then," Hoy said, "tell the jury what the condition of the room was, even after it was partially cleaned up."

"Why, this man's bowels had moved, and the room was in a terrible condition although it had been partly cleaned up, and the blanket was thrown over the radiator, but the room was in very, very bad shape. Couldn't be much worse." At the prodding of the prosecution, the witness went into further detail about the feces and vomit he saw. "The blankets were all dirty, the comforters were dirty; in front of the bed was all mussed up on the rug, and the chair which he sat in was also in very bad—had been mussed up."

Hoy asked Straub to demonstrate the best he could how Obendoerfer was curled up in the chair. With some difficulty in the witness chair, Straub drew his knees toward his chest, in a fetal position, grunting slightly as he did so. When a spectator giggled at the sight, Judge Bell fired a warning glance at the offender over his pince-nez.

Uncurled, Straub continued. "I said to him, 'Are you traveling alone?' and he said—like that—held up three fingers. He didn't answer, only muttered something, and I could not understand, and he held up three fingers."

"Your hand was shaking then," Hoy noted.

"That is the way *his* hand was going, very much so. My hand doesn't shake."

Just prior to checking out on the thirtieth and heading for Colorado Springs, Anna Marie told Straub that Obendoerfer "had a check of a thousand dollars he would get when he got to Colorado Springs," the hotel owner testified. It was his understanding that Obendoerfer "was going there on a chicken ranch."

Hoodin failed to shake Straub's testimony, although he tried, gaining an admission from the innkeeper that he never saw Anna Marie in Obendoerfer's room. Straub also admitted that a check for $10 that he cashed for her, which initially was returned for insufficient funds, later was made good. These were small, insignificant victories for the defense.

Hoy, who had retraced Anna Marie's steps in Chicago and Colorado, also conducted the interrogation of Colorado Springs Park Hotel owner Pell Turner. He read from the hotel's register for July 30, 1937: "Gg. Obendoerfer, Chicago, Illinois, Mrs. Hahn and son, Chicago, Illinois." The witness said he assisted Anna Marie in getting Obendoerfer up the stairs to his room.

"About two hours later I was going past the room. I noticed Mr. Obendoerfer was a very sick man."

"Did you see or hear anything at that time?"

"Yes. He was lying on the bed, moaning and groaning and squirming and seemed to be writhing in agony and pain."

Hoodin asked the court that the phrase, "seemed to be," be stricken from the record, but was overruled.

"What did you do then, Mr. Turner?" Hoy continued.

"I suggested to Mrs. Hahn that she take him to the hospital. I told her I wasn't running a hospital, and I thought he was too sick a man for either her or I to take care of him. I thought he needed medical or professional attention. This made Mrs. Hahn indignant, but, nevertheless, I went downstairs and in about ten or fifteen minutes she came down and told me to call a Yellow Cab, which I did, and she took him to a Protestant hospital. She asked for a Protestant hospital."

Turner said he recommended Beth-El Hospital, which is where she went. The next time he saw Anna Marie, he said, was the following day at the hotel when he asked her about Obendoerfer and how it was that they were traveling together.

"She told me she never saw him before in her life, but she just happened to meet him on the train between Chicago and Denver. She said he was a Swiss German and she, being of the same nationality, she could talk to him, and he was sick. She felt sorry for him and tried to take care of him."

Hoy asked if she said anything about Obendoerfer and the hospital.

"She told me she had taken him to the hospital and now she had washed her hands clean. It was up to the City of Colorado Springs to take care of him."

The next evening, Sunday, August 1, Turner spoke to Anna Marie in the lobby of the hotel. "I told Mrs. Hahn that Mr. Obendoerfer was dead. . . . And she says, 'Well, why tell me? I don't know the man. I never saw him before in my life until I met him on the train.'"

The following morning, about seven, the hotelier said, Anna Marie came down to the front desk to check out. "Then she asked me if she could check her baggage there . . . at the Denver and Rio Grande Western Depot." He told her she could.

When Colorado Springs police began their investigation and spoke to Turner, it was his recollection of Anna Marie's query that led them so quickly to Obendoerfer's wicker bag at the depot. They knew where to look.

Dr. Willard K. Hills attended to Obendoerfer when he came into Beth-El Hospital. Despite his repeated efforts, Dr. Hills could not get the old man to say his name, he testified. Anna Marie was in the room, and at one point "she stepped up there and asked him, 'What is your name?'"

The physician told the court that Anna Marie said she had met Obendoerfer on the train. "She said he had been awfully sick and had a bad time coming down [from Denver] on the train and then she said when he got off the train . . . 'he couldn't hardly walk and everybody laughed at him. . . . We [Anna Marie and Oscar] felt awfully sorry for him. We couldn't do anything else, could we?'"

Describing Obendoerfer as "critically ill" when he arrived at the hospital, Dr. Hills said the patient was pale, had "puffy" eyelids, and had a throat that was sore and inflamed, making it difficult to swallow. He also had scratch marks on his skin and "a motor paralysis," the Colorado physician said.

"These scratch marks that you speak of, doctor, where were they?" Hoy asked.

"Well, various places . . . on his legs and thighs, where his skin was slightly jaundiced, and he had . . . what we call a melanosis, which is a condition of deposit of pigment in the skin from toxic causes." In addition to the scratch marks, from a "good deal of itching," Dr. Hill also noticed that Obendoerfer had blisters on his genitals.

Was he "stuporous"? Hoy asked.

"Yes, he was, although you could rouse him by talking directly to him. He would make an effort to talk to you, but he couldn't articulate.

He couldn't say words in a clear manner so they could be understood." After failing to calm the restless Obendoerfer with sodium amytol, Dr. Hill prescribed doses of morphine, a much stronger drug.

The embalmer at the Law Mortuary, Harley Remington, testified that Anna Marie said she did not know Obendoerfer, that she met him for the first time on the train from Chicago. "She said that she thought she would be rid of him in Colorado Springs, that her son was annoyed with his [Obendoerfer] being along" on the trip.

When he received the body and the personal effects, Remington inventoried a pair of old glasses, matches, two tobacco cans with butts of cigars in them, and a bunch of keys—but not "one cent of money."

El Paso County Coroner J. Thomas Coghlan in Colorado Springs performed three autopsies on Obendoerfer. The first two, on August 4 and 5, did not reveal the cause of death, Coghlan told the court. On August 13, he removed Obendoerfer's liver, kidneys, and brain, placing each in a glass jar containing 10 percent formalin solution. "I took them all up to Dr. McConnell, up in Denver, a pathologist up there."

"Dr. Frances McConnell?"

"Dr. Frances McConnell."

Hoy asked his witness to look at the state's exhibits, numbered 29 and 30, and "state whether or not those are the bottles of embalming fluid that you took to Dr. McConnell?" Every member of the jury also looked at the grisly exhibits on the floor in front of them and just a few feet from where Anna Marie sat.

"They are," Coghlan said.

Dr. Frances McConnell testified in minute detail about her examination of the viscera and brain and the tests she performed on them. She found, she said, .520 grains of arsenic in the organs she examined. Hoy asked her to identify the jars on exhibit and to describe some of the common symptoms of arsenical poisoning. He then launched into another lengthy question.

"Now, doctor," the assistant prosecutor began slowly, "supposing a man who on July 20th is in good health, on July 29th has pain in his abdomen, running off at the bowels, there is extreme thirst; on July 30th has sore and inflamed throat and mouth, inability to swallow, jaundice, motor paralysis, is extremely restless and somewhat stuporous, and supposing that on August 1st the man died, and supposing that the postmortem examination revealed no apparent cause of death, and supposing that upon examination and chemical analysis of that man's liver, one kidney and brain, there is shown the presence of a little over a half grain of arsenic, could you from those facts form an opinion as to the cause of that man's death?"

"Yes, I would say he died of arsenical poisoning," the witness replied.

Following the dinner recess, Hoy called Edward J. Weckbach as his first witness. The assistant vice president of the Denver National Bank served Anna Marie when she first sought a loan "to buy a little farm near Denver." Twice on July 24 she visited the bank, attempting to secure a funds transfer from the Clifton Heights Loan and Building Company, Obendoerfer's Cincinnati bank, but Weckbach insisted that Anna Marie "bring her husband in and have him sign" for the $1,000 she sought. Through subterfuge and forgery, Anna Marie convinced the Cincinnati bank to forward $1,000 to Denver National, but when the money arrived on July 30, Weckbach refused to give it to her. He wanted a signature and proper identification from her "husband."

"What did she say about that?" Hoy asked.

"She said, 'I can sign it,' and I said no." Weckbach explained to the court that in Colorado a spouse couldn't sign for the marriage partner without explicit power of attorney.

"What did she say then? Go ahead. First of all, will you describe Mrs. Hahn at that time—her appearance?"

"I suppose she weighed about—she was quite a bit heavier I think then than now."

"That isn't what I had in mind, Mr. Weckbach." That brought smiles to a number of lips, including Anna Marie's. "What, if any, facial expression did you notice at that time?"

"Right along, the last three or four times that I had seen her . . ."

"I don't believe we are hearing you," said Hoy, who several times asked his witness to speak louder.

"The last three or four times that I saw her she seemed to be quite impatient—disturbed because these funds didn't arrive."

"Now, on the thirtieth, Mr. Weckbach, what about her appearance?"

"She seemed to be quite impatient, and she was disturbed because she couldn't take the money or the draft, and she suggested to me that the draft be sent to Colorado Springs to Mr. Obendoerfer." The money was to be addressed to general delivery there, he said.

Assistant County Prosecutor Simon Leis called Anna Palmer to testify. She lived at the same address as her brother, Albert. She described her brother as being "very sick most of the time" early in 1937. On the occasions when he visited Anna Marie, Miss Palmer said, he "came home . . . very sick to his stomach, and he would have to go very frequently to the bathroom immediately." He also appeared "so ashen looking, so funny looking in his face . . . weak in his knees. He seemed as though he couldn't walk very well without an umbrella or a cane," she said.

Court adjourned until Monday morning, giving everyone a two-day respite because of Hoodin's illness. All week he had continued to battle a bad cold; now he needed the rest Judge Bell granted.

11 | "DEATH IS FEARED, AND DISTRESS IS GREAT"

When the third week of Cincinnati's longest and most celebrated murder trial resumed on Monday, Walter J. Siegler, auditor of commercial accounts for Cincinnati's First National Bank, took the stand. However, the testimony was soon to become more gruesome than a recitation of bank records.

Hoodin, who felt better after bed rest but still evidenced signs of a lingering cold, didn't waste any time registering an objection. This time it was the introduction of a cashier's check that was made out to Palmer, endorsed by him and by Anna Marie, and deposited by her in the First National Bank. In the absence of the jury once again, Hoodin presented his argument.

"As I understand, if the court please, the statement made by Mr. Outcalt in his opening statement, he is going to show that she obtained money from all these old men by various means, and that those means were not honest means. Now, do you think this record should be cluttered up with a business transaction? . . . The only purpose of this thing is to do the very thing I have been shouting about for several days, namely, to prejudice the jury. If she got fifteen, seventeen hundred or two thousand dollars, what would that indicate in this case if that transaction was a perfectly legitimate transaction? . . . It does nothing but becloud the issue and cause this jury to have in their minds that she was taking money from elderly people."

Judge Bell ruled that it was not necessary to show that the defendant got the money by fraud. "A transaction may be perfectly legitimate," he said, offering a simple illustration of his point. "Suppose the court borrows from you five thousand, and you give it to me. In my mind, in an attempt to enrich myself and not repay the money, I destroy your life. I think it would be perfectly competent to go to the jury as to a question of my motive in destroying your life if they found I did destroy it. The objection will be overruled. Bring in the jury."

The star witness at the afternoon and evening sessions Monday was Dr. Robert A. Kehoe, a Cincinnati physician, pathologist, and physiologist with degrees from the University of Cincinnati, where he taught medical physiology. As he took the stand, Outcalt's assistants carried eighteen wrapped packages into the courtroom and placed them on the floor and table alongside Wagner's organs. All were within a few feet of the defendant. Hoodin, sensing what was about to unfold, jumped to his feet to object once again and was overruled once again.

At the outset of Kehoe's testimony, jurors filled with a hearty lunch strained mightily to stay awake during his slow, lengthy, clinical explanations of autopsies and the signs of acute arsenic poisoning.

The symptoms, Kehoe droned, "are alarming, they are uncomfortable, they come on quickly, and they bring with them a clinical situation in which death is feared and distress is great."

"Go ahead, doctor," Outcalt urged.

"The acute symptoms in some cases are most striking in the gastrointestinal tract, that is to say, in the whole alimentary tract, from the mouth clear through the intestines. The mouth may be sore and the throat may be irritated, but the stomach is almost certainly the most seriously involved portion of the tract, and this is the more true the larger the dose of arsenic that is given."

"I didn't understand the last part," Outcalt said, inviting the expert witness to launch into an even more complex and detailed description of what arsenic will do to a person's insides.

Kehoe explained how the poison mixes with gastric secretions, the retching that follows, and "profuse diarrhea . . . the discharge thin and whitish."

"Can you tell the jury, doctor, what is the accepted lethal or fatal dose of arsenic in the form of arsenic trioxide?"

"The lethal dose is somewhat variable for different persons, but from the records of cases that are available . . . a conclusion has been reached and generally agreed upon that the lethal dose is between one-and-a-half to three grains, with the statement that the absorption of three grains is capable of producing death in most individuals, regardless of size and their state of previous health."

Outcalt then unwrapped his eighteen packages of body parts taken from Palmer's body following a secret exhumation September 23. (It was commonly believed that Palmer had been cremated.) Holding each container up for all to see, the prosecutor asked, "Now, doctor, do you know what this is?" The jury now was wide-awake, spellbound by the grisly presentation. In the end, Kehoe said that his autopsies of organs from Palmer and Wagner revealed nearly six grains of arsenic trioxide in each body.

With Kehoe's testimony in the record, the prosecution had made its case that each of Anna Marie's pals—Wagner, Palmer, and Obendoerfer—had ingested lethal doses of arsenic.

Spectators had hope that George Heis would testify this day. Their expectations were high when he briefly appeared in court in a wheelchair during testimony, but prospects were dashed when he was taken home after the prosecution realized they would not need him quite yet.

The prosecution instead called to the stand Dr. Frank M. Coppock Jr., the county coroner, and two of Gsellman's elderly neighbors, Caroline Topicz, a cigar store owner, and Anna Spekert, who required a translator during her testimony in German.

In response to a question from Outcalt, Dr. Coppock, who the previous Wednesday had given testimony concerning Wagner's autopsy, now declared, "In my opinion, [Gsellman] died from ingestion of arsenic." He performed the Gsellman autopsy August 12, after the victim was disinterred.

Mrs. Topicz and Mrs. Spekert said that Gsellman appeared happy and in fine health the day before he died. He told them that he was taking a bride the following day.

TUESDAY, OCTOBER 26

A neighbor from Gsellman's tenement building, Minnie Schultz, was the prosecution's first witness of the day. The night before Gsellman died, she said she saw Anna Marie escort "a kind of weak" Gsellman down two flights of stairs to the second floor toilet and back again. "He . . . was leaning on the banister . . . and breathing a little hard. That was the last I saw of him."

Her husband, August, discovered the body the next morning. It was naked save for slippers on its feet. Schultz called the police. In the early afternoon, he met Anna Marie coming up the stairs. "I stopped her and told her, 'No use going up there.' The man died, and they had taken him away."

Anna Marie went up anyway, he testified, and when she came down from Gsellman's dwelling, "I asked her if the man had been ill that night."

"What did she say?" Outcalt asked.

"She said, 'Yes, he wasn't feeling well,' and I said, 'Why didn't he get a doctor?' and she said, 'He don't believe in them.'"

Patrolman Louis Pohl responded to the call from 1717 Elm Street. He ordered Gsellman's body taken to General Hospital, after which it was taken to the morgue. Loyal Martin asked the officer to describe the table he saw in Gsellman's room.

"There were two cups and saucers and a plate with butter on it and other dishes."

"Were there more than two places set at that table?"

"Well, it appeared it was set for two."

"Did you notice the room at that time, officer?"

"Well, the room appeared to me as if someone might have been looking for something."

"What do you mean by that, officer?"

"Well, there was a cupboard on the north side of the room, and it looked very much like somebody had been in there whatever—for what the purpose was I don't know, but it was kind of upset. . . . The table looked like there was—it was mussed up. I don't recall just how, but there was a lot of stuff . . . outside of the dishes."

"Papers, or things of that sort?"

"Well, there was papers and clothes."

After the body was removed, Pohl said he locked the door to the apartment and gave the key to the morgue attendant. Martin had made his point: Anna Marie had to have had a key to open Gsellman's door later in the day.

In his cross-examination, Bolsinger tried to get the officer to verify there were beer bottles on the table, but Pohl said there were none, just some bottles in the cupboard.

"You are positive of that?"

"Positive, yes, sir."

Veteran *Cincinnati Post* reporter Charles Ludwig and his photographer, Peter Koch, told of visiting Gsellman's room on August 13, one day after the victim was buried, then exhumed hours later. Securing permission to sort through Gsellman's personal effects, Ludwig described the discovery of the transit ticket on which Anna Marie had written, "Go home. I'll be there." The police had overlooked the key piece of evidence that linked Anna Marie to Gsellman on the day before he died.

"Our photographer was seated opposite me at the table . . . and we were looking through Gsellman's papers, and he [Koch] suddenly threw [an envelope] over to me and said something to me, called my attention to it. . . . I opened it and read it." Inside was the College Hill streetcar pass dated July 5, 1937. Handwriting experts at the FBI in Washington determined it was Anna Marie who had written the note on the back.

Yet another journalist, Wilber F. Carmichael, was called as a prosecution witness. The police reporter for the *Cincinnati Times-Star* recalled that on the day his rivals were at Gsellman's flat, he and two other reporters were at the lock-up, interviewing Anna Marie shortly after she had been indicted for Gsellman's murder.

"Will you just tell us what that conversation was?" Martin asked.

"Well, I visited the Women's Place of Detention at police headquarters with Lieutenant George Schattle, and she was called out. We stood there, talking about the weather [it was hot and steamy] and how she felt and . . . finally asked her would she name the men and women that she knew who had since either died or were ill."

"And what did she say?"

"Mrs. Hahn was standing behind the gate in the place, and we were on the outside, and she said she would name the people she knew, and started off by pointing to her fingers, and she mentioned Mr. Wagner. She mentioned Palmer. She mentioned Mr. Heis. She mentioned a man named Kohler, Obendoerfer, and mentioned a lady named Mrs. Koehler, and quit. That's all she named."

"What did you say to her then, Mr. Carmichael?"

"I asked her if it was not true she knew Mr. Gsellman, and she said it was not."

"What else, if anything, did she say?"

"I mentioned to her the fact that a man named Schultz from Elm Street had identified her as visiting Mr. Gsellman, and she said to me . . . 'Mister, that man lied when he said he saw me in Mr. Gsellman's house.' She says, 'If you claim I knew him, why don't you accuse me of killing all the old people that died?'"

Dr. Behrer, city chemist, recalled to the stand for the fourth time to identify poison in body parts, told of finding a total of 1.97 grains of arsenic in Gsellman's organs. In addition, his examination of the two pans found in Gsellman's room revealed 9.33 grains of arsenic in the one that had contained meat and 8.56 grains in the one that had had gravy.

After the lunch recess, the prosecution introduced its star witness.

12 | "YOU DID THIS!"

O ther than the defendant herself, no witness was more eagerly anticipated than George E. Heis, described by the prosecution as "the only living witness of a plot to slay for gain."

Chicago Daily News reporter Robert J. Casey humorously described Heis as "the big one that got away"—from Anna Marie, of course. Since consuming poison in food she prepared for him, Casey wrote, Heis "hasn't been around much except in a wheel chair."[1]

In his colorful reporting style, Casey portrayed Heis as "a pale, thin little man with expressionless gray eyes and a face animated only by a muscular twitching in his forehead. Save for the fact that he came into court in a new suit instead of in a collection of glass bottles, he seemed only a shade different from Jacob Wagner and George Gsellman and George Obendoerfer and Albert Palmer, who for a year have lain restlessly in cemeteries."[2]

It was a moment of high drama on a par with anything Hollywood could produce when the emaciated Heis entered the hushed, packed courtroom that Tuesday afternoon. He rode in a wheelchair pushed

1. Robert J. Casey, "Mrs. Hahn Hears Accusations by the Living One," *Chicago Daily News*, Oct. 26, 1937, 1.
2. Casey is credited by many as having begun his story about Heis, "Seven victims of Anna Marie Hahn were in court today, six in pickling jars and one in a blue serge suit," but no evidence could be found that he wrote that at the time.

by bailiff Charles Stagnaro, who positioned Heis close to the witness stand. Anna Marie sat almost within arm's length. Heis never looked at her, but she, her face almost drained of color now, couldn't keep her eyes off him.

The star witness fidgeted in his wheelchair, crossed and uncrossed his crippled legs, and played with the gold chain that hung from the lapel of his brown, plaid suit. Many times he aimlessly kicked at the several dozen multi-hued glass jars of evidence at his feet that contained parts of Gsellman, Palmer, and Wagner. When he rattled the jar containing a part of Gsellman's brain, Judge Bell summoned his bailiff, who whispered to the witness to stop doing that. Heis looked contrite. He uncrossed his legs, in doing so mindlessly kicking one of the arsenic-laced saucepans found on Gsellman's stove. Some who saw Heis's fidgeting seemed horrified; others smiled.

Assistant Prosecutor Leis began by questioning Heis about the first two visits Anna Marie made to his office and home (at 2922 Colerain Avenue) in June 1936. Ostensibly, both those visits were to discuss the purchase of coal.

"Now, at the time she came back the third time, what, if anything, did she bring with her?"

"She brought some bonds, Hungarian bonds, she claimed they were," Heis said in a voice that was surprisingly firm and strong. Unlike many of the witnesses who proceeded him, Heis had no trace of a German accent.

"What kind of a package were these bonds in?"

"She had them in a small package . . . rolled up and tied with a cord. She asked me if I would keep it for her in my safe."

"What did you tell her?"

"I told her, 'You got a big house up there, plenty of room to put them there.' She said she was afraid to leave them at her house, her husband might find them and steal them." Anna Marie shook her head in a silent denial.

Heis placed the package in his safe, as she requested. A short time later, she visited him again to let him know she was going to Buffalo, New York, to obtain a divorce from Philip. Several days later, she popped up on his doorstep again to inform him that "it was all over."

Leis questioned the witness about going to Brighton Bank with Anna Marie, withdrawing $200, and giving it to her.

"What did she say to you with reference to what she wanted that money for?"

"She wanted that money for those bonds to pay inheritance taxes and state taxes [on them]." On cross-examination, Heis added that he gave Anna Marie another $200 because, she said, the first amount of money was used to pay for her divorce.

On July 22 Heis gave her another $200 to pay more inheritance and state taxes, this time on a $7,000 trust fund she said she had inherited from an uncle. Heis understood she had placed the trust fund in his name at the Provident Savings Bank & Trust.

August was a light month; Anna Marie only borrowed $10 and $20 at a time, but in September she asked for and received $100. She said it was to buy a bond on a hundred shares of gas and electric company stock that she had received from an uncle. "She said, 'I am going to turn that all over to you,'" Heis said.

"Did she tell you what [the stock] was worth?"

She did, he said. He remembered her comment: "'One more point it has to raise, and it will be worth $14,000.'"

Also in September Anna Marie told Heis about a house and farm that she was interested in acquiring in North Bend, Ohio. It was listed at the courthouse for $12,000, she said. Her story was a complete fabrication, but Heis bought it.

"She said she needed some money for this, so I gave her some. One day she told me she had to go to court because of a lawsuit about the house. She came back and said, 'I won the case, the house is mine. Now I have to pay the lawyer $250 . . . for winning the case.'"

"What money, if any, did you give her then?"

"I gave her $250."

Heis explained that Anna Marie had promised to turn the house over to him, too. First, though, she told him she needed to pay for two hundred iron fence posts, wire, and wash posts that she bought for the farm in a sale. Heis obliged once again. Then she had problems with the hot water heater at the house. It was "all apart," she told Heis.

"She called up the Pittsburgh Heater Company . . . and they brought down two hot water heaters, and she picked out the biggest one," he recalled. "I asked her how much that big one cost. She said $135. I said, 'Did you pay for it?' She said 'No, I am going to pay for it tonight.' I said, 'Where are you going to get the money?' She said, 'From you,'" and she was right once again.

Within a few days, she was back with a story that she had "pretty near got arrested" because the sheriff wanted $134 paid on back taxes on the North Bend house. "I laughed at her," Heis said. "You will never get arrested for that." The laugh was on him, though; he gave her $100. She said she would get the rest some place else.

"How much money did she get from you altogether?"

"She got about $2,000." Heis looked sheepish at having to admit to the sum.

Leis tried to show that $1,200 of the $2,000 belonged to the Consolidated Coal Company, and both he and Outcalt argued that the pressure on Anna Marie to repay these funds hatched her murderous scheme. Judge Bell, however, disallowed the testimony, observing that where Heis got the money was irrelevant.

Leis resumed his questioning of the witness, returning to Anna Marie's visits in September. "What, if anything, did she bring to you, Mr. Heis?"

"She brought me something to eat."

"Before that, state whether or not you were a healthy man."

"Yes, sir."

"What kind of work were you able to perform before you took sick?"

"A hard day's work." Leis appeared to not hear the response, so Heis repeated it: "A hard day's work."

"Did you personally deliver coal?"

"Yes."

The prosecutor asked his sixty-two-year-old witness to describe his health in late September, early October. "I was awful sick," Heis said, describing his vomiting, a raw throat, and "the runs."

"How many times during the month of September did Mrs. Hahn bring you food?"

"Oh, two or three."

"And how many times in October?"

"Oh, once."

"Do you recall particularly what kind of food . . . she brought you?"

Anna Marie's cooking included veal chops, sliced peaches, and spinach; that's all Heis could recall.

"Did you talk to her with reference to the spinach that she brought you?"

"Yes, sir. I asked her if she put sugar in the spinach. She said, 'No, maybe the little boy [Oscar] did,' but she said she didn't."

"How much of that spinach did you eat?"

"About two forks full."

After eating a few of Anna Marie's culinary creations and then feeling lousy, Heis said he "ran her out" of his house.

"And what was the occasion when you ran her out?"

"She brought me a meal, and I told her I wouldn't eat it, I wasn't hungry, to leave it sit, I would eat it later. She said, 'Oh, you ain't hungry?' and naturally, as she went out, she took it away." Although Leis did not follow up his witness's response, Heis clearly intimated that Anna Marie removed the evidence from his home.

"Well, now, state your physical condition after you ate those meals."

"I got sick."

Leis asked Heis to demonstrate for the court how he displayed his weakened condition to Anna Marie.

"I went like this," he replied, holding out in front of him his weakened, shaking, bony hands. "I said, 'You did this!' She said, 'No, I did not.'"

Heis's physician, Dr. George Charles Altemeier, later testified that his patient "developed the symptoms of multiple neuritis, both in his legs and his arms . . . paralysis of the hands and the feet until finally, late in October, he had developed a well-marked wrist drop and foot drop." He concluded that Heis suffered from some kind of poison in his system—arsenic, "probably."

Margaret Tweedie, who lived on the same floor as Heis, told the court that in late September and early October he was "a very sick man," so sick that she cared for him and cooked for him after Anna Marie was "run out."

Bolsinger conducted the cross-examination of Heis, Hoodin having been earlier excused by the court because his cold was getting him down. Bolsinger first turned to the day Heis was in Anna Marie's home, eating her pancakes, when Philip came in.

"What did he say?" the defense attorney asked.

"He just says, 'Heis. Heis. Heis.' Then he comes in and he said, 'How is business?' I said, 'Pretty bad' . . . and he went in the next room" for a short time before leaving. This occurred in July, after the divorce, Heis said.

Bolsinger pointed out that the court usually grants a divorce decree, but there was none. The witness explained that Anna Marie had obtained the divorce in Buffalo, New York. "I am only telling you what she told me."

"You didn't put any faith in that, did you?"

"Well, I didn't know only what she told me. Another thing: It wasn't bothering me."

"It wasn't bothering you?" Bolsinger asked with more than a hint of incredulity in his voice.

"No, sir."

"Didn't make any difference to you whether she was getting a divorce or not?"

"No, sir."

After the prosecution's eighty-third witness was wheeled out of the courtroom, Leis told *Ohio State Journal* reporter Sarah L. Dush, "I hope she goes to the electric chair."

WEDNESDAY, OCTOBER 27

Dr. Altemeier, on the stand again as the morning session began, stuck to his diagnosis of Heis, despite a hammering cross-examination by Hoodin. The defense suggested that the same symptoms might have been caused by other factors, such as sleeping powders or drinking excessive amounts of home brew.

After the lunch recess, Dr. Willard Machle, a psychology professor and a toxicologist at the University of Cincinnati Medical School and assistant director of the university's Kettering Laboratory, tied Anna Marie to arsenic. His testimony all but sealed her conviction.

The link, as strong as fettering chains, was the small, white, crocheted purse that Anna Marie used daily in the summertime and the one that she had with her when arrested. Police confiscated it when she was jailed August 10. Hoodin argued long and hard to keep out of the trial any mention of what the purse contained, but his effort was in vain.

"I found 35 percent of poison in the lint of the purse," Dr. Machle said. He also discovered arsenic in the lining, on the metal clips, and on the outside of the handbag, which became state's exhibit 110. "The crystalline particles of death" was how *New York News* reporter George Dixon described the poison in the purse.

When Hoodin tried to secure an admission that the arsenic could have come from a lady's face powder, which does contain a modicum of arsenic, Dr. Machle replied, "You'd have to have eight or ten pounds of face powder to get that much arsenic from it." Several jurors smiled at the response.

The state introduced the purse into evidence, but not without a three-hour struggle. Judge Bell sustained Hoodin's objection that the state had not shown that the purse had not been tampered with after it was taken from Anna Marie upon her arrest. So, Outcalt was granted a recess while he rousted five additional witnesses to close the loophole

Similarly, Outcalt tried later to put into evidence the two salt shakers—one containing 82 percent arsenic trioxide—that Colorado Springs police found in Obendoerfer's grip recovered in the luggage checkroom at the train depot. Judge Bell sustained Hoodin's objection.

"It is a well-established rule in Ohio that a jury may not pile inferences on inferences to arrive at a conclusion," the judge said, "and the record does not show that the state has proved either that defendant checked this bag or that she placed the shakers in the bag." The shakers were out.

Outcalt called his next witness, Clarence E. Osborne, credit manager for Consolidated Coal Company, to bolster the State's contention that Anna Marie had "robbed Peter to pay Paul." In her case, it was robbing—and poisoning—Palmer, Wagner, Gsellman, and Obendoerfer to pay Consolidated Coal and Heis.

In his effort to get her to return Consolidated Coal's $1,200 that Heis had loaned his paramour, Osborne checked into her assets, namely the $16,000 she said she had in the bank and the North Bend home she said she had bought. Both were nonexistent, Osborne discovered. And when he asked her to liquidate the gas and electric stock, "she said the stock was in her son's name." Several checks and

When in court, Anna Marie always appeared impeccably turned out, thanks to her jail mates, who voluntarily arranged her hair, polished her nails, and pressed her clothes. Reprinted with permission of the *Columbus Dispatch*.

Judge Charles Steele Bell was tough, but he wept when he sentenced Anna Marie Hahn to death. Courtesy of the *Cincinnati Post.*

Hamilton County district attorney Dudley Miller Outcalt prosecuted "the greatest mass-murderess in history." Courtesy of the *Cincinnati Post.*

Capt. Patrick H. Hayes, a hardened Cincinnati detective, led the investigation into multiple murders. Courtesy of the *Cincinnati Post.*

The "living witness," George Heis, was sure Anna Marie Hahn had poisoned him. Courtesy of the Cleveland Public Library.

Defense attorney Joseph H. Hoodin and spectacled Anna Marie Hahn confer shortly before he put her on the stand. Special Collections, Cleveland State University Library.

Three days after his mother's arrest, Oscar Hahn poses at the police station with Anna Marie's husband, Philip, left, and defense attorney Hiram C. Bolsinger Sr. Special Collections, Cleveland State University Library.

Frederick L. Rike, left, Ohio penitentiary's chief engineer, and Warden James C. Woodard supervise a prisoner during the installation of "Old Sparky" in the prison's new death chamber, April 1938. Special Collections, Cleveland State University Library.

On December 1, 1937, Anna Marie Hahn walks into the Ohio penitentiary escorted by cigar-chomping Charles Stagnaro, Hamilton County Criminal Court bailiff, and Maude Burkhardt, Hamilton County Jail matron. Special Collections, Cleveland State University Library.

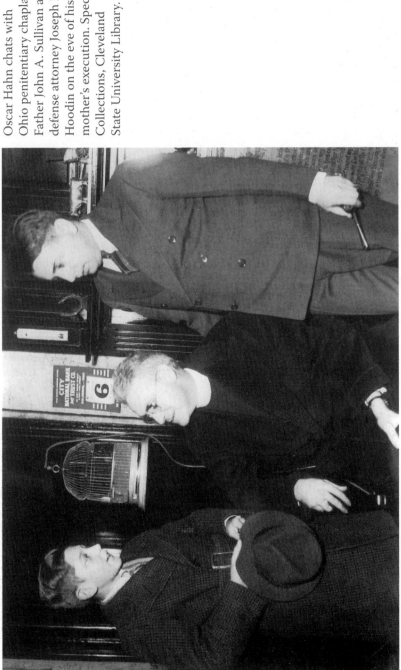

Oscar Hahn chats with Ohio penitentiary chaplain Father John A. Sullivan and defense attorney Joseph H. Hoodin on the eve of his mother's execution. Special Collections, Cleveland State University Library.

Anna Marie Hahn greets her
handsome son, Oscar, at the
outset of her Cincinnati trial.
Courtesy of Wide World
Photos/*Cincinnati Enquirer.*

Anna Marie Hahn's official
Ohio penitentiary photo-
graph, which hung on the wall
of the death chamber after
she became the 214th prisoner to be executed. Courtesy
of Charles C. Howard.

promissory notes from Anna Marie bounced before the company finally recovered $900, said Osborne.

Outcalt called Cincinnati homicide detective Walter Hart to the stand. Two days after Anna Marie's arrest, Hart and Assistant Prosecutor Gordon H. Scherer returned to her home and, without a search warrant, confiscated various items, including a pawn ticket from Denver that was tucked inside a magazine and a handwritten note that he found torn up in the wastepaper basket. The note in Anna Marie's handwriting used the same wording as Wagner's note to his bank, informing them that he had found his bankbook.

"I asked her why she wrote this letter," Hart said. "She said she wrote it out so Jacob Wagner could copy it."

Hoodin couldn't wait to cross-examine the witness.

"Did you ever use vile language in questioning her?" Hoodin stormed.

"I can tell you what I said to her, but I don't consider it vile." Hart said he asked Anna Marie if she had had intimate relations with the old men. "My investigation . . . indicated that she had."

"Those weren't your exact words," Hoodin snapped.

Hart looked at the judge to his right and directly into the faces of the petticoat jury. "Well, if you want to know exactly what I said, I will tell you. I said, 'Did you kill these old men by screwing them?'"

Hoodin recoiled. Anna Marie blushed and covered her face. The jury sat stunned. Spectators gasped.

"Your Honor!" the defense attorney shouted once again. "I move that his remarks be stricken!" But Judge Bell allowed Hart's earthy testimony to stand.

"Didn't she resent that kind of language?" Hoodin continued.

"She said, 'Don't talk to me like that.'"

The final two of the ninety-five prosecution witnesses were both handwriting experts. Albert D. Osborn of Montclair, New Jersey, had given expert testimony in the trial of Bruno Richard Hauptmann and other highly publicized trials of the day. He was described as "an eminent pen and ink expert." The second witness was the attractive Katherine Keeler of Chicago, who studied under Osborn's father, Albert S. Osborn. Her husband, Leonarde Keeler, invented an early polygraph that bore his name and headed up the Scientific Crime Detection Laboratory at Northwestern University School of Law.

Neither Wagner's will nor the note giving Anna Marie "power over everything" were, in Osborn's opinion, "good imitations of Wagner's handwriting. It is Mrs. Hahn's idea of his handwriting, but it is not a good idea." Furthermore, both documents were in English, Osborn noted. It was poor English, but English nevertheless—a language in which Wagner did not write.

"These writings of Mrs. Hahn show the usual characteristics of an imitation. They are slowly and carefully drawn. In one case you can see that the imitator [w]as going so slow that the pen actually was lifted from the paper, then placed back. It shows the natural inclination of the imitator to go back and patch."

Displaying photostatic copies of handwriting known to be Anna Marie's, enlarged sixty-four times, Osborn identified her handwriting in letters and cards to Philip, Palmer, Osborne, and bankers, and other documents, such as checks and the pawn ticket, all of which Outcalt succeeded in getting into evidence. Despite his vigorous attempt, on cross-examination Hoodin failed to shake Osborn's testimony.

Keeler's appearance at the trial was "a pictorial highlight in a succession of witnesses who may have been smart but were seldom beautiful," Casey wrote for his Chicago newspaper. Keeler also came with a slew of oversized charts that were displayed on easels. Judge Bell took a seat next to the jury so he could see them, too, as she described elements of Anna Marie's handwriting.

In four hours of detailed testimony about "downward shadings" and "upward swirls," her conclusions corroborated Osborn's. "The errors of the imitator or forger are due to his own habit," she said, "so that the errors he makes in one forgery are apt to be the same errors he makes in another." Keeler pointed to examples of such discrepancies in Anna Marie's handwriting.

THURSDAY, OCTOBER 28

As Keeler took the stand once again after the overnight recess, expectations were high that the state would rest its case after her cross-examination. That took but thirty minutes, with Hoodin gaining no ground. Keeler packed up her charts and headed back to Chicago.

When order was restored in the courtroom, Outcalt rose from his chair. "The state rests," he announced quietly.

"The court will not permit the state to rest at this time," Judge Bell said. "The defense has reserved the right to cross-examine two of the state's witnesses. I don't remember their names. Perhaps Mr. Hoodin does."

Hoodin didn't, but a quick search of the record revealed the witnesses were Captain Hayes and Dr. Marnell. He decided not to call either again. Judge Bell adjourned the court for twenty-four hours, directing that all motions would be heard Saturday morning.

13 | OSCAR'S STORY

A t the outset of the trial, Hoodin indicated he would call fifty-three witnesses for the defense. He came up fifty-one short.

Oscar, neatly attired in a natty striped tie and a double-breasted brown suit—his first with long pants—was the first witness called Monday morning in opening the case for the defense. This came as somewhat of a surprise, for when the trial adjourned Friday afternoon, Hoodin didn't have "the slightest idea in the world what the defense would be." He talked about calling expert witnesses and conferring with experienced criminal defense attorneys, namely William A. Thorndyke and Arthur C. Fricke, both of Cincinnati. He even mentioned that the defense might rest its case without calling a soul to the stand. "It's a delicate, technical problem," he allowed.

On Saturday morning the defense sought from Judge Bell a directed verdict of acquittal, arguing at length that the state had not proven its case. Hoodin noted that the bottle of arsenic Captain Hayes found was not proven to be Anna Marie's, her purse passed through many hands before being examined, Wagner could have committed suicide, and the prosecution failed to produce evidence that the defendant administered poison to anyone. "Unless that is proved, there is no case!" Hoodin loudly proclaimed. The state had "no evidence that a crime was committed!"

Outcalt addressed the court on Hoodin's suicide supposition. "If accident or suicide happens once, that may be considered by the jury, but when you add three other similar deaths, the suggestion of defense counsel becomes a mathematical impossibility."

Hoodin concluded by arguing that it was "a hard enough job to defend ourselves against one charge of murder, but that job is magnified five-hundred-fold when we are called upon to defend ourselves against five crimes. It's a job nobody can handle."

Judge Bell thought otherwise and on Monday morning denied the defense motion for a directed not-guilty verdict.

Now Oscar, whom reporters variously described as "wide-eyed," "precocious," "mannerly," and "nice looking . . . with an alert, intelligent face," sat in the witness chair. Hoodin began by asking Judge Bell if he wanted to test Oscar to be sure he understood the oath he took.

"How old is he?" the jurist asked, peering over his pince-nez at the handsome youth in the witness box.

"Twelve," said Hoodin. Curiously, Oscar later testified that he was eleven.

"Oscar, do you go to Sunday school?" asked Judge Bell.

"Yes."

"Do you know it is wrong for little boys not to tell the truth?"

"Yes."

"You know they are punished if they don't?"

"Yes."

"You understood the oath you just took?"

"Yes."

"You understand if you don't tell the truth, you will be punished?

"Yes."

Little did the court know that for years Oscar had told lies, many at the behest of his mother, to whom he clung.

Hoodin began his careful, gentle questioning, first about Oscar's chemical set in the basement of the Hahn home. Oscar said he and some neighborhood chums, including Junior Thornton, Jack Glazel, and Billy Johnson, played with chemicals. According to the witness, they salvaged bottles, test tubes, and hypodermic needles from the trash of nearby doctors, a hospital incinerator, and a funeral home.[1] Some bottles he stored in the basement rafters, Oscar said, which is where Captain Hayes testified he found a bottle of arsenic trioxide. The prosecution maintained that Anna Marie had put it there.

At Hoodin's prompting, Oscar next recalled the trip to Colorado with his mother and Obendoerfer. On the train from Cincinnati to Chicago, his mother handed out some sandwiches she had purchased in Cincinnati. She gave Obendoerfer two, Oscar said, and he served their travel companion some water and beer. After an overnight stay in Chicago, the trio continued on to Denver by rail.

During the train ride, Obendoerfer began to feel poorly. Several times Oscar brought him cups of water, although on the stand he continually used "we" to account for the actions he and his mother took.

"Oscar, did you hear any conversation between your mother and Mr. Obendoerfer on the way from Chicago to Denver, about his money?"

"Yes. . . . My mother asked him how much money he had to buy the [Colorado chicken] farm, or how much it cost or something like that, and he answered that he only had three or four dollars, and I just started to laugh. So my mother says, 'Why, farms cost more than that. We will have to see in Denver about a check or something, to send from Cincinnati to Denver.' So, in Denver my mother sent for the check, and she wrote his name down on a piece of paper."

By the time they arrived in Denver, Obendoerfer "wasn't feeling very well," Oscar admitted. He went for coffee and watermelon, which Anna Marie gave to the old cobbler in the room of the hotel. Oscar watched as Obendoerfer vomited and dirtied the bed after eating the watermelon. Oscar said he never saw his mother put anything in Obendoerfer's food, though.

Hoodin asked about the next train journey, to Colorado Springs. Oscar said he occupied his time by writing, cutting out paper, and

---

1. Shortly after Oscar's testimony, Frank E. Busse of the Busse & Borgmann funeral home near Oscar's home vehemently denied having disposed of any bottles that could have been picked up by the boys. "Inasmuch as the alleged testimony casts a reflection in the manner in which our funeral home is kept, the writer offers his services as a witness to entirely discredit such testimony," Busse wrote to Outcalt. Busse was not called upon to testify.

drawing. "I drew a skeleton head, and . . . he [Obendoerfer] picked it up and hollered, 'Witches! Witches!' and I started to laugh . . . and everybody on the train started laughing." Obendoerfer, clearly disturbed, folded up the paper and put it in his pocket.

"Now, Oscar," Hoodin asked, "what did he do on the way from Denver to Colorado Springs, do you remember?"

"Well, he wasn't feeling very good, and mother and him would talk every once in awhile and ask him how he was feeling . . . and he wanted a lot of water then, too. So I went and got him some more water and brought it up to him, and this was six or seven glasses I brought him [on the trip] from Denver to Colorado Springs. . . . He was beginning to feel worse, and he would sleep and wake up and look out at the scenery."

Upon arrival in Colorado Springs, Anna Marie sought out the Park Hotel, and she registered the three of them there.

"I went up to the [nearby] Antlers Hotel, there is a delicatessen in the basement, and I got [Obendoerfer] a sandwich and some coffee."

"Did you go up to his room with the sandwich and coffee?"

"Yes, I gave it to him."

"And were you there when he ate it?

"Yes."

"At that time did you see your mother or did you, put anything in the coffee or the sandwich?"

"No," the boy responded, adding as if coached, "The sugar was put in down at the café."

Arsenic in white powder form is odorless, virtually tasteless, and dissolves quickly, imperceptibly, in hot coffee, much the same as sugar.

Oscar again testified that he never saw his mother give medicine to Obendoerfer at that time. Mother and son undressed Obendoerfer and put him into bed before heading to dinner at a café the boy described as "a Manhattan." They returned after dark to find Obendoerfer asleep. The following night, after he and his mother had spent much of the day sightseeing, Anna Marie finally decided Obendoerfer needed medical attention, at the urging of the hotel proprietor, Pell Turner.

"Mr. Turner and Mother helped him downstairs to the cab, and we took him to the hospital," the boy testified.

On cross-examination, Outcalt attacked Oscar's story, particularly his time with Obendoerfer in the Denver and Colorado Springs hotels. Oscar recalled under questioning bringing the old man "six or seven glasses of water" at one time while at the Oxford Hotel. "I went and got them because I didn't want to run back . . . so often, but he didn't drink them all at once. He drank them slow."

"And then, when you got to . . . the second hotel in Denver, he was pretty sick, wasn't he?" the prosecutor inquired.

"Yes."

"In bed?"

"Yes."

"And you were there about five days, weren't you?"

"Yes."

"You say you brought the food up some of the time?"

"Yes."

"You say you brought up the watermelon?"

"Yes."

"Did your mother bring up some of the food?"

"Well, she went down with me when we got the watermelon. She walked down to the café with me."

"How about the other meals?"

"The sandwiches I brought up."

"You brought up every meal?"

"Not every meal. Mother carried the plate, and I the coffee and cream, and took it upstairs."

"He was drinking a lot of water there, wasn't he?"

"Well, he wanted a lot of water."

"And it was after the watermelon that he threw up, and lost control of himself?"

"Yes."

"That room was pretty dirty, wasn't it?"

"No, not exactly."

"It wasn't?"

"No."

"Well, you were there when the hotel man [Straub] told your mother that Mr. Obendoerfer was dying."

"No, I wasn't."

"Did you realize he was dying?"

"No."

"I object!" Hoodin said loudly, trying to break the pressure Outcalt was applying to the boy.

"The answer may remain," said the judge.

"Well, when he walked out of the hotel, it took your mother and the cab driver to get him into the cab, didn't it?"

"I know it."

"And he couldn't walk at that time, could he?"

"Not very well."

"Well, how did he get into the car—wasn't one on each side of him, to push him in?"

"They didn't exactly carry him, but he couldn't hardly stand up, and they had to hold him."

Outcalt returned to the evening arrival in Colorado Springs and getting the ill Obendoerfer into bed.

"And you laughed about that, did you, Oscar?"

"Yes, I thought it was pretty funny, because he believed in witches."

"He was pretty sick then, wasn't he?"

"Well, he wasn't feeling very well."

Over Hoodin's objection, the prosecutor turned to the day Oscar found the bottle of croton oil under the cushion of a chair in his home. The boy was asked to describe the bottle.

"Could you see what was said on it?"

"Yes."

"What did it say?"

"Well, I just seen the skull and crossbones, and I gave it to my daddy [Philip]. I knew it was poison right away." Several times the boy referred to his stepfather as "daddy," and Outcalt asked a question about "your father." All in the courtroom knew that Oscar was an illegitimate child.

Outcalt asked if Anna Marie was home when the bottle was found.

"No, she wasn't."

"Your father came home first?"

"Yes, and I gave it to him."

"And she was pretty mad about it, wasn't she?"

"Not exactly."

"That's what you said, wasn't it, Oscar?" Outcalt said, picking up a transcript of the interview Oscar gave the police in August.

"Well, she wasn't exactly real mad about it. She asked him where he got it, and I said I gave it to him."

Outcalt read from the police report. "Isn't this just exactly what you said down there [police headquarters] 'My mother got peeved when I gave the bottle to daddy'?"

"I didn't say that. I just said my mother—she didn't get exactly real mad, but she didn't like it because I gave the bottle to daddy. She didn't get real mad."

From her seat at the defense table, Anna Marie smiled at her son.

Outcalt also asked if Oscar hadn't told the police that he and his mother met Obendoerfer initially on the train to Chicago.

"Yes, sir."

"And the reason you told them that was because your mother told you to, wasn't it?"

"Yes."

With one question, the prosecution had all but negated the testimony of the first witness for the defense.

Next up, Anna Marie. Hoodin bravely told reporters his client was "eager and anxious to testify. She is going to be an excellent witness," he promised, adding that Anna Marie was "really happier than she has been in days and days. I have no worries in the world about her standing up under cross-examination. If she didn't wilt under the examination we have been giving her in private, and if she didn't wilt under the burden of seeing all those state exhibits piled up before her, as any *guilty* person would, do you think she ever will?"

Most observers thought not. Throughout her trial, Anna Marie appeared calm. At times she evidenced disinterest in the trial, some thought, but such was not the case. She spent many hours with her attorneys, reviewing her testimony and that of the prosecution witnesses. During some of the legal wrangling between the defense and the prosecution, she examined the law books on the defense table, following the cases Hoodin and Bolsinger cited.

"She has her emotions," Hoodin told the press. "I will say simply this: She is a woman, Anna Hahn is. She's just like any other woman. She's nervous. She never has been calm. She has her feelings, you can bet on that."

At the afternoon court session, her composure would be tested to the utmost.

14 | INNOCENCE PROCLAIMED

May it please the court, your honor," Hoodin said. "We call Anna Marie Hahn to the stand."

"ANNA MARIE HAHN."

The calling of her name by court clerk William E. Meyer sent an audible ripple of excitement through the stuffed third-floor courtroom and out into the hallways. By far the largest crowd yet—one court official estimated the number was more than a thousand—stood in the hard, marble-floored hallways with no hope of seeing or hearing a thing. The throng began gathering before 6 A.M., stepping over mops wielded by janitors rushing to finish their cleaning chores. This was the day that everyone had waited for since it became known the Blonde Borgia would stand trial. Even those who didn't have a ticket for a seat inside or a view of her through the doors of the courtroom wanted to be able to say they were there on The Day Anna Marie Told Her Story.

Judge Bell rapped his gavel several times, restoring silence in the aroused courtroom. Three of his Common Pleas Court colleagues—Judges Louis J. Schneider, Fred J. Hoffman, and Alfred Mack—joined him on the bench. Attired in the black robes of their office, they sat as interested visiting jurists.

The defendant, dressed nun-like in a navy blue serge suit, high-necked white satin blouse, and the ever-present white gold cross around her neck, resolutely walked to the witness stand, turned to half face the audience, and raised her right hand. She remained impassive as Meyer asked if she agreed "tell the truth, the whole truth, and nothing but the truth, so help you God."

"I do," she replied firmly, and sat down. She was as composed as if a charge of jaywalking faced her.

Hoodin took a deep, silent breath. He dreaded having to put his client on the stand, even though she had exhibited an icy calm throughout the proceedings. He knew on cross-examination an experienced prosecutor like Outcalt would find ways to slice through that angelic innocence, leaving his client in shreds, but he had no choice. Anna Marie had to take the stand for any chance to avoid prison—and the electric chair.

Hoodin began with gentle questions, exploring Anna Marie's early years in Germany and her first years in the United States, such as her marriage to Philip. It wasn't long, however, until the defense attorney gingerly approached the heart of the matter, namely the death of Jacob Wagner.

"I will ask you, when did you first meet Jacob Wagner?"

"Well, it was right after I had sold the store [the delicatessen, in 1935], Mr. Wagner come to my house, and he told me that he thought there was some relationship between us, and I had never seen Mr. Wagner before."

After that Wagner would occasionally work in her garden, she said, but she never knew where he lived. When, two years later, she received two letters from Baden-Baden, Germany, one for her and one for Wagner, she looked up his address and went to find him at 1805 Race Street. There she met Elizabeth Colby.

"You heard Mrs. Colby say that you said, 'Are there any old men living here?' Did you make that statement to her?"

"I did not."

After putting a note under Wagner's door, they subsequently met, and Anna Marie said she gave him the letter.

"Now, Mrs. Hahn, when you went into 1805 Race Street, did you ever say to anybody that you were Mr. Wagner's niece?

"I did not."

"What did you say about being his niece?"

"I told them we were supposed to be relatives."

Hoodin then jumped to the meeting at Kirsch's saloon, where Wagner said his bankbook was missing.

"I told him I would go to his room with him and help him find it," Anna Marie said. "We both went to the room and looked for it, and we found it."

"At that time, in that saloon, Mrs. Hahn, did he accuse you of taking the bankbook?"

"Well, he didn't exactly, but then the way he told the bank that I was in his room, and maybe they had taken it up that maybe I took it."

"Did he tell you he had been down to the bank about the bankbook?"

"Yes, he did."

"What was it he told them?"

"He had stopped everything, and told them that I was at his room."

"And what did you say to him about it?"

"Well, I didn't feel very good about it, and I told him he should go to the bank and tell them that he found it."

"Did you get angry about him accusing you of it?"

"I did. Yes, I did," replied Anna Marie, looking hurt.

Although witnesses testified to having seen her in Wagner's room the following day, a Sunday, Anna Marie said she didn't visit Wagner until Monday when she found him lying in bed, ill. On Tuesday he was still "very ill," she said, so she called a doctor, Dr. James H. Clift, on Tuesday evening.

"Did you have a conversation with Dr. Clift, [asking him] whether or not Mr. Wagner was going to die?"

"No, I didn't."

"Did you have any conversation with Dr. Clift about being a nurse?"

"No, sir."

The defendant responded to the questions softly, calmly, and with only the slightest German accent. Several times the court asked her to speak a little louder so the entire jury could hear her testimony. Spectators strained to hear her every word.

She recalled Dr. Richard Marnell visiting Wagner the next day and ordering him to the hospital. Before they left in the ambulance, Wagner "gave me his bankbook and told me that I should take a thousand dollars from his account and have it transferred in my name so I could pay the bills and take care of everything." He also gave her a note for the bank, she said.

At the bank the day Wagner died, Arthur J. Schmitt, assistant vice president at Fifth Third Union Trust Company, refused to honor the $1,000 check Anna Marie presented "because it was written in pencil," she said. She returned shortly with a check Schmitt had filled out for her for Wagner to sign, but she had signed his name to it.

"Mr. Wagner's name I signed, because I was certain that Mr. Wagner wanted me to do it, because he wanted me to have that money to take care of his bills."

Winding up his questions about Wagner, Hoodin asked his client:

"Did you at any time that you knew Mr. Wagner put anything into his food or drink in the nature of poison?"

Anna Marie squarely faced the jury and calmly, softly, replied, "I have never done such a thing."

Hoodin then moved on to questions about Albert J. Palmer, whom Anna Marie described as "a very fine man. . . . He was very good to me and to my boy. He was more like a father to me and to my boy. . . . There wouldn't be anything I wouldn't do for him." She described accompanying Palmer to the Elmwood Place betting establishments, preparing meals for him at her house, and visiting him in his home perhaps "two or three times a week."

"Now, Mrs. Hahn, when you gave Mr. Palmer food at your home, which you and Oscar ate also, did you ever put any poison in that food?"

"Why, no."

"Did you ever put poison in anything that you have given to Mr. Palmer?"

"I never have."

"Now, when you were at Mr. Palmer's house and ate there, did you put anything in the food?"

"Never."

"Or in his drink?"

"No, sir. I have never done that." Again she responded directly to the jury that sat in front of her, perhaps only fifteen feet away.

George Gsellman was the next subject Hoodin questioned his client about. She testified that Gsellman was a friend to her "Uncle Charlie," Charles "Karl" Osswald.

"My uncle told me Mr. Gsellman had at one time a lot of money," Anna Marie told the court, "but through his wife and children he had lost everything, and he was too old to work. So my uncle had loaned him $450 to take out an income policy . . . and told Mr. Gsellman he should pay that money to me if ever he would die," which Osswald did shortly thereafter.

On May 1, 1937, or about two years after she said she met Gsellman, he gave her $136, and the following day she gave him a receipt for the money. They next saw each other on Monday, July 5, she said. Gsellman came to her home and "told me he had borrowed money on the [income policy] insurance and that he wanted to return that money he had borrowed from my uncle." On a transit pass she said she found in the street that day, Anna Marie wrote, "Go home, I will be there," and gave it to Gsellman. The note meant she would be there sometime the following week, she said, not that day, not July 5, a holiday.

That afternoon Anna Marie took off for Elmwood Place for some action on the horses. She told the court she recalled the day because of the holiday and because she won about $140 on a horse named "Money Getter." Neither she nor the court recognized that she had the nag's name wrong: "Mad Money" was the horse that won that day at Chicago's Arlington Park and paid $14.20, $4.80, and $3.20. Ten dollars on the nose would have paid $142.

Anna Marie insisted that she came right home afterward and went to bed because she didn't feel well.

"Were you at Mr. Gsellman's house on July 5 between 4:30 and 8:30?" Hoodin asked.

"No, I was not." She testified that she went to see him "Wednesday," getting the day of the week wrong. She meant Tuesday. Gsellman's neighbor, August Schultz, informed her that Gsellman had died. "I was so surprised. I couldn't believe it after seeing the man at my house that Monday. I couldn't hardly believe that he was dead."

"Did you ever go there [to Gsellman's home] after that, Mrs. Hahn?"

"No, I didn't."

"Mrs. Hahn, did you at any time cook any food for Mr. Gsellman?"

"I never did."

"Did you ever at any time put anything in anything that Mr. Gsellman ate or drank?"

"I never seen Mr. Gsellman eat or drink anything."

Hoodin asked his client why she had denied knowing Gsellman when questioned by police.

"I was afraid to tell them that I knew him because I knew they would say I maybe have killed him."

Anna Marie next recalled for the court the day a heel came off her shoe and that retired cobbler Georg Obendoerfer had repaired it for her at his home. She stayed for more than an hour, chatting in German about a trip to Colorado that she had planned with Oscar "to see the mountains."

"He asked me if I would mind if he could go along with us. Well, I didn't want to say no, so I told him it would be all right."

On Wednesday, July 21, the trio took a taxi from her home to the Union Depot to await the train, Anna Marie recalled, but she left Oscar and Obendoerfer there for more than an hour while she returned home to find her watch. She said her husband had hidden it "because I was reckless." That prompted Hoodin to ask:

"Mrs. Hahn, will you tell us please, are you on real good terms with your husband, or have you been?"

"No, we have not."

After more than three hours of tense, dramatic testimony by the accused, Judge Bell called a supper recess. When the evening session began, Anna Marie once again took the witness stand. Not a single spectator seat was empty. Visitors who held the little white admission tickets for the afternoon session were forced to vacate the courtroom, and holders of evening session tickets were seated. Many more remained in the hallways.

Under her attorney's gentle guidance, Anna Marie recalled the first leg of the trip to Chicago with Oscar and Obendoerfer. All of them had eaten sandwiches earlier, but Oscar and his mother went to the dining car later. Obendoerfer, she said, declined to go. He told her he couldn't afford it.

"I said, 'Well, you have money with you.' He said, 'Well, I tell you, I have only $4.85 with me.' I was surprised a man taking a twelve hundred mile trip with $4.85. So, I told him . . . if he needed money he could send for some."

Hoodin then jumped right over the overnight stop in Chicago, landing in Denver on Friday, July 23 where she registered the three of them at the Oxford Hotel. By then, Obendoerfer "didn't feel so well," she said. While in Denver, she tried to help Obendoerfer withdraw $1,000 from his bank in Cincinnati and have it transferred to the Denver National Bank. On his behalf, she wrote a letter to Harry H. Becker, director of the Clifton Heights Savings and Loan in Cincinnati, signing it "A. Felser."

"Now, will you tell the court and jury, Mrs. Hahn, why you signed your name, 'A. Felser'?"

Squarely facing the jury with her hazel eyes, Anna Marie calmly replied, "I didn't want anything to do with the transaction."

By Sunday, Obendoerfer's condition had worsened, she admitted. She obtained slices of watermelon at his request, she said, but he became sicker.

"I figured that the watermelon was too cold, that he chilled his stomach," Anna Marie explained, and he "messed the bed."

"Mrs. Hahn, did you at any time put anything into that food that you gave to Mr. Obendoerfer?"

"No, sir."

"Did you put poison in that food, Mrs. Hahn?"

"No, never. I never gave poison to anyone."

"Did you put poison on that watermelon?"

"I didn't." She nervously sipped the glass of water by her side.

On Friday, July 30, the three travelers headed by train to Colorado Springs, despite the fact that "Mr. Obendoerfer was very sick," as Anna Marie recalled. At the Park Hotel she registered all three of them, noting that they were from Chicago. She said the hotel owner, Pell Turner, told her, "This man should be in a hospital. He looks like he is very ill." So, with Oscar in tow, she took Obendoerfer to Beth-El Hospital. There she again registered him as being from Chicago, because "I didn't want to be responsible for any bills," she testified.

Obendoerfer died Sunday, August 1, while Anna Marie and Oscar were touring the Colorado Springs area to "see the sceneries." The following day, they returned to Denver. At the Midland Hotel she cashed a check for $10 and received $30 by wire from her husband in response to her request. She, in turn, had sent him a postcard on which she noted what a "nice time" she and Oscar were having.

Hoodin then skipped to "the living victim," George Heis, who had been trundled into court in a wheelchair to testify that Anna Marie had poisoned his food. Under her attorney's questioning, she admitted preparing food for the coal dealer, both at her home and at his, for a month or more. She also admitted to having borrowed some $1,200 from him to pay her bills but denied she had promised as security some gas and electric stock and a home in North Bend, Ohio.

Once again Hoodin asked the key question: "Did you ever put poison in Mr. Heis's food, Mrs. Hahn?"

"I have never done that," she replied, looking squarely at the jury yet again.

With the word poison on his lips, Hoodin asked Anna Marie about the bottle labeled "Croton Oil—Poison X" that her son found tucked in a chair. He gave it to Philip, who refused to return it to her. The bottle eventually ended up in the hands of the Cincinnati police. She testified that she had bought it at Carroll Deming's pharmacy in College Hill because she was in need of a physic. Once home, she took the wrapped bottle out of her purse, laid it on the easy chair, "and forgot all about it."

The final questions Hoodin had concerned the purse she was carrying when arrested, and which, according to the prosecution, contained arsenic—a lot of arsenic. Anna Marie resolutely denied that she ever carried arsenic in the purse, just money, a compact, a powder puff, and "several clean handkerchiefs."

Many in the courtroom agreed that Anna Marie had acquitted herself well. According to Virginia Gardner, sob-sister reporter for the *Chicago Tribune,* the defendant "avoided frippery" in her manner of dress and appeared poised and gracious, "as if she were making a little intimate talk before a women's club." The jury, to which Anna Marie addressed many of her responses, remained impassive but attentive—very attentive.

After a brief recess, during which news photographers were permitted in the courtroom to take photos of the defendant seated on the witness stand with her attorneys, Outcalt began his cross-examination.

Under rapid-fire, pointed questioning by the prosecutor, Anna Marie held her ground for a time, denying any and all allegations that she tried to obtain money from Obendoerfer; that his diarrhea, nausea, and severe stomach pain that rendered him a virtual invalid were symptoms similar to those she saw in Wagner, Palmer, and Heis; and that once he was in the Colorado Springs hospital where he died, she professed that she hardly knew the man.

Outcalt, described by *Chicago Daily News* reporter Casey as "sarcastic, impolite and apparently well-informed," peppered the wilting defendant with questions concerning Obendoerfer's condition while at the Midland Hotel, owned by Louis Straub. After observing Obendoerfer, Straub felt the elderly gentleman should be in a hospital.

"You knew that Mr. Straub was concerned about Mr. Obendoerfer's health, didn't you?"

"Not that I know of."

"Did you say that he thought the man was very sick, that he thought he was dying?"

"He didn't say he was dying; he said he was ill."

"He said he should go to the hospital. He said he was a councilman in the City of Denver?"

"Yes, he did."

"He said he could get him into a city hospital, didn't he?"

"I don't remember him saying that."

"But you didn't put him in a hospital?"

"Mr. Obendoerfer told me he wouldn't go to a hospital because he didn't have any money."

"You knew that there was such a thing as a charity hospital?"

"Yes, I did. He didn't want to go."

Anna Marie testified that Obendoerfer had relatives in the Denver area, but she couldn't find them. Outcalt continued, his questions coming thick and fast.

"Did you agree that Mr. Obendoerfer should be put in the hospital?"

"Yes, I did."

"But you didn't do it?"

"He didn't want to go."

"He couldn't talk then, could he?"

"Oh, he could so!" Anna Marie's eyes flashed at the prosecutor. "Why, he could talk."

"Wasn't he only able to make signs with his fingers?"

"Mr. Obendoerfer could speak as plain as I could and can right now," she snapped.

"You weren't there in the room when Mr. Straub went up to the room and tried to talk to the old gentleman, were you?"

"I had taken a trip through the mountains with my son."

"You left Mr. Obendoerfer there alone in the room while you and your son went and took a trip through the mountains?" Outcalt asked incredulously.

"I went out there on a vacation," she replied, flashing fire once again. "I didn't go out there to take care of someone else."

Outcalt quickly glanced at the jury. He knew he had scored some points for the state.

He shifted his questioning to Colorado Springs, where Anna Marie registered Obendoerfer as a charity patient at Beth-El Hospital, and her meeting there with the attending physician, Dr. Willard K. Hills.

"Didn't Dr. Hills ask you this man's name, and didn't you say, 'I don't know'?"

"I had him registered at the hospital," she replied.

"I am asking you a question, Mrs. Hahn. Didn't Dr. Hills ask you what his name was?"

"Yes."

"He did?"

"He did."

"You said you didn't know?"

"I told Dr. Hills that I didn't know very much about the man, but I had registered his name on the hospital chart."

"You say that you admit that you laid over this bed and asked this man what his name was?"

"I wanted Mr. Obendoerfer to tell the doctor himself what his name was."

Outcalt looked briefly at the jury, disbelief on his face, and took up his questioning about her visit with Dr. Hills the next day, the day Obendoerfer died.

"Let me ask you if this didn't happen. Didn't you ask Dr. Hills if he had seen Mr. Obendoerfer that morning, and didn't he tell you that he had?"

"Yes."

"Then, didn't you ask him if he had found out what his name was—the name of 'the old patient'?"

She denied having asked that.

"Then, didn't you repeat the statement that you made the evening before, that you didn't know him and that you felt sorry for him in his crippled condition? He couldn't take care of himself, and you couldn't leave him that way, so you sent him to the hospital."

"Mr. Obendoerfer was ill after leaving Cincinnati with me. . . ."

"I am asking you, didn't you make the statement that I just referred to to Dr. Hills?"

"I didn't," the defendant replied, now nervously tapping her polished nails on the rail of the witness box. "I told Dr. Hills that I felt sorry for the man, that I couldn't leave him alone."

"I will ask you, didn't you ask Dr. Hills that morning if he had found out yet what was wrong with him?"

She did, she said.

"Didn't you know by that time what was wrong with him?"

"I didn't."

"You said that you didn't recognize what was wrong with Mr. Wagner?"

"That's right."

"By the time you came to Mr. Obendoerfer, he had the same symptoms that Mr. Wagner had, didn't he?"

Hoodin jumped to his feet to object to the question, arguing that Outcalt was trying to compare one case with the other.

"Where a person sees two persons sick," Judge Bell ruled, "it seems to the court that it is entirely proper to ask whether both persons had the same symptoms." He overruled the objection, to the dismay of the defense. Outcalt proceeded to link the symptoms question from Obendoerfer to Wagner to Palmer to Heis, inexplicably skipping Gsellman. Anna Marie professed ignorance in each instance.

With a flair for the dramatic, Outcalt maintained that after the defendant sent and served meals to Heis, he became bedridden. "At the end of October, Mr. Heis held out his hands, trembling"—Outcalt thrust his out, shaking them almost in Anna Marie's face—"and he said, 'You did that!' didn't he?"

"No, he didn't, because I never gave that man anything to harm him."

"You knew that Mr. Heis accused you of poisoning him, didn't you?"

"The first time I heard that was when Mr. What's-His-Name [Clarence E. Osborne] from the Consolidation [sic] Coal Company came and he told me, and I felt very bad about that, because I didn't think that Mr. Heis would say such a thing about me."

"One of the things that Mr. Osborne told you at that time, Mrs. Hahn, was that he would try to prevail on Mr. Heis not to institute action against you if you paid this twelve hundred dollars?"

"Mr. Osborne never said that."

Jumping around again, Outcalt returned to questions concerning Obendoerfer's death and Anna Marie's meeting with Harley Remington, an embalmer with the Law Mortuary in Colorado Springs.

"You told Mr. Remington that you didn't know him [Obendoerfer] any more than any man on the street."

"I didn't."

"You didn't?"

"No, sir. I never said that."

"Did you say to him, 'Why tell me?'"

"No, sir."

"Did you say to Mr. Remington that you thought you would be rid of him [Obendoerfer] when you got to Colorado Springs?"

"No, sir."

"You were rid of him in Colorado Springs, weren't you?" the prosecutor said as he walked away from the accused, confident that he had driven home another nail. Anna Marie's denial was inconsequential.

Although she admitted knowing that Obendoerfer had money in the Clifton Heights Loan and Building Company in Cincinnati—she had tried to get $1,000 transferred from there—she couldn't tell the court why she had not told Beth-El Hospital officials or the embalmer that Obendoerfer had sufficient funds to pay both. Nor did she recall telling Denver banker Edward J. Weckbach that she was Mrs. Obendoerfer and that her "husband" couldn't come into the bank because he was "way out on the edge of town." In fact, both the Oxford and Midland hotels in Denver were within a few blocks of the Denver National Bank.

Turning back to the day Obendoerfer lay in "extremely critical condition" in the hospital, Outcalt pounded Anna Marie about her actions that day.

"You knew he was dying then."

"No, I didn't." Her voice quavered a little.

"You were out to the hospital on Saturday?"

"Saturday morning. . . . He was sleeping."

"Did you enjoy yourself that day?"

Hoodin's objection was overruled.

"I have told you," Anna Marie said with obvious annoyance, "that we went out there on a vacation, and that I wanted to take in all the sceneries and the trips I possibly could, and naturally I did enjoy them."

There was a touch of testy smugness in the reply.

"I see," said Outcalt, pacing in front of her to put himself in front of the jurors. "And that was the day that you wrote Philip, your husband, 'Having a nice time. It is kind of chilly up here. We are throwing honest-to-goodness snowballs. Love'?"

Anna Marie smiled. Outcalt did not.

"That is true, yes," the accused replied. "We were at Pikes Peak, and it was snowing at that time."

The long day ended with a brief cross-examination of Anna Marie's dealings with the Curtis Jewelry Company, a Denver pawn shop. She denied using the name Marie Fisher. "That's a different thing again, which doesn't correspond to this at all," she said.

Outcalt disagreed with her statement; Hoodin defended it, and the two attorneys argued the issue outside the presence of the jury. In the end, Judge Bell ruled that asking the defendant about names she used "was a proper question."

Outcalt held up as evidence a pawn ticket from the Curtis shop dated August 3, 1937. Anna Marie peered at it through her eyeglasses, which she wore throughout her testimony. "Did you pawn some jewelry out there in the name of Marie Fisher?"

"They were not for me," Anna Marie insisted. "They were for a girl that I loaned money to."

"Where does she live?"

"I met her in Colorado Springs—my son and I. On Sunday afternoon we took a walk through the park and that girl had come from a different city and she sat with us . . . and she told me she wanted to go to Cincinnati."

"What city did she come from?"

"From Texas she came."

"From Texas?"

Anna Marie nodded. "I didn't ask her what city. Maybe she told me but I don't remember."

"Mrs. Hahn, when you were arrested, this note and envelope . . . the envelope addressed Curtis Jewelry Company, were in your home, weren't they?"

"Yes, they were."

"They are both in your handwriting?"

"Yes.

"Did you write, 'Send my rings by Air Mail, General Delivery, Covington, Kentucky. Respectfully, Marie Fisher'?"

"Because the girl wanted me to sign her name."

"Mrs. Hahn, did you write that?" Outcalt asked, his voice increasing in volume.

"I did, yes, sir."

After more than five arduous hours on the stand, Anna Marie was visibly exhausted. The hour was late, too, so Judge Bell adjourned the court, noting that the trial would resume Wednesday morning. Tuesday was Election Day.

15 | "DO YOUR DUTY!"

During her first day on the witness stand, Anna Marie got nothing but a hammering from Prosecutor Dudley Miller Outcalt. The next day she got a vote.

On November 2, Election Day, a Cincinnati voter wrote in her name for a municipal judgeship, and election officials recorded it.

The jurors also voted on Election Day. Bundled in coats, hats, and gloves, and accompanied by their bailiffs, they trooped as a group by bus around to their voting precincts. John Granda's was the last stop. His wife and daughter waited for four hours for him to show up, just for a hug and a kiss. Upon viewing this scene from the bus, the eleven ladies of the jury began to chant, "We want Johnnie! We want Johnnie!"

"If they want him, they can have him," said a bemused Mrs. Granda, "but he will be back with me before long." Her husband blushed.

H. Fuller Stevens, the affable manager of the fourteen-story, 1,000-room Hotel Gibson at Fifth and Walnut streets, tossed an election-night dinner for nearly two dozen members of the press covering the trial. During the evening, both Judge Bell and Prosecutor Outcalt dropped by, but the defense team did not. It was more concerned with how Anna Marie would withstand another day of Outcalt's scorching cross-examination when the trial resumed on Wednesday.

Actually, the day in court proved to be somewhat anticlimactic. Hoodin had successfully argued that the defense had little or no money to pay the $300 per day expenses of its sole expert witness, toxicologist Dr. William Duncan McNally, an associate professor of medicine at the Rush Medical College, University of Chicago. Therefore, the court agreed to interrupt the prosecution's case and the questioning of Anna Marie to first hear McNally's testimony immediately upon his arrival from Chicago. He flew into Cincinnati's Lunken Municipal Airport Wednesday afternoon and, under a police escort, was whisked at seventy miles an hour to the Hamilton County Courthouse.

As the former Cook County coroner's chemist, McNally claimed to have examined thousands of corpses for poison, some of them riddled with "lead poisoning" from Chicago's gangland wars. In an authoritative voice, he testified that drinking too much home brew or any number of rather common illnesses could have caused Heis's symptoms. Hoodin handed McNally Anna Marie's crocheted purse, which defense counsel had suggested could have been manufactured with arsenic in the lining. After examining it carefully, inside and out, the witness agreed, noting that "some clothing is loaded with arsenic" to protect against insect infestation.

When his time came to cross-examine the defense witness, Outcalt questioned virtually everything McNally had said, even reading a passage from the professor's own recently published textbook, *Toxicology*. It made clear that paralysis was indeed one of the prime symptoms of arsenic poisoning.

"What is a lethal dose of arsenic?" the prosecutor asked.

McNally's response coincided with previous expert testimony. "One-and-a-half to three grains," he replied.

As for Anna Marie's purse, Outcalt had but one question for McNally.

"If you found material that you could pick out with forceps, you would not consider the possibility of contamination from the material of the purse, would you?" he asked.

"No, I would not."

"Thank you, Dr. McNally. No further questions."

The testimony of the only expert witness for the defense appeared to veteran court observers to be more favorable to the prosecution.

At the noon recess and before the jury filed out of the courtroom, an angry Judge Bell had a statement to make. He had been informed, he said, that when the jurors arrived at the courthouse that morning, some "coward" had hurled at them "a vile insult," which he later identified as "a bunch of rats."

"If that occurs again, it is the wish of the court that you report the matter promptly to one of the bailiffs and have that person brought before the court. . . . Anyone who calls any name or uses vile language toward this jury will be brought before the court, and his punishment will not be light."

Perhaps to relieve the tension in the courtroom, Hoodin found it necessary to stand and apologize to the court for having said "Good morning" to the jurors. Judge Bell smiled and said he did not view such greetings by the defense or prosecution as contempt of court.

However, the "vile insult" wasn't the only unpleasantness associated with the trial. Hoodin revealed that three callers, each with a foreign accent, had recently threatened his life should Anna Marie go free. The matter was turned over to the police.

Just as the afternoon session resumed, a fire broke out at the nearby Garden Supply Company on Main Street, filling the courthouse corridors with the acrid smell of smoke. Despite their discomfort, however, few among several hundred waiting for the chance to get into the courtroom budged from their place in line. Once again every seat in the courtroom was occupied.

With a somewhat pale Anna Marie back on the stand, Outcalt resumed his devastating attack, pounding away at her credibility. He picked up where he had left off Monday evening, questioning the defendant about the pawn ticket and her use of the name Marie Fisher.

"You told me you had pawned the rings so that you could lend some money to a girl. How much did you lend her?"

"Ten dollars."

"Now, Mrs. Hahn, when you were in Colorado Springs you were so short of money that you had to wire your husband for money, and he sent you $30."

"Yes."

"And in Denver a few days after that you found it necessary to ask a hotel to cash a check for $10, and still you say you loaned $10 to a girl you met in a public park?"

"Well, she said she wanted to get home, and I thought I would help her."

"Where was she from?"

"Covington." Quickly realizing that she had contradicted her previous testimony, Anna Marie corrected herself. "That is, she was from Texas, but she was going to Covington."

Asked if that was the only time she had used an assumed name, Anna Marie acknowledged that on occasion she had used her maiden name, Filser, and on occasion, spelled it Felser, with an "e." The prosecutor had laid another trap and opened the door to telling the jury the name of yet another victim of Anna Marie's care.

Outcalt produced a document that gave Anna Marie power of attorney to gain access to the safe deposit box of Olive Louella Koehler at the Provident Savings Bank & Trust Company in Cincinnati. "Marie Felser" witnessed the document.

Hoodin immediately objected to the introduction of Mrs. Koehler's name. At Hoodin's request, the jury again left the courtroom before he began his argument. The state, he said, had not been able to prove that the seventy-nine-year-old widow, who died at Longview State Hospital on August 19, had been poisoned. Therefore, her name should not be introduced to the jury.

"Mrs. Hahn is no angel," the young defense attorney admitted, blowing his nose into a white linen handkerchief, "and we do not say that she hasn't done things that I personally would not have done. But her character is not at stake in this trial. This is simply a case of Mr. Outcalt loading the jury's minds with prejudice to the point where the smartest lawyer and the smartest defense and the most innocent person in the world could never get out."

Judge Bell overruled the objection, and before the jury once again, Anna Marie admitted that she had indeed signed the document as a witness, but she denied that she also had signed the name of the second witness, "Lee Radley." Lee Radley was never identified, however.

Repeatedly Anna Marie answered the prosecution's questions with "I don't know," "That's not true," or "I don't remember." When questioned about money that she said she had loaned various individuals, Anna Marie several times refused to name the borrowers, because she didn't want to "bring anyone else's name into this."

Outcalt turned his focus to the bottle of croton oil that she purchased "for a physic." It later was found in the Hahn home by her son, Oscar, and hidden from her by her husband.

"Did you know that croton oil was a poison?" he asked.

"No."

"You didn't know that three drops of croton oil would kill a man?"

"No. How would I know?"

"Mr. Deming, didn't he tell you what the dose of croton oil should be?"

"No," she replied. "I might have taken it and killed myself."

Observers had expected Outcalt to delve deeply into the deaths of Wagner, Palmer, Gsellman, and Obendoerfer, but he asked Anna Marie relatively few questions about each of them. He focused instead on her relationship with the mysterious Ray, who took her and Oscar on "vacation" to Kentucky immediately after Wagner's funeral.

"Now, this man Ray, Mrs. Hahn," Outcalt began, his voice increasing in volume. "He's a gambler over in Newport, isn't he?"

Hoodin jumped to his feet yet again, objecting loudly to the question. Newport, a Kentucky community just across the Ohio River from Cincinnati, was for years considered the area's vice capital. "Overruled," said the judge.

"Yes." Anna Marie spoke quietly now, fingering the crucifix that hung around her neck and nervously rapping her fingernails on the arm of the witness chair. She glanced quickly at her defense counsel for support, eliciting a reassuring smile from Hoodin.

"Now, haven't you been over to Newport and played the hazard table where this Ray is a professional gambler?"

Uncertain where her accuser was going with this subject, Anna Marie answered cautiously. "I have."

"That's all," Outcalt said abruptly, striding back to his table, confident his cross-examination had painted just the right picture of the defendant.

Just prior to shutting down for the night, Judge Bell agreed to Hoodin's motion that the bottle of croton oil would not be accepted into evidence, since the prosecution did not establish that the oil was used in any of the deaths. It was a small victory for the defense.

"The state rests," Outcalt quietly announced.

"The defense rests," Hoodin stated. The spectators shifted in their seats. The trial was all but over.

Anna Marie looked blissfully at the jurors as they filed out, the hint of relief on her wan face.

Thursday morning final arguments began, each side having been allocated up to five hours. Once again the courtroom was packed to capacity, with a large overflow crowd in the hallways. Outcalt was up first, arguing for two-and-a-half hours for the state. His remaining time would follow the defense summation.

Outcalt impressed the press with his oratory. "He has a good court-room presence, a clear, crisp, oratorical delivery, a logical mind and a long memory—none of which in this case did the defendant any good," Casey wrote for *Chicago Daily News* readers.

"Five months ago yesterday," Outcalt began, almost in a hushed tone, "Jacob Wagner died in agony. Five months ago tomorrow he was placed in his grave. We have come to investigate the circumstances. We have come to learn how it was brought about and upon whom the responsibility must rest for what we believe the evidence must show to be an atrocious crime."

He recalled for the jury Anna Marie's random search for her "uncle" in Wagner's apartment building. She said relatives in Germany had written to her because they didn't know his address.

"Mark that!" Outcalt told the panel. "He had lived at 1805 Race Street for years. She had lived at 2970 Colerain Avenue for a comparatively short time. But in the odd workings of her mind, it seemed credible that Wagner's relatives in Germany should have known her address and not his."

So, the defendant left a note under Wagner's door, and "when she learned Wagner had a small amount of money saved for his old age, that marked the beginning of the end for him," the prosecutor said.

Outcalt also reminded the jury of Wagner's "missing" bankbook and the forged entries in her own bankbook that were "done with a purpose." She produced her own bankbook that indicated a balance of $16,000, when, in fact, she had but a few dollars in that account. Anna Marie's story that Oscar had made the false entry while practicing his typing didn't hold up, Outcalt said. Yet, "she deceived Frank Kaessheimer, who was a businessman," said the prosecutor, "and that meant that whoever made those entries was clever. It was no little boy."

The defendant created another ruse with forged notes and checks to get Wagner's money out of the bank, even after Wagner had died, Outcalt reminded the jurors. When the possibility of her arrest arose, she "found" his bankbook, she called the bank to say it had been found and produced a note from Wagner exonerating her, all in an effort to avoid the police.

"Would to God he had followed the advice of his friends and gone to the police," said the prosecutor, looking toward the heavens. "If he had done that, you and I wouldn't be here. Jacob Wagner would be living in his little room at 1805 Race Street; George Gsellman would be living quietly in his little room at 1717 Elm Street, and Georg Obendoerfer would be puttering around in his little garden at 2150 Clifton Avenue.

"But she prevailed on Jacob Wagner, and Jacob Wagner died. When she wrote this note for him to copy," Outcalt said, holding it aloft, "she wrote not only an alibi for the bankbooks but for the murder she was to commit!"

Outcalt recalled how each of the victims—Wagner, Palmer, Gsellman, and Obendoerfer, plus the "living victim," Heis—had been blinded by Anna Marie's affections and how she then set upon them to gain control of their money, one way or another. And when she got what she could from each of the old men, she poisoned them.

"She murdered Wagner to get his money, and when she failed to, she killed Gsellman for his, and when that was not enough she killed Obendoerfer for his.... I know all these crimes were connected by the pressure placed on her to repay the money," he said. The final "proof" of her deeds was the discovery "in the rafters of her cellar seventy-seven grains of arsenic, enough to kill twenty-six people!"

Striding quickly to where the diminutive defendant sat and pointing his finger at her, Outcalt thundered, "Anna Hahn is the only one in God's world that had the heart for such murders! She sits there with her

Madonna face and her soft voice, but they hide a ruthless, passionless purpose the likes of which this state has never known!"

As she had throughout his summation, Anna Marie just stared at Outcalt in contempt. If looks, rather than poison, could kill. . . .

Then Outcalt hit her with a haymaker that she obviously never expected. Tears came to her eyes when he brought Oscar's name into his final argument, claiming that she used her son as her alibi.

"When Heis complained that his spinach tasted sweetish, Anna said she had put no sugar in it, but Oscar might have done so. It was Oscar again when arsenic was found in her cellar—Oscar was playing with the poison that had been in his chemical set. Oscar bought the food [for Obendoerfer]. Oscar put sugar in old George Heis's food. She blames all these incriminating, inescapable circumstances on Oscar."

It was a penetrating indictment, one that Outcalt knew would pierce the defendant's very heart and remain in the minds of the jurors. With the prosecution's two-and-a-half hours used up, it became the defense's turn to paint its own picture of the accused; Outcalt would get another shot at Anna Marie after the defense's five-hour summation.

The tall, bespectacled Bolsinger, who throughout the trial had played a support role to his law partner, Hoodin, introduced the final arguments for the defense, arguments that would consume all the hours allotted. In a short, disjointed statement, Bolsinger described life as "a set of circumstances. . . . Every one of us has at one time done wrong [such as running a red light], but we haven't been caught or been compelled to face a jury." Then he sat down. Hoodin, looking younger than his thirty years, rose to make the principal argument.

Gazing warmly into the impassive faces of the jurors, Hoodin spoke softly of the strain the trial had placed on everyone, yet "somehow we were brought closer together, and we have come to know each other." The rasp in his voice revealed his personal strain, the result of the cold that still lingered. He smiled and continued. He would not, he said, contend "that Mrs. Hahn is an angel or a righteous woman. But keep in mind that because a person has gambled, because a person doesn't get along well with her husband, because a person went on with a person named Ray isn't any indication that that person committed murder.

"You will recall I asked you in the original examination whether you would hold anything like that against her. I am asking you again to please consider this case from the evidence . . . and please don't take into consideration the little wrongdoings Mrs. Hahn has done."

Repeatedly describing the prosecutor as "an actor," Hoodin accused Outcalt of clouding the evidence. "Every smoke screen he can put before you to stop you from determining the issues in this case, he does," the defense counselor said. "He asks about her associations with Ray, and asks if Ray isn't a gambler. Her character is not at issue. What does it help you in knowing that she went somewhere with a man named Ray? He's trying to show you that because she associated with a gambler, she must have killed Jacob Wagner."

If she had killed Wagner and forged his will, "she would have written that Wagner desired to have his remains cremated and scattered the ashes to the winds, and no toxicologist or chemist, with all the marvels of science, would ever have discovered that Jacob Wagner died of arsenical poisoning.

"I say to you frankly," Hoodin continued, "that I believe there is arsenic in the body of Jacob Wagner. But I don't know how it got there and neither do you because the state has not presented any testimony to help you decide that most important point."

The state only proved that Anna Marie received money from Palmer, he said, not committed murder. The same with the Gsellman case—purely a money transaction. As for Obendoerfer, he "drew $350 from the bank—no evidence what he did with it—but Mr. Outcalt wants you to believe that because Mrs. Hahn had $250 in the bank it must have been Obendoerfer's money."

Heis's condition did not come from poison administered by his client, Hoodin maintained. "George Heis is no more suffering from arsenical poisoning that I am. His condition was brought on by drinking too much home brew!"

The young, diminutive defense attorney challenged the jury to remember what they had done on a particular date in an effort to lend credibility to his client's testimony that she remembered very little when questioned by Outcalt. "How many can answer what you did on June 3, even if something happened in your life that day? I wonder if you could recollect the exact date. I couldn't, and our legal minds are supposed to be trained to lots and lots of things."

After five hours of summation and near exhaustion, Hoodin came to the climax. "God tempers justice with mercy," he whispered, tears in his eyes. "I know you will return Mrs. Hahn to Oscar so she can take care of him."

Anna Marie wept openly, dabbing at her eyes with her twisted handkerchief. The jurors, looking grim, were obviously touched by the argument. Two of them cast their eyes to the floor, lest anyone see their watering eyes.

"You are going to hear Mr. Outcalt demand the death penalty," Hoodin whispered. "It's within your power to take that spark of life from Mrs. Hahn. It's in your power to give her mercy. It's in your power to free her.

"Ladies and gentlemen, I ask you to send Mrs. Hahn back to Oscar. Give him the opportunity in life he deserves."

Outcalt began his final summation by turning the tears to smiles for many when he noted that his name had been mentioned so often in Hoodin's closing argument "that I sometimes wondered if this were not the case of state versus Outcalt."

He pointed out to the jury that it would be "a mathematical impossibility that all these deaths could be due to a mistake or accident." Because each in their old age had sought the comfort and consolation of a woman, he said, Anna Marie was able to do what she did.

"I don't think I am exaggerating when I say in this woman we see the most heartless, cruel, greedy person who has ever come within the scope of our lives!" the prosecutor all but shouted.

"Counsel for the defense has asked why we have brought this woman's gambling activities into this case . . . and why we sought to prejudice the minds of this jury with slurring references to her association with 'a man named Ray.' I will tell you why. It is to show you that she constantly took that eleven-year-old lad, behind whose form she now seeks to stand, to handbooks. It is to show you that she took that boy, whom her counsel now asks you to return to her 'so that he may have a chance in life,' while she went on a five-day trailer trip to the mountains of Kentucky with her gambling paramour.

"I say to you, ladies and gentlemen, that if there is one chance for that boy, it is to erase from his mind forever the memory of such a mother!"

Thoroughly warmed now to his task, his voice even louder and his face even redder, Outcalt described the sort of woman who sat unperturbed at the defense table just a few feet away.

"She is sly. She made it her business to develop associations with lonely old men who had no relatives.

"She is avaricious, for no act was too low for her which might have resulted in her gaining a slight financial advantage.

"She is cold—as cold-blooded as no woman you or I ever saw. No other woman could have sat in this courtroom and listened for four weeks to the damning testimony that she heard with no show of any emotion.

"She is heartless, or she would not have been capable of dealing out deaths of agony to these old men."

Picking up the "arsenic" purse in evidence, Outcalt waved it high in front of the jury. "In this purse you see as much a lethal weapon as if she had held a smoking gun in her hand," he said. To prove that Anna Marie had bought the arsenic was not as important as to show that she possessed it, "and that we have done," he said.

The state prosecutor saved for last his most dramatic moment.

"In the four corners of this courtroom there stand four dead men," Outcalt said, looking about the silent, spellbound chamber. "Jacob Wagner!" he cried out, pointing to the far corner. "George Gsellman! Georg Obendoerfer! Albert Palmer!" he shouted, stabbing his finger in the direction of a corner with each name.

Outcalt quickly strode to the front of the defense table and singled out the pale, frightened defendant, all but putting his finger in her face. "From the four corners of this room, bony fingers point at her and they say to you, 'That woman poisoned me! That woman made my last moment an agony! That woman tortured me with tortures of the damned!' And then, turning to you, they say, 'Let my death be not entirely in vain. My life can not be brought back, but through my death and the punishment to be inflicted on her you can prevent such a death coming to another old man.'

"From the four corners of this room those old men say to you, 'Do your duty!'"

In a voice that began as a whisper and rapidly rose to its full power, Outcalt ended his plea. "I ask you, ladies and gentlemen, to find Anna Marie Hahn guilty of first degree murder as charged in the indictment!"

His job was done. Jurors and spectators alike, absolutely stunned by the forcefulness of the prosecutor's attack, now took a breath, cleared a throat, or shifted position. Anna Marie never looked more pale, never more frightened, than in those final minutes of her trial.

In his fifteen-page charge to the jury, Judge Bell said it had three verdicts to consider: Guilty without a recommendation of mercy, making the death penalty mandatory; Guilty with a recommendation of mercy, resulting in a life sentence; or acquittal. Hoodin asked that a second-degree murder verdict or one of manslaughter be included in the court's charge, but Judge Bell swiftly denied the motion.

After four weeks, the longest murder trial ever in Cincinnati was nearing its conclusion. The end was in the hands of the petticoat jury.

16 | A LITTLE MADNESS

When the jury returned its surprising guilty without mercy verdict, it set off a flurry of activity in Cincinnati and Columbus, including a promise from the defense to appeal Anna Marie's case "all the way to the top" of the judicial system.

Many who followed the Blonde Borgia's trial—that included virtually everyone in Cincinnati—thought Anna Marie would be convicted of poisoning Jacob Wagner and spend the remainder of her life in prison, but few expected the jury to impose the ultimate penalty—death in the electric chair. A headline in the *Cincinnati Enquirer* noted prevailing opinion: "Penitentiary Officials Doubt That Blonde Ever Will Go to the Electric Chair."

Upon learning of the verdict, Philip Hahn briefly met with reporters. Throughout the trial it was clear to one and all that he was no longer close to his wife—a dash of arsenic in the stew will do that—but outwardly he continued to stand by her side.

"No matter what has happened, I'll stick by my wife," he said, with eyes filled with tears. "This has been almost too hard to take."

He rarely was present in the courtroom during the trial, even though he was working nights at Western Union and might have been able to attend the day sessions. As the trial progressed, he kept abreast of most major developments by tapping out in Morse code the stories reporters sent with Western Union each evening to newspapers throughout the land.

When Judge Bell dismissed Foreman John Granda and the eleven women on the jury with him, a swarm of reporters and photographers rushed to the jury room to determine how the panel had reached its verdict. It was "bedlam," the *Cincinnati Enquirer* reported.

The jury took two ballots. The first came at their meeting on the morning of November 6 when they unanimously and quickly agreed that Anna Marie was guilty, but one vote was cast with a recommendation of mercy. The panel reviewed some of the testimony and took a second ballot at noon. The vote was unanimous: no mercy.

Anna Thompson, who turned sixty-five the day deliberations began, initially voted for mercy. She explained that she had a daughter, Aurdelle, the same age as Oscar. "I just couldn't bear the thought of that boy going through life with the memory that his mother had been executed. But when we talked it over, it seemed better for the boy to be taken away from his mother. So, I voted with the rest." During the reading of the verdict, however, she cried.

Several agreed that the defendant's purse that was shown to contain arsenic was the most damning of the 137 prosecution exhibits placed in evidence. "We knew that nothing could come into that purse through that piqué lining," said juror Marjorie Bishop, the wife of a tailor and a seamstress herself. "I know that the insides of purses are made of cotton piqué, finely woven. Nothing goes through them."

The poison in the purse was "the deciding factor" for him, too, Granda said. "It indicated premeditation." He also noted Anna Marie's stoicism throughout the trial. "If I had been in her shoes," he said, "I would have shown plenty of emotion, believe me."

On several occasions during the trial, Granda looked up and found Anna Marie gazing at him. "At those times I wasn't sure whether she was guilty or I was," he said. "There was something—like a little madness—in her eyes."

Oscar's fate without his mother also was discussed. "We thought of this boy growing up, perhaps on the verge of success, and then having the fact of his mother having died in the electric chair to darken his career," explained Emma Cassidy, a great-grandmother and the wife of a thespian. "Then we considered Mr. Outcalt's statement that only if the memory of such a mother was erased forever from his mind would Oscar have any chance for a normal, happy, successful life."

About her more-than-three-weeks on the jury, Mrs. Cassidy said, "I don't think I could have stood this another day, and I don't want to do it again."

Stella Tragesser, an assistant bank cashier, said "Mrs. Hahn had a way of studying each of our faces, . . . and it was her cold stare that made me wonder what she really thought of each of us." Tragesser did not find the defendant "beautiful" or even particularly pretty, but "rather nice looking, and, while she was extremely cold, there was something about her that attracted you."[1]

It also was revealed that the thirteenth juror, alternate Frederick Juergens, was "the life of the party" during the panel's twenty-three days together. Often he would produce his accordion and liven up the scene at the Hotel Metropole. As the alternate, he did not participate in the jury's deliberations.

Ella Black, a middle-aged widow, "had no reluctance about voting for the death penalty. We're all close friends here now, too. We've had such good conversations. You know, this experience is a highlight in our lives." Frances Sullivan agreed. She revealed that the panel had formed the AMH (Anne Marie Hahn) Club and would henceforth meet annually at the Hotel Metropole on October 11, the date the trial began. "We've had a lot of fun . . . in these weeks," she said. Within days, however, others on the panel vociferously denied that such a club had been formed. It never did meet.

As the jurors left the courthouse together, one Chicago reporter described them as "giggling nervously" as they posed one more time for photographers. Huddled together on a cold November day, the group "looked like a woman's club which had just come from a murder mystery movie."[2]

Newsboys already were on the street, shouting out the headlines on the latest editions. "Mrs. Hahn found guilty!" "Anna Hahn to die for murder!" "Mrs. Hahn denied mercy by jury!"

1. Stella Tragesser, "Hahn Trial to Be Vivid Memory!" *Cincinnati Enquirer,* Nov. 19, 1937, 12.

2. "11 Women Doom Anna to Chair," *Chicago Herald and Examiner,* Nov. 7, 1937, 1.

The newspapers that had reporters at the trial published editorials and opinion columns on the verdict. Alfred Segal of the *Cincinnati Post* noted, "Mrs. Hahn may derive consolation from the fact that she couldn't have expected any less. . . . Her crimes will be in local conversation a long time to come . . . and she will be mentioned not for cleverness but for surpassing cold-bloodedness that played with lonely old men and when through with them, poisoned them."[3]

The *Cincinnati Times-Star* editorial pointed out that "the majesty of the law has been asserted in Cincinnati. . . . When sentence is pronounced upon Anna Hahn she will be the first woman in Hamilton County to have been condemned to death. But the crime for which she was tried was one of the most shocking in local history."[4]

The conviction of Anna Marie "will help to fortify one's confidence in the jury system," Cleveland's *Plain Dealer* noted. The editorial described her crime as "particularly diabolical." Still, it continued, "many were frankly surprised that the jury brought in the verdict it did," given the fact that the defendant was a pretty, young mother and the jury was primarily female. "One wonders if the verdict would have been the same had the jury not been mainly of women."

The *Columbus Dispatch* observed—correctly, as it has turned out—that Anna Marie "left a trail of death and human misery in her wake, the full extent of which, perhaps, will never be known."

It was Anna Marie who now was in misery in the jail. She ate and spoke very little all weekend. Even when Oscar and Bolsinger came for a fifteen-minute visit she hardly said a word. (Philip tried to visit her, but she had him turned away.) She cried while singing a hymn at a Sunday service in the jail. Neither a personal visit from jail chaplain Reverend Alexander Patterson nor the arrival of a $5 bouquet of roses from an anonymous "Good Samaritan" failed to console her. More tears flowed when she opened a letter from her mother, who made no mention of the trial.

Fearing a suicide attempt, her keepers increased the watch and

3. Alfred Segal, "Mrs. Hahn," *Cincinnati Post*, Nov. 8, 1937, 8.
4. Editorial, "The Hahn Trial," *Cincinnati Times-Star*, Nov. 8, 1937, 6.

moved out her cellmate, Mabel Hill. One rumor had it that Anna Marie would take her life with poison she had hidden inside her crucifix. Such was not the case, jailer Andrew Frank said.

So unexpected was the verdict that authorities had made no plans to incarcerate a woman headed for the electric chair. Anna Marie wanted to remain in the Hamilton County Jail, to be near Oscar, but that was out of the question for anyone sentenced to death. It was suggested that she be taken to the Columbus City Jail or the Ohio Reformatory for Women at Marysville, about twenty-five miles northwest of Columbus, but the warden there thought Anna Marie's presence would be "disruptive." Authorities discovered later that Ohio law did not allow death penalty prisoners to be incarcerated at the reformatory, either. The remaining choice was the Ohio Penitentiary in Columbus, which had the electric chair but no facilities whatsoever for a female inmate.

A week of debate ended with Warden James C. Woodard's decision that the penitentiary's first female prisoner in twenty-one years would be placed in a cell constructed for her on the third floor of the prison's hospital. Convict labor, wearing black-and-white-striped prison garb, hastily remodeled an area that had been used as a dormitory for a dozen or so convicts working the night shift in the prison's power plant. A heavy wire mesh screen enclosed the 27 x 21–foot area, which was almost three times what she had enjoyed at the Hamilton County facility and much larger than the 5 x 7–foot cells occupied by male prisoners on death row.

On the Monday following the verdict, Hoodin and Bolsinger filed a motion for a new trial, and Judge Bell scheduled a hearing for a week later, November 15. According to the defense motion, Anna Marie did not deserve the death penalty, based on the evidence; there was misconduct by the prosecution; and there were irregularities in court procedures.

"The prosecutor's misconduct itself was so flagrant as to warrant a new trial," Hoodin charged during his two-and-a-half-hour oration in Judge Bell's courtroom, crowded with visitors again. He called Outcalt's closing argument "inflammatory." His introduction of the names of Gsellman, Obendoerfer, and Palmer were a "surprise" to the defense, Hoodin maintained, and therefore never should have been introduced.

"Mrs. Hahn was not tried for one offense but for five," Hoodin said, including Heis. "I don't think Mrs. Hahn got a fair trial."

"My conception is," Outcalt snapped, "that when my duty has been best done, it is least pleasing to defense counsel."

When Hoodin pointed out that the state did not produce a single eyewitness in the Wagner case, Outcalt responded.

"If the state should be required to produce an eyewitness in poison cases, all persons who have been convicted as poisoners were convicted unjustly." Outcalt added that the state had been "scrupulously fair in presenting the evidence."

"What do *you* think is going to happen?" Warden Frank asked Anna Marie as he escorted her back to jail after the hearing.

"Oh, I suppose the motion will be denied," she responded. It was.

On the morning of November 27, upon appearing before Judge Bell for the last time, she heard her fate.

Following many hours rereading the trial transcript and reviewing the law, Judge Bell produced a thirty-two-page opinion that he provided both sides rather than read it in court. In it he said he found the evidence "so overwhelming that no verdict other than guilty could have been reached by the jury. The verdict is not contrary to law." The defense's argument that the client was tried for five offenses was, in the judge's opinion, "an incorrect statement of the situation." He cited Ohio law that held the introduction of "any like acts or other acts of a defendant" was admissible. Finally, he found no misconduct on the part of the prosecuting attorney.

Speaking in court and summarizing his ruling, Judge Bell stated that "the court has arrived at the conclusion there is no prejudicial error in the record, and that the motion should be, and is, overturned."

Turning his attention to the red-eyed, diminutive woman standing at the bar before him the jurist asked, "Do you have a statement to make, Mrs. Hahn?"

"I have," a strong and determined Anna Marie replied. Looking squarely into the eyes of Judge Bell, she declared, "I am innocent, your Honor."

"You stated that to the jury, Mrs. Hahn, and the jury found against you." He paused momentarily to give Anna Marie time to add to her statement. When she did not, he turned to reading her death sentence.

"It is ordered, adjudged, and decreed by the court that the defendant, Anna Marie Hahn, be taken hence to the jail of Hamilton County, Ohio, and that within thirty days hereof the sheriff of Hamilton County shall convey the said defendant to the Ohio Penitentiary and deliver her to the warden thereof, and that on the tenth day of March, 1938, shall cause a current of electricity of sufficient intensity to cause death, to pass through the body of the said defendant, the application of such current to be continued until the said defendant is dead."

Judge Bell then added: "And may God, in His infinite wisdom, have mercy on your soul." He fought with his emotions, only giving up once he had returned to his chambers. There, in private and behind a locked door, he cried.

As she had throughout her long ordeal, Anna Marie remained impassive during Judge Bell's death knell, but once back in jail she collapsed into loud sobbing. Maude Burkhardt, the jail matron who accompanied Anna Marie to court and back, wept alongside her prisoner. When Anna Marie felt faint, Dr. William T. Lindsay, the jail physician, quickly came to her side.

Three days later, defense counsel was back before Judge Bell, requesting a stay, pending further legal maneuvering by the defense. The judge ruled it was a matter for the Ohio Court of Appeals, which received an appeal for a stay later that Tuesday.

Bolsinger also lit a fire, of sorts, by "leaking" to the local press that there were "new developments" in the case that would prove to be "a sensation." The defense had received an anonymous letter from a jealous woman Wagner knew, Bolsinger said, and she was responsible for his death. It read in part: "I just can't stand this tearble thing my consious is driving me crayz. I am the one Poisoned Mr. Wagner, not Mrs. Hahan . . . heaven knows she is innocese."

While the defense distributed copies of the letter to reporters, Outcalt debunked it, saying that it was "written by some crank." Wagner had no interest in any other women other than Anna Marie, the prosecutor said. The secret killer issue fizzled in a few days, then surfaced again when Outcalt received another "hoax" letter from "someone with a perverted sense of humor," he said. The letter said, in part: "Poor, dear Mrs. Haan didn't not do the orful murder of Mr. Waggner. And that brave lady who commed forth to confess she done it—she is a liar; she didn't do nothing of the sort. . . . I hate to admit it, but I killed Mr. Waggoner myself . . . so let Mrs. Haan go."

Judge Bell, Hoodin, Bolsinger, Outcalt, and others received numerous letters and postcards from throughout the country following the trial. "If you let that Hahn woman free, we [will] blow up the courthouse!" was one of the threats received. Another wrote to criticize the jury and its verdict. "They more than murdered that poor little boy [Oscar]. I was in court and witnessed the distressing tragedy of a child's love for a criminal mother. . . . It's enough to make the boy hate the world forever." A third told Judge Bell, "You have no idea of the favorable opinion your handle of the case has engendered, not only for the law but also for Cincinnati." Pearl M. Hoon of Cincinnati requested a seat at Anna Marie's execution. "In making up your list of witnesses to the electrocution of Mrs. A. M. Hahn, please include me. I certainly wish to witness that," she wrote, adding that she had had "no end of embarrassment due to the similarity of names."

Anna Marie received mail, too. Clifford Ennis of Clarendon, New York, wrote to inquire if she would be interested in placing Oscar "in a good home, a place where he can grow up without his relationship being a handicap. . . . This offer is sincere, motivated by the desire to do good, and I have a fondness for boys."

George Berry of Latoma, Kentucky, offered to make a $25 donation to Anna Marie's defense fund if she would acknowledge her appreciation "by knitting a sweater for a boy eight years of age."

Wednesday morning, December 1, Bolsinger, Sidney Brant, and Sidney Kahn argued before the appeals court that Anna Marie be permitted to remain in the Hamilton County Jail during her appeals process. Outcalt argued that already the case had cost the county dearly—an estimated $10,000—and now the prisoner was properly a ward of the state and should be incarcerated at the Ohio Penitentiary.

Presiding judge Simon Ross and judges Stanley Matthews and Francis Hamilton agreed. Their ruling from the bench was that the prisoner should go to the penitentiary forthwith.

"Oh, no! No! They can't do that!" Anna Marie cried upon hearing the news on the radio.

The penitentiary was ready to receive Anna Marie, so Sheriff George A. Lutz decided to move her to Columbus that very afternoon, within the hour, in fact. At the jail, Mrs. Burkhardt helped Anna Marie gather up her few personal things and pack a small valise that still bore steamship stickers from her travels. A deputy sheriff picked up Oscar at the Washington School and brought him to his mother's side. After a few minutes together, they walked arm-in-arm down the stairs to the waiting sheriff's black sedan, Oscar carrying the case. Both were smiling.

"Are you going to miss your mother?" she asked her son as parting neared.

"Not so much," he replied, teasing her even now. "It don't do any good."

"Be sure to be a good boy and mind your grandparents and your father," she told him, holding his face in her hands and kissing him. This time there were no tears—at least, not until Oscar was out of sight. Then she softly cried.

Anna Marie left Cincinnati squeezed into the backseat of the sedan between Mrs. Burkhardt and Julia Kies. Because a December chill was in the air, all three wore heavy fur coats—Anna Marie's was her favorite blocked lapin—so it was a tight fit. Mrs. Kies's husband, Deputy Sheriff Raymond B. Kies, drove with bailiff Charles Stagnaro beside him in the front seat. In the bailiff's pocket were Anna Marie's commitment papers and her death warrant. A second car, carrying Sheriff Lutz, Deputy Chief George J. Heitzler, and William J. Wiggeringloh, chief of the Hamilton County police, followed through the streets of Cincinnati. "I'll be back here for another trial," Anna Marie said quietly but firmly. Once beyond the city limits, the second car sped ahead. The three officers were headed for an Ohio Sheriff's Association meeting in Columbus.

In Cincinnati, Bolsinger released a statement from Anna Marie that he had written out in pencil for her in her jail cell. She thanked her jailers for her good treatment during the one hundred and thirteen days she spent in their care. She also proclaimed her innocence once more. "I feel at this time that my innocence will be established as I am innocent of the crime charged against me. I hope and pray that the party having any knowledge of the crime will get in touch with my attorneys."

The two-and-three-quarter-hour drive north on what was known as the Three-C Highway (linking Cincinnati, Columbus, and Cleveland) traversed gently rolling farmland through Montgomery, Wilmington, Washington Court House, and Mount Sterling to Columbus. The trip was quiet but not quite uneventful. About halfway, outside Wilmington, Stagnaro noticed a rather pale-faced Anna Marie had put her head on Mrs. Burkhardt's shoulder. (Both Mr. and Mrs. Kies told reporters the prisoner had fainted.) Stagnaro, whose cigar smoke filled the sedan and may have been the cause of Anna Marie's swoon, ordered a brief stop at a roadside stand to get her a cup of black coffee.

As dusk approached, the car arrived in downtown Columbus and turned onto Spring Street. The ominous Ohio Penitentiary loomed just ahead.

17 | CITY OF SCOUNDRELS

The 103-year-old Ohio Penitentiary in Columbus looked like a penitentiary should. Its weighty blocks of Ohio limestone rose three stories, creating a forbidding countenance in gray—dark and brooding. The largest penal institution in the world when it was built possessed a "massive grandeur," said one historian. It stood as "a silent and frowning warning to the observer of the majesty of the law and the consequences which are sure to follow and overtake those who insult or violate its imperial dignity and sovereign mandates."[1]

Behind walls thirty-six inches thick were 4,189 bank robbers, burglars, rapists, murderers, ruffians, and thieves.[2] It was a city of scoundrels, and all were male, even the guards. Now there was inmate Number 73228—Anna Marie Hahn—the lone female, who joined the pen's list of celebrated prisoners.

Inmate Number 30664, for example, was William Sidney Porter, better known as the short-story writer, O. Henry. Convicted of embezzlement of a Texas bank, he was imprisoned on April 25, 1898. During his three years and three months inside, he wrote the first of the short stories that would make him famous.

1. Marvin E. Fornshell, *The Historical and Illustrated Ohio Penitentiary* (Columbus, Ohio: self-published, 1908), 9.
2. In April 1955, the penitentiary inmate population reached a record 5,235. The facility was closed in 1979 and demolished in 1998.

Other notorious inmates through the years included gangster George "Bugs" Moran; Confederate general John Hunt Morgan, who in 1863 made the prison's most famous escape; Cleveland's Solly Hart, public enemy No. 1, who served twenty years as the warden's chauffeur; and Dr. Sam Sheppard, who was imprisoned for killing his wife in suburban Cleveland in the 1950s.

As Anna Marie and her guardians arrived at the prison, a December evening chill descended on Columbus. It had been a long and trying day for the prisoner, but now she would enter what would be her home for the remainder of her life.

A small crowd, mostly reporters and photographers, had waited for several hours for her arrival. When at 5:15 P.M. the cry went up, "Here she comes!" everyone rushed to the car. Flashbulbs popped repeatedly as the diminutive Blonde Borgia stepped from the vehicle, Stagnaro on one side of her and Mrs. Burkhardt on the other. "But what drew the eyes of all," wrote Charlotte Sherwood of the *Columbus Citizen*, "was her hair: beautiful blonde hair, almost red in the light, that fell nearly to her shoulders."[3]

Warden Woodard and prison physician Dr. Eugene D. Clarke accompanied Anna Marie and a gaggle of officials and journalists through three iron security gates, across the yard to the prison hospital and up three flights to the cell that had been built for her in the tower. She dropped her coat on the bed and plopped down in a chair, exhausted and tearful. She never noticed that her name and prison number already had been hung on the wire mesh surrounding her spacious cell.

The furnishings were luxurious in comparison to what other death-row prisoners had. There was a white cast-iron bed, a rocking chair, a large table where she could eat her meals and write her letters, a second chair where she now sat, and next to the bed a small table on which someone had placed a Bible. Two large but somewhat threadbare rugs covered a portion of the wood floor. The "private" bathroom, installed for her use only, wasn't a room at all but wide-open so the prisoner would be visible at all times to the matrons, who occupied an adjacent, open room of their own.

3. Charlotte Sherwood, "Sun Fades, Raw Dusk Wind Whips Anna Hahn, Who Braves Pen Reporters, Then Weeps Alone," *Columbus Citizen*, Dec. 2, 1938, 1.

The ten windows were draped with muslin curtains, the first in the history of the penitentiary. From only one, looking east, could Anna Marie see beyond the prison wall. Barely in sight were elevated railroad tracks but not "The Bridge of Sighs," the nearby railroad trestle spanning the Scioto River at Scioto and Spring streets. It was said that at night, when all was quiet, prisoners heard the clickety-clack of trains crossing the bridge and sighed.

The first four matrons, hired at $100 a month each to guard Anna Marie day and night, were introduced to her upon her arrival. She shook each woman by the hand and repeated each name. "You'll have no trouble with me," she told Kate Swift, Esther A. Lyle, Adelaide Schultz, and Harriet C. Mercer. Mrs. Lyle and Mrs. Schultz were both widows of former Ohio Penitentiary guards. Mrs. Swift had been matron to Julia Maude Lowther, the only other woman sentenced to death in Ohio's electric chair. Lowther, who was imprisoned in the Columbus City Jail rather than the penitentiary, won a new trial in 1931, pleaded guilty to a general charge of homicide, and received a life sentence at the Marysville reformatory. Mrs. Mercer was the alternate and relief matron. If any matron ever needed immediate assistance, she could ring an alarm solely for Anna Marie's area. The matrons also had a telephone.

After a quick examination, Dr. Clarke pronounced the prisoner fit. Mrs. Burkhardt said a tearful good-bye, promising Anna Marie that she would visit her again, but there is no record that she ever did so. Grace Woodard, wife of the warden, stopped by for the first of many visits. She took an immediate liking to the state's newest and most notable death-row inmate. But then, Anna Marie always had had that innate ability to charm everyone she met. "She is the bravest woman I ever saw," Mrs. Woodard said after her initial visit. She also revealed that several who prepared Anna Marie's first supper in the penitentiary—bacon and eggs, potatoes, bread and butter, peaches, and coffee—cried while doing so.

Although her husband announced that Anna Marie would receive no special privileges over the coming months, Mrs. Woodard saw to it that she did. For example, Anna Marie wore her own clothes, not the standard, striped prison issue.

In the morning, the Protestant chaplain, the Reverend Kleber E. Wall, stopped by with copies of the *Christian Herald, Reader's Digest,* and *National Geographic.* She invited him to return often. She also received a visit from Bertillon superintendent Samuel M. Current, who fingerprinted and photographed her for the penitentiary's records.

She spent her first Sunday quietly. She listened to a church service on the radio and ate a dinner of steak, mashed potatoes, and peas. It was the same meal served to the other inmates in the dining hall she never would be allowed to enter. Warden Woodard reported that she was "getting along just fine," and that the first visit on Saturday from Oscar, Philip, and Hoodin did not appear to upset her.

For Philip it was a difficult time, too. He knew his wife did not wish him to be there. On the other hand, she wanted to make sure that he and his parents were taking good care of Oscar, which they were. "Until this trouble came, Oscar thought I was his real father," Philip said, and outwardly they appeared to have a good relationship.

He told a *Cleveland Plain Dealer* reporter that he had tried to "keep my self-respect. I've always been, well, dapper, like the papers said. I've kept right on with my work, going everywhere and being seen, because I've done nothing to be ashamed of. I've tried to take care of Oscar as a father. So, you see, I cannot talk about his mother—well, anyway, not more than I have to. Perhaps one of these days I'll have plenty to say."[4] One of those days never arrived.

Shortly after his wife took up residence at the penitentiary, Philip received a package from her. It contained four neatly folded, expensive pink silk slips and the pearl-buttoned white satin blouse she had worn for her trip from Cincinnati to the Columbus prison. Maggie Hahn explained that her daughter-in-law "was afraid they'll ruin them in the prison laundry."

Anna Marie's incarceration was barely three days old when Assistant State Fire Marshal Harry Callan, accompanied by Columbus Fire chief Edward P. Welch, took prison authorities to task following a tour of the facilities. Callan announced that the forty-two-year-old hospital

---

4. Regine Kurlander, "'I'm Not Ashamed,' Says Philip Hahn," *Cleveland Plain Dealer,* Dec. 30, 1937, 13.

building was "a terrible firetrap," a charge initially denied by Warden Woodard. Still fresh in everyone's mind, however, was the April 21, 1930, blaze—set by three prisoners in an escape attempt—that claimed the lives of 322 inmates. Woodard soon agreed with the fire marshal's assessment, including the recommendation that the all-wood hospital building in which Anna Marie resided be abandoned. Planning for a new death row that would include new accommodations for Anna Marie began immediately.

Anna Marie had barely settled into the humdrum life of a death-row prisoner; now she would have to move. She had not been occupying a cell on death row itself; that was on "L" block near the west wall, and the electric chair was in a small, brick building in the southeast corner of the prison. Warden Woodard planned to put Anna Marie, the condemned male prisoners, and the electric chair together on the second floor of the prison chapel, which was deemed relatively fireproof.

When she did move, her furnishings moved with her into a wire mesh cell a mite smaller but "nicer" than what she had had, the warden said. A few feet away, but out of sight, were eight small cells for the men on death row. The electric chair occupied the room beyond the cells, behind a soundproof wall.

"There is nothing 'nice' about it," commented Anna Marie. "It's only closer" to the electric chair.

The changes afforded Frederick L. Rike, chief engineer at the prison, the opportunity to automate "Old Sparky," which had taken 206 lives in a span of four decades. For many years it was held that inmate Charles Justice built Ohio's electric chair while serving time for burglary and larceny. Just legend, say historians, although he may have performed some electrical work on the chair. What is true about Justice is that after winning parole, he committed murder, returned to the penitentiary, and was executed in the chair on October 27, 1911.

According to Warden Woodard, inmate Harry Glick, a cabinet-maker, built the chair in 1896. Two years later Glick was released, but in 1912 he also returned to the prison after fatally shooting of a police officer. Glick died in his cell five years later.

By the luck of the draw, seventeen-year-old William Haas of Cincinnati, known as "the Boy Murderer," inaugurated the era of death by electrocution. His execution had been scheduled for April 20, 1897, but a burned-out dynamo in the electric plant supplying power to the untried chair gave Haas one more day of life.

"The eyes of all Ohio were turned upon this first experiment in using God's weapon to kill a man," H. M. Fogle wrote in "The Palace of Death."[5] There was considerable interest in the first use of the chair, "not only throughout the state of Ohio but the entire civilized world [and] arguments pro and con were advanced. . . . The advocates of this new method knew, of course, that everything would depend upon the result of this night's work."[6]

As a result of the delay, Ohio's first use of "Old Sparky" became a double—and successful—execution. Convicted murderer William Wiley, also of Cincinnati, went to the chair moments after Haas's corpse was removed from it. The two convicts had drawn lots to see who would go first. Haas lost, yet gained a measure of fame as a pioneer.[7]

Rike rewired the old chair so that the current was automatically applied in three successive and measured doses. By pressing three buttons simultaneously, three guards in the transformer room one floor below activated the chair. The guards knew one button was "hot," but not which one.

Had the United States Supreme Court not agreed to hear an appeal on her behalf, Anna Marie would have been the first in the automated chair. Instead, it was Thomas B. Williams, a twenty-year-old convicted murderer, on June 27. While tightly strapped into the device, he sang several verses of "This Is a Mean Old World," tapping out the rhythm with his left foot. He followed that number with one verse of "Lead Me On" before the warden halted the macabre, impromptu performance and proceeded with the execution.

Hoodin and Bolsinger turned every page in every law book to win Anna Marie her freedom, or, at the very least, an escape from the death sentence. Remuneration no longer was possible. Anna Marie had mortgaged her home for $5,000 for the defense team, but that's

5. H. M. Fogle, *The Palace of Death* (Columbus, Ohio: self-published, 1908), 136.

6. Ibid., 145, 146.

7. Ronald L. Reinbolt, 29, was the last to be executed in Ohio's chair, on March 15, 1963.

all there was. The law firm had spent $8,000 of its own money, yet it continued on with admirable doggedness.

Having won an indefinite stay for his client on March 3, pending the conclusion of the appeal, Hoodin appeared before the seven judges of the Ohio Supreme Court in Columbus on March 25 to seek their review of the trial. Although Anna Marie was not present for the fifty-minute hearing, once again many female spectators were.

"This woman was tried as a hunted animal," Hoodin said of his client. Reiterating many of the same points he made before Judge Bell in November, he said Anna Marie had been denied a fair trial because the prosecution's introduction of other poisonings linked to her "so inflamed the jury that they were unable to get to the true facts of the case."

Outcalt denied that any evidence had been improperly introduced. "Each one of those crimes is tied up together," he argued.

In a unanimous seven-word decision on April 13, Ohio's highest court declined to review Anna Marie's conviction. "There is no debatable constitutional question involved," the court ruled. It set May 4 as her new date with the electric chair.

"I had a feeling the court would rule against me," Anna Marie said upon hearing the news from Warden Woodard and the Catholic prison chaplain, Father John A. Sullivan. Loud wailing could be heard well after they had left her cell. By the time Hoodin, Bolsinger, and Sidney Brant arrived, she had composed herself once again. They brought her a few dollars so she could buy cigarettes, but she refused it, asking that lilies be purchased for Father Sullivan's altar for Easter services.

One option the defense team considered was an application for commutation of her sentence, but Anna Marie "is hardly interested in a commutation," said Hoodin, so he returned to the Ohio Supreme Court April 22, seeking a new hearing on constitutional issues. Within the week the high court denied the request, after which Anna Marie changed her tune. She told Hoodin "that if my life were spared, I could show all these people that I did not do the things that they say I did. I think that they would find out sometime that I didn't do them. I could show them that I was not the woman that I was painted [to be] at my trial."

Hoodin needed Ohio Supreme Court Chief Justice Carl V. Weygandt to sign off on an appeal to the United States Supreme Court.

When he could not be located immediately, Hoodin filed for a stay of execution with the office of Ohio's governor, Martin L. Davey. A day later Weygandt scheduled a hearing for Tuesday afternoon, one day before the scheduled execution date.

With an eleventh-hour hearing set, the defense team let it be known that it had new evidence that would "bust this case wide open."

In an extraordinary, unprecedented action, state welfare director Margaret Allman, who was responsible for state prisons, told the newspapers that Anna Marie would be available for a cell-side interview May 2. Hoodin feared his client wasn't up to it and asked Mrs. Allman to reconsider, but she refused.

Forty-eight hours before she was to die, more than twenty-five reporters from as far away as Chicago and New York sat and stood outside the wire mesh of Anna Marie's cell. At Hoodin's insistence, only Charles Rentrop of the *Cincinnati Post* and Joseph Garretson Jr. of the *Cincinnati Enquirer* were allowed to question the prisoner, relaying questions posed by the remainder of the press corps.

Anna Marie wore a high-necked white satin blouse, with her crucifix, and a navy blue skirt. Her nails were polished a neutral pink and her hair waved loosely. She wore no lipstick and only a light dusting of powder over a hint of rouge.

On her desk was a vase of tulips and roses, a crucifix, her rosary beads and Bible, several books with German titles, and some letters she had received. There also were a number of photographs of her son in her cell as well as pictures of the infant child of defense attorney Brant and the smiling faces of several children and motion picture actresses, whose pictures were cut from magazines.

At the outset, Anna Marie told the reporters that she did not feel she had received a fair trial.

"In what respect?"

"In every respect. The prosecution brought things into my trial to blacken my character without reason. They told lies about me."

"But, Anna, didn't you admit some of those things on the witness stand?"

"We all do things in life we shouldn't do. Not all of us are perfect."

"How do you feel now about having so many women on the jury?"

"I did not know women could do such a thing to another woman. After being a mother myself, I didn't think any woman could do such a thing." In hindsight, she said, an all-male jury would have been better.

"How do you feel about dying?"

"If I am not going to live, if I have to go, I will be ready. . . . I would not be afraid to die. I have no fear whatsoever."

The reporters took her at her word, having observed her steely resolve since the day of her arrest. Throughout her imprisonment, she refused to reveal the turmoil inside her. She was, in fact, afraid of death, but she also was convinced that her conviction would be overturned or her sentence commuted.

"Do you see a chance to save your life?"

"I feel there may be a chance yet. I never have felt any other way."

"Anna, are you innocent?"

"I am."

"In whom do you place your hope for life?"

"In the governor. I have always admired the way he makes speeches and has handled his office. He will be fair in this. I still believe they do not want to take my life. It is not for myself that I want to live. It is because when I am gone the stain will be on him," she said, looking at a picture of her son on the bedside table.

Anna Marie said she had begun writing about her life, but stopped. "It was so sorrowful that nobody would believe it. The public would not want to read it."

She said she had heard through the prison grapevine about the three executions since she came to death row.

"Well, Anna, what was your reaction?"

"I had a great feeling for Everett Jones because he never had a chance in life. I, too, never had a chance. I feel that I have had nothing but sorrow in my life."

"But wasn't that sorrow of your own making?"

She shrugged. "No."

"How did it come about?

"There are a lot of things that happened in my life."

During each of the executions, matron Esther Lyle later explained, "Mrs. Hahn froze up and her whole attitude was one of extreme tension for several hours." The remainder of the time she had displayed "amazing fortitude," Mrs. Lyle said.

In the first five months of her incarceration, Anna Marie received more than five hundred letters, mostly from well wishers. Eight more arrived on the day of the mass interview but none from her family in Germany, she said. An elderly man in Kentucky offered to take her place on death row. "It's a shame to take the life of a pretty young woman," he said. A woman in Kentucky wrote to say she was making a personal appeal to Ohio's governor on Anna Marie's behalf. Another asked that the lapin fur coat Anna Marie wore upon entering the penitentiary be willed to her.

"The idea! I won't do it! Just because she wants my coat! I do not think it was a nice letter."

She was asked if she had written her final farewell to her mother. There was silence, save for faint strains of music from the prison band rehearsing in the yard. Anna Marie looked down at her hands, then glanced at Hoodin, who said nothing.

"I'd rather not answer that," she said softly. Nor did she care to comment on the fact that she no longer wore her wedding ring. She had allowed Philip to visit but twice since her arrival at the penitentiary, she said, adding that he could come again if he wished. He never did. The split was complete.

Oscar and his welfare were her only interest, she said. She revealed that he wanted to be a surgeon or a chemist.

"Would you want him to study in Germany?"

"No."

"Because of Hitler?"

"Suppose?" she replied, smiling. Anna Marie had made it clear in the past she did not support Adolf Hitler and the Nazi regime that came to power after she had left Germany.

One reporter wanted to know about the flakes of arsenic found in her purse, a damning piece of evidence presented by the prosecution. Anna Marie said she had no idea how they got there.

"I didn't have any idea what arsenic was before my trial. I don't believe there was any arsenic in that purse. I certainly didn't put it there if there was. I didn't purchase the purse until July." It was that month that she traveled to Colorado with her son and Georg Obendoerfer, who died there from arsenical poisoning.

Anna Marie also spoke scornfully of Detectives Patrick H. Hayes and Walter Hart, whom her defense counsel accused of making "vile" comments to her. "I remember Captain Hayes and Detective Hart very well, indeed," she said, adding sarcastically, "They are very fine gentlemen."

It was alleged by authorities that she had received $70,000 or more from her victims, but she denied receiving any amount of money whatsoever.

"That's just like the thousands of other lies they told about me," she said. "Those statements that I received all that money from the men are not true. Do you want to know about my big fortune? I haven't a cent in the world, and I never did have a cent that didn't come into my hands in a perfectly honest way."

Rentrop asked which horse Anna Marie liked in the Kentucky Derby, a race to be run that Saturday. Although during her trial she admitted to having bet often on horse races, "I haven't any pick," she replied. "I don't even know who is running."

When the extraordinary interview ended, Anna Marie shook hands with a few reporters she recognized from her trial and sat back down in her rocking chair. The last of the journalists to leave heard her crying softly.

The following day, Anna Marie obtained copies of the Columbus and Cincinnati newspapers that carried the interview and read each avidly. She smiled when she read that *Columbus Dispatch* reporter Kay Murphy viewed her as a "phlegmatic enigma," whose face gives no clue as to "what goes on behind her almost passive countenance."

She also received a visit from Hoodin, who pleaded with his client to tell the truth. She insisted that she had been telling the truth all along.

"If you want me to admit that I poisoned those people, and you promise that you'll save me, Mr. Hoodin, I'd rather die in the electric chair."

That specter was removed, temporarily at least, when Judge Weygandt stayed the execution pending an appeal to the United States

Supreme Court on constitutional grounds. "Whew! What a relief," said Hoodin, who immediately asked the Court to review the conviction. Because the Court was in summer recess, it would be fall before it rendered its decision.

Anna Marie heard the news of Weygandt's stay—or she almost did—on the radio in her cell. "You listen. I can't," she told the matron, cupping her hands over her ears. When she saw the matron smile, Anna Marie smiled, too. Another reprieve, but as the months of waiting went by, the daily death-row routine wore on her. The sewing she so enjoyed—projects including a pair of embroidered altar cloths for Father Sullivan and a bedspread and chair covers for herself—all but stopped. She favored the radio—she preferred classical music—and newspapers more than novels now. Other than occasionally scrubbing the floor of her cell on her hands and knees, she exercised little. Consequently, she gained weight on prison fare.

"She paces up and down her cell like a wild, caged animal, smoking one cigarette after another," said matron Kate Swift. "Often she stops to stare at the ceiling for minutes, only to resume her pacing. Then she stops and stares at the wall or floor. Sometimes she continues this until 3 or 4 o'clock in the morning."[8]

The spring and summer of 1938 was a relatively quiet period for the woman who, by July, had been on death row longer than any of the men incarcerated there. She met two new matrons, Rene A. Tipple and Josie O'Bleness, who replaced Mrs. Swift and Mrs. Schultz, both of whom left the penitentiary. Mrs. O'Bleness's late husband, Frank, was a witness to Ohio's first electrocution in 1897. Now his widow faced the prospect of watching Ohio's first electrocution of a woman.

Out-of-town newspapers that had reporters in Columbus for the twice-canceled execution dates now waited for a third date to be set. Still, oddities occurred, such as the story about one Andrew Gunther, forty-one, of Milwaukee and Chicago.

Gunther arrived in Cincinnati, where he told police that a woman he knew as Anna Baumann was, in fact, Anna Marie Hahn. He said

8. Kate Swift, "Matron Reveals How Anna Hahn Awaits Chair," *Columbus Sunday Dispatch*, November 20, 1938, B-1.

he had met her after responding to her classified advertisement for matrimony. They met in Chicago on June 16, 1936, he said, and after they had spent several days together, the woman, who Gunther described as German-born, took a particular interest in his financial affairs. "She said before she married him, he would have to put equal [dollar] amounts in [the] bank," Cincinnati police notes reveal. "He put in $790.00, and they were to be married Friday [June 19]. He was all ready [but] she did not show up. He went to [the] bank and found Anna had drew [sic] out all but $9.00. He swore out a warrant."[9]

After telling this story to the police, Gunther next showed up at the penitentiary, asking to see Anna Marie. Warden Woodard became suspicious. His prisoner said she had never heard of Andrew Gunther. The warden, who refused to make his prisoner available, suspected Gunther was a Chicago newspaper reporter seeking an exclusive interview with Anna Marie. When Woodard showed Gunther the prison's Bertillon photograph of her, he was not able to identify her. Woodard sent the man packing, and he never was heard from again.

When, on October 10, the United States Supreme Court rejected Anna Marie's appeal for a hearing, she took it hard..Hoodin thought she was in "apparent shock." He and Bolsinger plotted their next legal maneuver. Their client wanted them to "take every step possible" to save her life.

Judge Weygandt set December 7 as the new date for her execution.

The Blonde Borgia—a moniker that she said stabbed her "right in the heart"—conducted her final death-row interview with Cincinnati and Columbus reporters on the morning of November 22. The reporters found her "cheerful" as she sat in her rocking chair in a brown silk polka-dot dress covered by a flowered brown smock. She still found it hard to tell the truth, though.

"I am going to tell you for the first time what I really went to Colorado for. It was to obtain a cancer-cure formula developed by Oscar's father, a Viennese physician," who, she said, was "one of the greatest doctors in the world." She said she worked beside him in his laboratory. Shortly before departing for Colorado, she obtained the formula from Germany, she said, continuing her tangled tale.

9. Captain Patrick H. Hayes, personal notes, undated.

"I went to Colorado to find the brother-in-law of Oscar's father, who is also a doctor and who I thought could help me introduce the formula. When I reached there, I learned that the doctor had gone to Arizona with his tubercular wife. His wife has since died."

Why had she not mentioned this at her trial, a reporter wanted to know.

"Oh, they wouldn't have believed me, and they would have accused me of experimenting on those old men. I know this sounds crazy, but crazier things than this have happened."

During her time as a matron, Katie Smith became convinced that Anna Marie was knowledgeable about various medical compounds and their potency. In a secret hiding place in her home, Anna Marie said, was a formula for a medicine that had cured Oscar of infantile paralysis in Germany.

Anna Marie described as "silly" the inferences that she was romantically linked to Obendoerfer.

"I could have had all the young men I wanted," she said. "They had no right to infer that there was anything immoral in my associations with him or any of those other men. In all my life, I have never done anything immoral."

The reporters wanted to know if it was true that she had written her life's story. Actually she had begun to do so shortly after taking up residence in the penitentiary, using a typewriter loaned to her by Ann Duffy, secretary to Ohio attorney general Herbert S. Duffy (unrelated to Ann), but the machine was removed and the project was abandoned after prison authorities raised a flap over her having it. Miss Duffy said she only was trying to do "a good turn." Mrs. Smith later revealed that Anna Marie believed what the do-gooder wanted in return was the prisoner's story. "All that you have talked about is getting this story," Smith quoted Anna Marie as having said to Miss Duffy. "You have never mentioned what you'll give me for it."

At the press conference, though, Anna Marie made no mention of this. Instead, she said she gave up on the writing because she was "too nervous to keep my mind on it, but when I get to Marysville, I will write the story, and it will be almost unbelievable."

On the morning of Thanksgiving Day, most of the prison population attended a ten-act vaudeville show, a dance-band performance, and two wrestling matches. The noontime dinner that followed included roast pork and dressing, sweet potatoes, cranberry sauce, mince pie, and coffee, topped by cigars for all. Anna Marie didn't get a show or a cigar, but she did eat the same meal—alone in her cell.

"I am at peace with the world," she said, convinced that the governor would commute her sentence.

18 | FAREWELL

If capital punishment is to remain a part of Ohio law," the editorial in the *Cleveland Plain Dealer* began, "there should be some restraint, legal or moral, set up to prevent such an exhibition of maudlinism and positive cruelty as marked the last hours of Anna Marie Hahn's misspent life."[1]

The "exhibition" that the newspaper found so distasteful, so "beyond the realm of decency," stemmed from thirteen-year-old Oscar Hahn's last hours with his mother and his public pleas for her life, all noted in considerable detail by the curious press.

Anna Marie's attorneys had made multiple appeals to authorities to stay the execution and win a commutation of her death sentence. They had been successful in winning stays twice before—in March, when the original execution date was the tenth of that month, and again May 4, when, at the eleventh hour, her case was allowed to go to the United States Supreme Court. In mid-November, just three weeks from the newly scheduled execution date of December 7, Ohio governor Martin L. Davey was asked to commute the sentence.

The governor was not under a lot of pressure to do so. His office was not flooded with mail appealing for the life of the only woman incarcer-

1. Editorial, "Sorry Exhibition," *Cleveland Plain Dealer*, Dec. 9, 1938, 10.

ated on death row. In fact, an aide to the governor described the mail protesting the execution as a "thin trickle." Davey did receive one letter from a Youngstown, Ohio, women's club, however. The ladies asked that he "give Mrs. Hahn's son his mother for a Christmas present."

Certainly the voice of Anna Marie's husband, Philip, was not heard. He remained in Cincinnati, where rumors circulated that he already had become infatuated with another woman.[2] Anna Marie's family in Germany was all but silent, too, although her sister, Katti, did write to say that their distraught mother had suffered a heart attack.

Frau Filser, now seventy, told all who asked that her youngest daughter was innocent, but few asked. The Filsers in Fuessen, long respected and influential, all but withdrew from view at the time, unable to face the disgrace Anna Marie had brought to the family name.[3]

The lone voice was Oscar's. Six days before his mother was to die, attorneys Bolsinger and Hoodin brought the boy to Columbus for a clemency hearing at the statehouse. They had asked to see the governor himself, but they appeared instead before Daniel S. Earhart, executive secretary to the governor, who presided at clemency hearings.

"I want them to see me and to know that I am a good son," Oscar said prior to his testimony. "I want them to know I am the kind of a boy who could not have been raised by the kind of a woman they say my mother is."

The December 1 hearing lasted more than three hours, but Oscar, put on the stand and questioned by Hoodin, testified for only five minutes.

"What do you think about the charges against your mother, that she poisoned seven men for their money?"

"I don't think she ever did that. She has been a good mother. I don't want her to die. I don't think there ever could be a mother as good as she is. Nobody can ever take her place."

"Do you know what will happen to your mother if Governor Davey refuses to grant clemency?"

2. Philip Hahn remarried after Anna Marie's death.
3. The small community never had recorded a murder.

"Yes, sir," the boy replied, focusing his deep blue eyes on Earhart, sitting close by. If his mother's life were spared, he added, "it would be the greatest Christmas I ever had or ever will have."

If a pin had dropped in the hearing room, it would have been heard. Hamilton County prosecutor Carl Rich waited a moment, then rose from his chair, looked at the shine on his shoes, took a couple of measured steps, and said, "We respectfully urge that executive clemency be denied to this woman. Oscar is a fine boy, but this woman, his mother, is a mass murderer in every sense of the word. She does not deserve clemency."[4] The youth showed no emotional response to the harsh words.

Describing Anna Marie's trial as "the greatest farce in history," Hoodin attacked the press, the petticoat jury, the "living victim" Heis, Captain Hayes, the evidence, and the prosecutor, Outcalt, whom he described as "bloodthirsty" and politically motivated.

"Dudley Outcalt attempted to build his political future on the skeleton bones of a woman," said Hoodin. "He stepped over the body of Anna Marie Hahn to become a judge of the Hamilton County Common Pleas Court."

As for Heis, he had been seen walking about Cincinnati, Hoodin declared, which was true. A reporter for the *Cincinnati Post* found the sixty-three-year-old former coal dealer in his backyard, chopping wood. Other than having lost weight and no feeling in his feet, Heis claimed to be fine. "If I had the say-so," he told the reporter, "she would go to the chair."

The governor felt the same. After he had received a report from the clemency hearing, Davey issued a two-page written statement in which he declined to intervene. The governor, who left office a month later, having lost reelection, said his sense of chivalry "rebelled against the idea of allowing a woman to go to the chair," but he went on to describe Anna Marie as "cold-blooded" and "without a quiver of emotion or any remorse or any repentance."

4. In the November 1938 elections, Dudley M. Outcalt handily won a seat on the Court of Common Pleas. Carl Rich succeeded him as Hamilton County prosecutor.

Davey said he felt "sorry for the boy, but I think his own mother has been most unfair to him. She has bequeathed him nothing to be proud of."

The *Ohio State Journal* editorial praised the governor, who had "lived up to his reputation of being a man of courage."[5] The *Cleveland Plain Dealer* also approved of the governor's "hard decision" and noted: "Ohio law recognizes no difference of sex in the matter of capital crime. Women who have fought for and won equality with men in virtually every field of life cannot well complain if they are held equally responsible for their violations of law."[6]

During the final days, members of the press jockeyed for position at the execution. For the first time in Ohio, two women reporters—Sarah L. Dush of the *Ohio State Journal* and Dorothy Todd Foster of the *Columbus Dispatch*—were to be allowed to walk with Anna Marie from her cell to what death-row prisoners called the "good-bye door" leading to "Old Sparky." For a time, though, reporters from the powerful Scripps-Howard chain of newspapers, including the local *Columbus Citizen*, were banned from witnessing any part of the execution.

The Scripps-Howard flap began December 1 when the *Citizen* published an item that Margaret Allman found personally degrading. It chided her frequent absences from her cabinet post as state welfare director, which had nothing to do with the Hahn execution. Allman called the article "asinine" and directed that Scripps-Howard reporters be barred from witnessing the execution as a result.

"I am one of those sweet-tempered women," Mrs. Allman said at a press conference, "but when I get going, I am a holy terror."

However, the incident died quickly after lawyers for the newspaper chain pointed out that a provision in Ohio's General Code permitted a reporter from each of the daily newspapers in Columbus to attend all executions. It was the only bit of silliness in what was otherwise a grim week.

Neatly dressed in a tan suit with a white shirt, a brown, patterned tie,

5. Editorial, "A Man of Courage," *Ohio State Journal* (Columbus), Dec. 7, 1938, 4.
6. Editorial, "To the Chair," *Cleveland Plain Dealer*, Dec. 7, 1938, 12.

a belted, dark gray, checked overcoat, and a child's fedora, Oscar traveled alone by bus from Cincinnati to Columbus on the morning of December 6, the first day he was given "free" access to his mother's cell. Each of several visits could last an hour or two, Warden Woodard said.

Hoodin met Oscar at the bus station at noon, and shortly before 2 P.M. they went together to the penitentiary, where in advance of the official announcement a reporter quietly slipped Hoodin word of Davey's decision. Hoodin didn't immediately mention the unsettling news to Oscar. Together they passed through the series of steel gates and up to the second floor, home of death row. Hoodin asked the boy to wait at the top of the stairwell, within a few yards of his mother's spacious cell. The attorney needed a few moments alone with his client to inform her of the governor's decision.

"I've got bad news for you," her attorney said even as he approached the cell. He saw Anna Marie through the mesh partition before he reached the iron cell door that squeaked on its hinges a little. She wore dark blue cotton pajamas, and fear showed on her face. Once inside, Hoodin put his hand on her shoulder as if to steady her. "He will not intervene. He won't commute your sentence."

The words were hardly out of his mouth before Anna Marie screamed, "Oh, my God! I didn't think he could do that to me!" She pulled away from Hoodin, buried her face in her hands, and collapsed into the rocking chair. "He should let me live for my boy!" she shouted in despair and in fear.

Anna Marie's piercing cries were heard clearly in the stairwell. Matron Josie O'Bleness pulled Oscar closer to her. "Be brave, Oscar," she said, "and make your mother be brave." Hoodin returned to the boy's side and told him the same distressing news. Oscar, who throughout his mother's ordeal had been every bit as strong as she, now gave in to the tears, too.

When Oscar was admitted to her cell, he literally ran into his mother's arms and each tried to comfort the other, yet saying little. With tears streaming down her face, Anna Marie held her son in her lap, stroking his blond hair and rocking back and forth gently. She brushed back hair from his forehead and continued to weep, even wail. "Don't, mother, please don't," Oscar said. For him, she held back her tears the best she could.

After a few minutes—it seemed much longer—he showed her the model airplane he had made. She admired and praised him for his craftsmanship. The large model of a single-engine seaplane, the length of his arm and framed out in balsa wood, had won a prize at a Cincinnati hobby show a few days earlier. Anna Marie was very proud of her son, a boy whom she had directed to be an unwitting partner in her murderous deeds.

Watching the boy and his mother cling together, cry together, was "pitiful, truly pitiful," a touched Mrs. O'Bleness said. She didn't want to watch, but it was her job to do so. The matrons were on high alert, fearing that the prisoner would attempt to take her life—and that of her son's, too. "She was tricky," Mrs. O'Bleness said. "I wouldn't have trusted her for a moment then."

After less than an hour together, Oscar left his mother, never having removed his overcoat, as if he didn't intend to stay long. Now, with the approval of Hoodin, he was summoned to meet with the crush of newspaper reporters and photographers who pressed into Warden Woodard's office. Smiling shyly and chewing gum, Oscar walked in with Father Sullivan and Hoodin, and with his coat still on and hat in hand, he posed for pictures with the two men. Then he sat down and announced, "I'm not to say anything until Mr. Hoodin tells me to." Hoodin, standing beside him, smiled. Just behind Oscar, a canary silently watched the scene from its cage. On the wall above the youth's head was the number six, the date shown on a City National Bank & Trust wall calendar. A sea of fedoras closed in as the journalists pressed forward to catch Oscar's every word.

Always the little gentleman among adults, Oscar answered every question politely, although he looked up at Hoodin a couple of times to make sure he should respond. He handled English very well, with only an occasional hint of his native tongue.

"She was the best mother in the world to me."

"My mother would never do anything like that. How could anyone so kind, a woman so good a mother to me, do anything like that?"

"I would like to see the governor to ask him if he could do anything else for my mother, because I don't think she did anything like that."

"She told me to be a good boy, and everything would turn out all right."

A reporter asked him about his treatment by other children in his sixth-grade class at the Washington School in Cincinnati. "They're alright," he responded.

"You certainly are a brave little boy," the reporter said. Two or three of the other reporters nodded their assent.

After the interview, Father Sullivan, Oscar, and Hoodin returned to Anna Marie's cell and spent the remainder of the afternoon with her. Also in the cell from time to time were Mrs. Woodard and Mrs. O'Bleness.

Oscar remained with his mother until just before suppertime, when Hoodin escorted the boy to the nearby Deshler-Wallick Hotel at Broad and High streets in downtown Columbus. After dinner, they retired there, Oscar reading a book before bed and Hoodin reviewing his legal options for once again halting the execution. There seemed to be few, but Anna Marie had told him, "I have the utmost faith in you. Let's hope for the best."

When a reporter in Cincinnati informed Philip of Governor Davey's decision, he simply replied, "I am very sorry, friend. I have nothing to say."

At the prison, Anna Marie became truly hysterical after her son left. Overwrought, she sobbed loudly, kissing Oscar's picture over and over again, tears streaming down her face. "Oh, God! I wish I might live for him, for my boy!" In between sobs, she puffed on one cigarette after another and paced the cell. Only for brief periods did she sit in the rocker or lie on the bed.

When she fainted and fell to the floor, an alarmed Mrs. O'Bleness summoned one of the death-row guards, who carried the unconscious prisoner to her bed. There, with the aid of spirits of ammonia, the matron was able to revive her charge, but Anna Marie continued to cry throughout the night. She had no appetite and never touched her dinner.

Mrs. O'Bleness, who was quite fond of the Blonde Borgia, would not see her again that night. Matrons Mrs. Lyle and Mrs. Tipple relieved

Mrs. O'Bleness at 10:30 P.M. Together they kept a close eye on their near-hysterical prisoner, who, they agreed, had lost all hope of being saved from the chair. Several times during the night, as the clock ticked ever closer to her death, she cried out, "My God! What about Oscar?" At 1 A.M. Anna Marie passed out again. Mrs. Tipple called prison physician Dr. George W. Keil, who revived her with spirits of ammonia and black coffee. Later Mrs. Woodard brought a cup of tea.

Although Anna Marie got no rest and her eyes were red and puffy, Wednesday morning she carefully fixed her hair and straightened herself up for Oscar's visit. The day before she had manicured her nails, painting them with a natural polish because she thought it "more appropriate" than the red blush polish she usually wore. She also had packed a small, black overnight bag with her few belongings, believing at that time that the governor would spare her life, and she would be transferred to the Women's Reformatory in Marysville.

Before Oscar arrived with the defense team at 8:30 A.M. Wednesday, she was allowed out of her cell to attend brief services in the Catholic chapel, conducted by Father Sullivan. Only twice since arriving at the penitentiary 372 days earlier had she been "freed" from her death-row cell. Once she had her teeth checked at the prison hospital, and she attended a service in the chapel in March, immediately prior to the stay of her first date of execution.

Mother and son spent most of the day together, although matrons and Father Sullivan were always nearby. The warden and then his wife briefly dropped by as well. Again Oscar asked Warden Woodard if he could see the governor, but the request never went forward. Hoodin told the press he would take the boy to see Davey that afternoon, but it never happened. The governor had made his decision.

Anna Marie and Oscar ate lunch together at a wooden table where she occasionally would write. She hardly touched her fried ham sandwich. It would be her last meal, although she was offered a chicken dinner.

Anna Marie enjoyed a radio until the last days. Then the warden ordered it removed so his prisoner could not listen to news reports of her impending execution. That very afternoon the matrons took down photos of Oscar from the stark brick wall where they'd hung.

"We thought it best," said Mrs. Lyle, who served as a matron during Anna Marie's entire stay in the penitentiary.

Then came the most awful time for all.

"Mrs. Hahn. It's time for Oscar to leave," Mrs. Tipple said. It was 4:45 P.M. Anna Marie looked up at her, pleading for a few more minutes, but already the "no visitors" deadline set by the warden had passed. Anna Marie kissed her son's face repeatedly, quickly. "It's time," the matron said again, not without compassion, but she had to wrest the boy away from his mother's embrace.

"Don't take him away!" Anna Marie screamed in a voice so loud it startled those nearby. "Don't take him from me! DON'T TAKE HIM FROM ME!"

Mrs. Tipple stepped in between Anna Marie and her son so he could leave. Father Sullivan moved in to assist the matron and quickly led the tearful Oscar from the cell and into the care of Bolsinger. Anna Marie screamed and cried and pleaded and became violent. She "viciously" attacked Mrs. Tipple in a desperate effort to get out of the cell and to her son. Mrs. Tipple called to Mrs. Lyle for help. Together they got Anna Marie onto the bed, where she was injected with a sedative to calm her.

Oscar's eyes were red and his face drained and drawn as Bolsinger and Assistant Deputy Warden Colonel William J. Walker sped out the front door of the prison, shielding the boy.

"Have a heart! Have a heart!" Bolsinger pleaded with the photographers who pressed toward them.

The boy used his mother's dark brown lapin coat, which he had over his arm, to partially hide his face from the press. His mother had worn the coat last when she entered the penitentiary the previous December. One or two women had written to Anna Marie, requesting that she give it to them, since she would need it no longer. The two men and Oscar crossed Spring Street and climbed into Walker's car for the short drive to the Deshler-Wallick Hotel.

Bolsinger took the boy up to Room 766. It was just 5 P.M., and the winter's darkness shrouded the city, yet neither one turned on a light. Oscar shucked his shoes and curled up in an overstuffed chair.

Bolsinger sat opposite him, watching his charge. "Let's not turn on a light," he said. "This is restful."

"Yes, sir."

A knock came on the door. It was a local newspaper reporter, Edward Bliss of the *Columbus Citizen,* who the attorneys agreed would join Oscar for the awful, final hours.

The room was quiet, even awkward. Nobody knew what to say, or even if anything should be said.

"It is hard to think of anything to say to a boy whose mother is going to be killed, and you know it and he knows it," Bliss would write.

He asked Oscar what he remembered about his birthplace, Fuessen, Bavaria. The boy recalled a big castle in the mountains and very little else.[7] He reminded the visitor that he was only five years of age when he came to the United States with his mother by boat. He remembered that.

Bliss and Bolsinger engaged in trivial talk, quietly, allowing Oscar to be alone with his thoughts. Bolsinger knew that the U.S. District Court was weighing a last-minute appeal for a writ of habeas corpus. Hoodin had filed the petition that afternoon with Judge Mell J. Underwood, stating that Anna Marie's incarceration was in violation of her rights to life and liberty under the Fourteenth Amendment to the Constitution. More specifically, Hoodin said his client was tried and convicted by "an irresistible wave of public passion," as evidenced by the crowds in the courtroom and the courthouse corridors each day of the trial. Furthermore, the defense maintained that the prosecution inflamed those passions by word and deed before a jury that from the outset had determined Anna Marie's guilt.

After an hour or so in the hotel room, Bolsinger suggested that they get some supper nearby, which they did. Oscar ordered two fried eggs with toast, a custard, and hot tea, all of which he devoured as heartily as any growing boy would. The seemingly tranquil time was shattered, however, by a newsboy's loud shouts on the street outside.

"EXTRA! EXTRA! Anna Marie Hahn must die!"

---

7. Oscar's reference was to the Neuschwanstein Castle within sight of Fuessen.

Immediately, the two men knew that all efforts to win a stay for Anna Marie, to spare her life, had failed. Neither wanted to look at Oscar, who appeared frightened and ashen. All three quickly walked back toward the hotel.

"Ed. Please take Oscar back to the room and collect our things," Bolsinger said. "I'll go get the car and meet you in the lobby."

The reporter and the boy quickly collected what had been brought there and headed for the elevator. When it finally arrived on the seventh floor, it was jammed with noisy, happy people. Suddenly the cage grew silent as its passengers made room for two more. Oscar had been recognized. Bliss, with Oscar's model plane in hand, held it high so that its delicate frame would not be crushed. Only after they left the elevator and walked through the mezzanine did an aileron fall off. "Just put it here in my pocket," Oscar said, patting the side of his coat.

Oscar returned to the prison at 7:15 P.M. with Bolsinger and Bliss. They drove unnoticed into the wagon stockade, a vehicle entrance on the north side of the penitentiary, and walked down the wide hallway past the prison offices and through a gate of iron bars into the prison yard. A ruse had been used to herd the reporters and photographers into a back office until the three visitors were inside and beyond the view of the press. Oscar had hoped to see his mother yet again, but Warden Woodard firmly denied his request. The condemned were not allowed visitors as the time of execution drew near.

Earlier, and for the last time, Hoodin visited his client to tell her he had exhausted all avenues to save her life.

"Can't you do something?" she wailed, rocking back and forth in her chair. "Can't you let me live just until Christmas?" Hoodin didn't answer her questions, telling her instead that everything possible would be done for Oscar's happiness and well-being.

As Hoodin slipped out of the cell for the last time, Oscar crossed the deserted prison yard. He looked up, toward his mother's second-floor cell. A thin crack of light, peeking out from behind drawn shades, could be seen, but that was all. They waited for perhaps five minutes for Father Sullivan to arrive and take them to the prison chapel for a few minutes of prayer. Oscar kept his eyes on the window, except when a TWA plane, its red and green lights flashing, flew low overhead, on its way from the Columbus airport nearby to a destination unknown.

Father Sullivan, who had just left Anna Marie's cell, too, walked out into the moonlit yard and put his arm around the boy's shoulders. "Your mother is feeling better," he told the youngster, comforting him with the message, yet fighting to control his own emotions. The priest led them to the chapel, where he and Oscar knelt together in prayer in front of the altar adorned with a cloth Anna Marie had embroidered. "Dear God, please save my mother," the boy said quietly. Bolsinger and Bliss also kneeled, but the reporter found it difficult to pray. He was busy making notes.

After three or four minutes of prayer, the group went back into the yard, where Oscar again looked toward his mother's cell.

"May I see my mother again?" he asked the priest. His voice was not pleading, but it was full of emotion. The boy was close to tears.

"No, Oscar," Father Sullivan said softly but firmly. "You know how it was this afternoon. You don't want to make it any harder for her."

Oscar had no reply, but the tears he had managed to bravely keep back now flowed freely down his cheeks.

Oscar did not see the people who had gathered on Spring Street, outside the towering, gray prison walls. He was taken back out through the wagon stockade. As the youngster left, he turned back toward the prison but once, tears in his eyes.

With the silent youth beside him in the front seat of the sedan, Bolsinger drove quickly away, heading south on the Three-C Highway toward Cincinnati.

Oscar Hahn also "died" that cold December day in 1938; his name was changed and his past erased as he went to live with another family somewhere in the Midwest. There were one or two vague reports subsequently—one that he had served in the U.S. Navy during World War II and another that he had been killed in the Korean War—but the bright, handsome German-born youth who loved his mother with all his heart was gone forever.[8]

8. The day after Anna Marie died, one of Hollywood's biggest stars, George Raft, invited Oscar to spend the Christmas holidays with him at his Beverly Hills home. "The thought of that kid haunts me," the actor said. His invitation was declined.

19 | "IT'S TIME"

Dr. Fred C. Swing buttoned up his heavy wool overcoat as he left the Palace Theater downtown. He had just seen *Angels with Dirty Faces*, a 1938 gangster film starring James Cagney, Pat O'Brien, and Humphrey Bogart. Billed as a "taut, tidy melodrama," the movie ends with Rocky, Cagney's tough-guy character, going to the electric chair. "Oh, please! I don't wanna die!" Rocky pleads. "Oh, please! Don't let me burn!"

Now Swing, a former Hamilton County coroner, walked briskly along the dark streets to the Ohio penitentiary to witness a woman "burn."

A quiet crowd of perhaps one hundred curiosity seekers—it would grow almost tenfold by execution time—had gathered outside the prison's Spring Street entrance. Police kept traffic moving through the area, although more than a few motorists wanted to linger outside the massive walls. Reporters and photographers had been milling about the penitentiary since midafternoon, waiting to hear if Anna Marie had won yet another stay of execution.

Shortly before 7 P.M. the news arrived that Judge Underwood had denied the last-ditch appeal. For the journalists attending the execution, Warden Woodard provided an evening meal in his quarters. Guards frisked all witnesses entering the penitentiary. No cameras were permitted.

The majority of those who knew firsthand the Anna Marie Hahn story and had witnessed her icy calm in times of great stress believed that when she sat in the chair she would be just as composed, just as cold, as she had been throughout her trial and incarceration. Kate Swift, who spent ten months as prison matron to Anna Marie, told the *Columbus Dispatch* that she was convinced that when it came time for the execution, "she will walk there [with her] head up, showing no emotion whatsoever."

When Rene Tipple asked Anna Marie to write a letter to Warden Woodard for her, asking that he excuse her from accompanying the prisoner to the death chamber, Anna Marie chided her for her lack of intestinal fortitude. "I have more courage than you. I am not afraid to die. I have such courage that I know no fear."

Josie O'Bleness revealed, however, that in "her last twenty-four hours, Anna Hahn changed from the poised, confident, proud, and even vain woman she had been continuously since she was first arrested into a little witch—a demon with a wild look in her eyes. When she knew the jig was up, she became the true Anna."[1]

Joseph H. Hoodin, Sidney Brant, and Sidney Kahn arrived at the prison shortly after seven. Woodard excused himself from the dinner table to accompany the three attorneys to Anna Marie's cell. Within a few minutes he returned to his dinner guests, tears in his eyes. "The situation is pretty good over there," he said, but he lied. Anna Marie was hysterical. Prison psychiatrist Dr. George D. Woodward and the matrons tried to calm her, to little avail. Hoodin and Kahn returned shortly thereafter, also in tears. Brant stayed in Anna Marie's cell, and she clung to him, begging for help. He put his arm around her shoulder in comfort. How blanched and frail she was, he thought. Father Sullivan, who wore a purple stole, knelt by the seated Anna Marie, holding her hand as he spoke the holy viaticum.

"Oh, Heavenly Father, I can't go! I want to see Mr. Hoodin! I won't go until I see Mr. Hoodin!"

---

1. Josie O'Bleness, Kay Murphy, "True Anna Hahn Seen as Last Day Slipped by, Matron Says," *Columbus Dispatch*, Dec. 8, 1938, B-8.

"Mr. Hoodin won't be here," Colonel Walker softly told her. "He can't come now."

It was 8 P.M. "It's time," Walker said quietly.

"No! I am not going!" the condemned woman shouted.

"Oh, yes, Anna, you are going," Walker firmly replied. "You might as well make up your mind." Mrs. O'Bleness and Mrs. Lyle helped the prisoner to her feet.

The thirty-three witnesses, each a bearer of a pink admission card that read, "Dec. 7, 1938. J. C. Woodward, warden," already were seated in the death chamber. The card became a grim souvenir for some. For the first time in many years, folding chairs were set up for an execution; such was the interest in Anna Marie's death. On a nearby table, copies of the *Ohio Penitentiary News* went unread. The *News*, an internal periodical, never reported on executions, anyway.

Walker led the entourage out of the Anna Marie's cell, followed by Father Sullivan and Mrs. Tipple. Mrs. O'Bleness and Mrs. Lyle kept pace behind, each holding an arm of their sagging prisoner. Brant, newspaper reporters Dush and Foster, and three guards brought up the rear. "I walked the road of anguish with Anna Marie Hahn last night," Dush of the *Ohio State Journal* wrote for her newspaper. She and Foster, of the *Columbus Dispatch*, were the first female reporters to accompany a condemned prisoner to the death house.

The procession moved agonizingly slowly toward the good-bye door that led to the chair. On the way, it passed the cells holding eleven condemned men: George Wells; Harry Chapman; Henry Dingledine and his father, Harry Dingledine; Albert Lippe; John Williams Cline; Harvey L. Roush; Lafe Williams; Frank Tracy; Stephen Figuli; and Willie Caldwell. All would follow her path to the chair except Wells and Lippe, whose sentences were commuted to life.

Wells, twenty-two, took a particular interest in Anna Marie's walk, because his execution, for killing an Akron grocer during a holdup, was scheduled for one week later. As it turned out, Wells was the only one of the eleven to leave the penitentiary alive. After the governor commuted his death sentence, he was granted parole on June 15, 1966.

Figuli, twenty-one, went to the chair two weeks after Anna Marie. During her year on death row, ten men were electrocuted.

As she passed each cell, the condemned men bade farewell to a woman they were seeing for the first and last time. "Good luck," one said. "God bless you," said another.

"Good-bye, boys," Anna Marie replied, never looking at any of them.

For her farewell appearance, she chose faded blue pajamas, a flowered brown smock she had made while in the penitentiary, rolled down stockings, and street oxfords on her tiny feet.

It was 8:07 P.M. when the good-bye door to the enormously bright, white chamber swung open, sucking the last bit of courage from Anna Marie. There, facing her squarely, was the state's instrument of death. She took but three of the thirteen paces toward "Old Sparky," then collapsed into a heap on the floor, moaning, crying. Two khaki-clad guards rushed over to the door to help the matrons and prison physician Dr. Keil raise the prisoner from her knees. Together they carried her into the chair, despite her struggle to be free.

"Oh, no! No! Oh, no!" she cried, legs thrashing.

Dr. Keil, the senior of three physicians present, waved a small vial of smelling salts under her nose. The condemned had to be conscious to be executed.

"No! No! Don't do this to me!" she screamed, her voice sending a chill through the witnesses and prison personnel alike. The death chamber was designed to be soundproof, but the men on death row, still standing, heard her shrieks.

"Oh, don't! Please don't! Think of my baby!"

Experienced hands quickly fastened the leather straps around her wrists and ankles.

Anna Marie struggled, and whimpered, and pleaded and wailed.

She quickly glanced around the room and spotted the witnesses. One was *Cincinnati Post* reporter Charles Rentrop, the only witness she elected to be there. (The condemned could choose three witnesses.)

"Isn't there someone to help? Can't you think of my baby? Anybody? Just anybody? Please help me!"

The waist strap, cinched tight, pulled her back against the chair, restricting her writhing. Her legs, too short to reach the rubber-matted floor, dangled freely still.

She spied gray-haired Warden Woodard standing off to one side. "Mr. Woodard," she screamed, "don't let them do this to me!"

"I'm sorry, Mrs. Hahn. We can't help it, you know," he replied, his eyes filled with tears. He failed to disguise his distaste for the task ahead, and yet, when earlier asked by news photographers to pose with an empty "Old Sparky," he did so willingly.

Anna Marie's golden locks, once so perfectly coiffured, were now in disarray. At the urging of Mrs. Woodard, the hair had been combed to cover the small, round patch the matrons had shaved on Anna Marie's head. "It will provide some dignity," Mrs. Woodard explained. Now a guard pulled the locks aside, placed a copper disk on the shaved spot, and fastened a chinstrap to hold the disk in place. Anna Marie screamed in terror yet again, writhing wildly in the chair. Dr. Keil wafted the smelling salts under her nose once again. Nearby sat a bucket of water, to be used should the prisoner's hair catch on fire.

In a pitiful wail, Anna Marie acknowledged her predicament. "No one is going to help me!" With her stockings rolled down and her pajama leg slit up to her knee, a guard quickly fastened an electrode clamp to the calf of her right leg. She looked at Father Sullivan. "Come closer, Father," she implored. "Won't you help me?"

The priest, tears in his eyes and Bible in hand, put a comforting hand on hers, now securely strapped to the arms of the chair. In between sobs she remembered the lethal position she was in. She warned the cleric, "Don't touch me. You might be killed." His was the last face she was to see.

A guard slipped the fitted, black leather mask, with an opening at the nose, over her face. She now was in the shadow of death.

Standing aside, Father Sullivan began the Lord's Prayer.

"Our Father, who art in Heaven . . ."

Between sobs Anna Marie repeated the phrase, as did the three matrons and several others in the death chamber. Most mumbled a few words, transfixed on the macabre scene in front of them.

"Hallowed be Thy Name . . ."

"Hallowed be Thy Name . . ."

"Thy kingdom come, Thy will be done . . ."

"Thy kingdom . . ." Anna Marie's voice cracked. ". . . will be done."

"And forgive us our trespasses as we forgive those who trespass against us . . ."

Just muffled moans came from behind the death mask.

"Lead us not into temptation but deliver us from evil . . ."

"Lead us not into temptation but deliv . . ."

A light behind the chair flashed from green to red. Mrs. Lyle quickly closed her eyes, not wishing to witness the initial surge of electrical current. Anna Marie's body stiffened and slightly rose out of the deadly chair. Her thumbs turned upward. She made no sound.

A frightful whirring—sounding "like a Fourth of July sparkler," a reporter wrote—filled the room as 1,950 volts surged through Anna Marie for ten seconds. A wisp of smoke, ghostly in character, curled toward the ceiling. The voltage automatically dropped to 500 volts for forty seconds, then surged to 1,950 volts for another ten seconds. Father Sullivan and Brant turned their heads away. "The odor of burning flesh permeated the room," wrote James L. Kilgallen, reporter for the *New York Journal-American.*

Dr. Keil stepped forward. Placing his stethoscope on her chest, he listened for a heartbeat. He conferred briefly with Dr. Woodward and Dr. John I. White, each having also examined the lifeless form. After his examination, Dr. White whispered to his associates, "The heart is still beating." They waited twenty or thirty seconds, then Dr. Keil listened once again for a heartbeat. Suddenly he turned to the witnesses and forcefully pronounced that "a sufficient current of electricity has passed through the body of Anna Marie Hahn to cause death at thirteen-and-a-half minutes after eight o'clock."

Father Sullivan administered extreme unction, anointing Anna Marie's forehead. "I am surprised she broke," Warden Woodard said, noting that nobody before her in the chair had protested as violently as did Anna Marie. He wiped his moist eyes. "I had expected her to remain cool."

Thirty-two years of a twisted, even macabre, life had been snuffed out. "Old Sparky," having seated only men for more than forty years, had claimed its first woman. Three days later Anna Marie's prison photograph, an ugly portrait that revealed none of her attractiveness, hung on the death-chamber wall alongside those of the 213 men the state had previously executed.

Immediately following the execution, the O'Shaughnessy Funeral Home on East Town Street picked up the body and prepared it for a limited viewing the following day. Nearly one hundred persons, who had learned where the body had been taken, were allowed to pass by the open casket, most of them seeing Anna Marie for the first time. The morticians had curled her hair and attired her in a white Palm Beach suit with white buttons and a white silk knitted blouse that the matrons had picked out from Anna Marie's limited prison wardrobe. Almost at the last minute, a large floral display of gladiolus, bronze chrysanthemums, and red tea roses arrived. "With deepest sympathy—Friends in Cincinnati" the card read. Everyone assumed that the flowers, the only ones by the casket, had come from the defense team.

Some weeks earlier Hoodin had asked the Filser family in Fuessen if they wanted Anna Marie's body returned to her home in Bavaria. It was best that the State of Ohio bury her, they said.

Father Sullivan, deeply moved by the events of the previous twenty-four hours, conducted a brief, private service at the funeral home. Hoodin, Brant, and Kahn were there, along with Mrs. Woodard and matrons O'Bleness, Tipple, and Lyle. Bolsinger remained in Cincinnati with Oscar, as did Philip.

Anna Marie is buried at the Catholic Mt. Calvary Cemetery, within a stone's throw of downtown Columbus. In accordance with Canon Law of 1917, she was laid to rest in unconsecrated ground because she had shed blood. In 1983, however, all the ground in the cemetery was blessed. A very simple, weathered headstone, made by inmates at the penitentiary, marks the grave today at Cathedral Single C, Row 9, Grave 8, but her name is no longer discernible on it.

After months of spirited public discussion during Anna Marie's trial and incarceration, the execution was almost anticlimactic, although a woman in Cleveland sitting on a jury in a first-degree murder case was so overcome with emotion by reports of Anna Marie's death, that she was excused from the panel. A few politicos felt the legislature should abolish capital punishment. "A monstrosity of revenge," said one; but another correctly predicted that any bill to do so "will be laughed at and will not have a chance."

For years after, Father Sullivan wept before family and friends when he spoke of Anna Marie.

"Anna Hahn wasn't all bad," Mrs. O'Bleness commented the following day. "She had many good qualities that have been forgotten in the light of her crimes. She was kind, of a sweet disposition, charitable, gentle, and immaculately clean about her person—until that last day when she became a lost soul, unkempt and untidy. . . . But, in spite of her remarkable disposition, there was that indomitable wild streak in her that led to her downfall."[2]

2. Ibid.

20 | THE CONFESSION

Rumors that Anna Marie had written a confession sprang up even before the switch was thrown on "Old Sparky," shocking the life out of her.

Hoodin knew that his client had been writing something. Several times on visits to her cell in her final days, she said she would have something for him. He suspected it was a confession, but he wasn't sure. On his last visit, shortly before she walked to the death chamber, Anna Marie told him to gather up four envelopes, containing "certain papers." He started to ask her what was inside, but she was so overcome with emotion that she was virtually incoherent.

"Can't you do something? Can't you do something?" she asked over and over again between sobs and wails.

"It was the most pitiful thing I ever saw in my life," Hoodin said.

Two days later, the attorney told Cincinnati journalists that if the envelopes contained a confession, "maybe the public and the newspapers will never get it." In any event, he wasn't going to open anything, he said, until he had had a chance to rest from the ordeal of the trial. Hoodin put the envelopes in his safe at home.

Bolsinger heightened the interest in a possible confession when he announced that Anna Marie had left no will, "because she had nothing to will."

Mrs. Lyle, who walked Anna Marie to her death, advised Hoodin to tear out the lining of Anna Marie's fur coat, which Oscar had carried out of the penitentiary after his last visit with his mother. Anna Marie had suggested to her that she had sewn something of value inside the lining, but Hoodin's search revealed nothing.

A week passed since the execution, and there was still no word as to what the envelopes contained, although the attorneys had opened them on Monday, December 12. What Hoodin and Bolsinger were waiting for was word that there was a buyer for Anna Marie's confession, if, in fact, that is what she wrote. They hired New York attorney Emmanuel Rosenberg to shop the "confession" around to large newspaper syndicates with the proceeds to go to Oscar for his upbringing and education. Weeks before the execution, offers of several thousand dollars had been made for her story but no deal was struck at that time.

The amount of money Rosenberg sought was widely believed to be $75,000 ($1.4 million in 2005), a huge sum at the time. So huge, in fact, that none of the syndicates purchased the rights. A motion picture company stepped forward, bought the papers for an unannounced sum, and peddled the rights to several newspapers individually, such as the *Cincinnati Enquirer* and the *Ohio State Journal* in Columbus. Anna Marie's twenty-page, handwritten confession began in the newspapers dated December 19, 1938.

Even in her waning hours on earth, Anna Marie was unable to write the whole truth, once again taking liberties with the facts and often denying her guilt. "It was another mind that made me do these things," she wrote. "I didn't do them."

[The following confession, which Anna Marie left behind, contains a number of eccentricities in grammar, punctuation, and spelling.]

I don't know how I could have done the things I did in my life.

Only God knows what came over me when I gave Albert Palmer that first one, that poison that caused his death.

Up in heaven there is a God who will judge me. He will know and He will tell me how it came about? He will tell me what caused me to do the same things to Mr. Wagner, Gsellman and the last one, Mr. Obendoerfer. I never knew myself afterwards, and I don't know now.

When those poor men got sick I tried to do everything for them. I sat at their bedside nursing them. When I stood by Mr. Wagner as he was laid out in the funeral home, I didn't know how it was that I didn't scream out at the top of my voice.

I couldn't in my mind believe that it was me, Anna Marie Hahn, who loved people so well and wanted friends all the time, that could have put Mr. Wagner there. I can't believe it even today. I couldn't believe it when, in court there, people came to the room and told the jury how they said these men died. I was sitting there hearing a story like out of a book all about another person.

As things came to my mind now and as I put them on this paper I can't believe I am writing about the things I did myself. But they must be about me, because they are in my mind, and I know them. God above will tell me what made me do these terrible things. I couldn't have been in my right mind when I did them. I loved all people so much.

Now I am so close to death; death is all around me. I have been here for what seems another lifetime already, several other people in this place have been called out. I have been here at Columbus since before Christmas. It has been a long time. It has been just like another lifetime. I have had so much time to think. I have lived and died with each one of the others who have been taken out of their cells here to meet their death.

The days have been long and the nights have been longer. I have tried to forget sometimes about myself, but I can't. I have stretched out on the bed in my cell with my eyes wide open, trying to dream of the kind of life I would live if I had it all to do over again instead of being here and facing death.

I read my Bible for some understanding of my case. My mind goes back over my early times when I was a small girl at home with my family. I get some magazines and listen to the radio. The stories that I read and the plays on the radio are just like my case. They are all make-believe. I can't believe that I am here instead of outside with my boy and being a mother to him, watching over him, seeing that he will grow up right to be a great man.

For a little time these stories and the radio take me away from everything. But always my case comes back to me. No matter how hard I try to forget, I am always reminded of death.

Those poor men in the other part of this house. They cry out in the night times mostly. Some of them cry out to God for forgiveness. Sometimes they say that if they only had it to do all over again. Those men and boys know I am here, and they send candy and say hello to me. But we people here are always thinking about death. We can't get away from ourselves and what is in store for us in a little while.

When I raise my head to look through the bars to the sunshine and the sky outside I am reminded of death. There on the wire screen of my cell hangs a little sign. It is my name, Anna Marie Hahn, and my prison number. I try to look around it to the blue sky and sunshine, but I can't. It makes a blot on the outside. It is just like a tombstone marker. It always brings me back to why I am here.

Those poor men, I wanted to help them so much, but I did something to them. I don't know why I did it, but maybe sometimes God will tell me about myself.

I always think of my boy. I got his picture here all the time with me, and I dream dreams for him being a great man. I want to be such a good mother to him. Then I think of my own mother and my family in Germany. My own birthday is not so long ago; the first one I ever spent in a prison. Never when I was a little girl did I ever think that someday I would be in prison.

I was born in Fussen, Germany, on June 7, 1906. My parents were well-to-do, good German people that were always thinking about their children and that they should be raised right and get the best that they could given them.

I received my schooling in Fussen and partly in Holland. My parents send me to boarding school so I should learn to grow up to some day be a good wife to a good man and mother to some fine children. I led my girlhood life the same like any other normal girl whose family wanted the best for them. But for 15 years up to before all this happened to me, I never enjoyed good health. I sometimes think that it is because of the terrible accidents that happened to me. I am sure they are some of the cause why my mind changed so that I did those terrible things that they say I did.

I was badly injured in a bicycle accident. Twice I was knocked unconscious by skiing and ice skating. That must have done something to my head that I didn't know of and can't explain now, except that because of my poor health from those accidents I did them. Another time, when I was a young girl, I got blood poison and was in the hospital for five months. They thought I was going to die several times. Maybe it would have been better if I had died. Then I wouldn't have know all the troubles that I got now. I also had a goitre operation. All of these things must have changed my mind so that I could do the things that happened.

I was 17 years old when I met Dr. Max Matchek in Munich. Those were some of the happiest days of my life. He was such a grand fellow, and we were attracted to one another right away. We fell in love. It was the kind of love that every young girl thinks about, this love at first sight. I went out with him many times, to dances and other places where young people enjoy themselves. He could dance so well, and he held me so tight and whispered love to me when we were dancing. I was happy then.

He said we would get married some day and could be so happy. I believed him, just like any other girl believes in a fellow she has learned to love. He was always talking about getting married soon and that he loved me so much. I loved him. So I gave in to him. We kept meeting each other often, and he was so sweet to me and held me so tight. I believed what he said.

Then one day I had to tell him that I was going to have a baby, and that we would have to get married right away.

When I told him that, right away there was a big change in him. I couldn't understand it at first. I told him that it was our love baby, and that when we got married everything would be alright and our baby would be our love baby. Then he told me that he couldn't marry me, that he already had a wife in Vienna.

Something happened to me right then. It was just like a mountain falling on me, not killing me but just smothering me and crushing me. I remembered how I cried then. I don't remember what I said. It was just such a terrific moment. No one except a person who has had this thing happen to them will ever know what a thing like that does to a young girl. I had been so full of love for Max, and he had said he loved me so much and said that we would be married and live happy. Now that couldn't be. The man to whom I had given myself in such a full love belonged to another.

Then Max suggested that I should get rid of the unborn baby. Max, he told me that. He wanted me to destroy the thing that I believe that God through love had given me. The baby that was to be mine with my first true love. He wanted me to get rid of the unborn baby and told me how I could do it. That was a terrible day in my life.

No matter whatever will happen to me now, there will never be another time like that. I thank God that I did not listen to him. I thank God that I let my baby live. No matter what mean things people, who did not know all about my case and how everything happened to me, say about Anna Marie Hahn, they can never say I killed my baby.

Thank God that in a foolish moment like when I gave in to Max that I didn't kill my unborn baby. The little pleasure that I have gotten out of life has been from my boy. He is such a fine boy. Everybody that knows him says he is so bright and such a little gentleman. He learns so good in school. Some day, I hope he will be a great man, and many nights now since I got into this trouble I pray to God, who knows all, that people will not hold against him the things that his mother did.

Since I have been in this trouble he has been allowed to see me. And while he is with me life becomes so bright. I know that Oscar loves his mother, that he always will, and that nothing ever will change his love. When he is taken away from me, my life becomes so black again and these bars seem to crush me, and I begin thinking again. If I could only have been myself and not another person when I did these things in those moments when I was not myself.

When I was 22 years of age I left Germany. I could no longer stand those things that people were saying about my misfortune. My boy was almost 5 years old, and I was afraid that he would understand the things people were saying about me and my boy. I came to the United States to my Uncle Max Deaschel to see if I could make a home for my son where no one would ever know anything about his being born out of wedlock. I came to Cincinnati.

But I did not want my uncle to support me, so I obtained work at the Alms Hotel. I wanted to make my own living and enough to support my boy so that I could give him the mother's care that every boy should have. I wanted to get him away from those people back home who whispered things about my misfortune. These things were hurting my mother, who was caring for my boy. I wanted to shield my mother and my son.

I met my husband, Philip Hahn, at a German dance. He was nice to me and said he loved me and wanted to marry me. I was afraid at first when he talked about marriage. Then I told him that the only way I would marry him would be that if I could bring my boy to me from Germany. He said that it would be alright and that he understood. I could bring my boy to me and that he could have someone to call father.

So I married my present husband. Then I returned to Germany for my boy and brought him back to America with me.

I was happy and proud that my boy had someone to call father. We lived in College Hill. We started in business, for I had plans for my boy. I wanted to make enough money to send him to all the schools to give him the best education. But business was bad, it was the bad times. And we lost our business. Then we went to live with Mr. Kohler at 2970 Colerain Avenue. He was a friend of my father's in his early boyhood. He was sick with a cancer, and I nursed him like I would my own father.

He had this cancer, and it was this that caused his death. I swear on everything I hold dear that I had nothing to do with his death. He told me many times that because I was kind and good to him that he would not forget me in his will. When he died he left me his house of his own free will and because I had treated him like a daughter.

I went in business again, always thinking about my boy that I would have money to raise him up properly. But business was bad again, and this time before I lost everything in business I sold it to pay my debts. In a little while, though, this money went. My husband had been out of work, and I started worrying about my boy's future. I became crazy with fear that my boy and I would starve. I signed some notes for my husband. Because I had signed these notes, they threatened to take my Colerain Avenue house away from me, to sell the house over my head and throw me and my boy out into the street.

Then it was I started gambling and playing the race horses. I went to a place out in Elmwood where you could play the races just like at the race track. I wanted to make some money for my boy.

It was there that I met Mr. Palmer. We became friends because we went home the same way each day. There were many days when he would stop at the house on his way out to Elmwood and take me with him. Because he seemed to be a friend, I told him I was going out there, playing the races, to get money to protect my boy. He offered me assistance. He told me that I would have to come to his house to get the money. I was crazy with fear and needed this money, so I went. He made me loans, and I paid much of it back. Then when I didn't pay it back fast enough to suit him, then it was that he wanted me to be his girl.

All my early troubles of my girlhood in giving in to a man came back to me. It did something to me. It turned my head. He threatened me that if I didn't do what he asked he would see his attorney to get the rest of the money that I loaned from him. I told him to please wait awhile and give me a chance.

But he wouldn't let me alone. He came to my house and threatened me again. He had brought some oysters and wanted me to go home with him. God knows that I did not want to kill him, and I don't know what put such a thought in my head. I can't remember how it was. I only know that suddenly I remembered that down in the cellar was some rat poison. I had seen it one day when I was in the cellar. I don't know how it got there. Something in my mind kept saying to me, give him a little bit of this and he won't trouble you anymore.

It was then that he again insisted that I be his girl friend or he would have to have his money at once. I told him that I couldn't pay him right away. Again he threatened me, and I don't know what made me do it. But I slipped some of the poison in the oysters. I told him to go on home, and he left, at the same time threatening what he was going to do to me.

I didn't see him again for some time, two weeks, I think it was.

All the time I was worrying. Nobody will know my troubles. I prayed that everything would be alright.

As the time went on, and I did not hear from him, I began hoping that the thing I did was only a bad dream and that he was not going to sue me and make trouble for me. Then it was that his sister called me up and told me they had taken her brother, Mr. Palmer, to the hospital.

I visited him just as soon as I could, and he was very nice to me. He told me he was sorry the way he had treated me. He told me he would not make trouble for me.

I prayed that he would get well. Nobody knows the things that went through my mind. I told the nurses and doctors to do everything they could to make him well, but on Holy Thursday Mr. Palmer died.

Only I knew why, but I couldn't understand what made me do such a thing.

Mr. Palmer was laid out on Easter Sunday. For weeks after he was buried I felt that I would lose my mind because way down in my heart I really did not want this awful thing to happen to him.

I know now that when I put that poison in the oysters I wasn't in my normal mind; no one could do a thing like that. I never had felt unkind to anyone and always tried to help those that were in trouble. Always I kept thinking about what I had done and why I did it.

It must have been fear for my family's future to just make me do it. Only God knows why I should have done and why I did this thing and some day He will explain what was in my mind that made me sin so.

I don't know how I kept going with this thing on my mind. But I always brought myself around by saying that I had my boy to live for and bring up. I said that nobody should ever know what I had done and that I would live it down by doing the right thing to everybody.

I had met George Heis while I was still in business, just before Mr. Palmer died. I had borrowed some money from him to pay Mr. Palmer.

Mr. Heis held some of my notes for the money I had borrowed, but I didn't poison him. Mr. Heis is alive and well today and that is proof that I didn't poison him. God knows that I didn't.

I was getting along nicely, and that terrible experience with Mr. Palmer was going out of my mind, like a dream.

Jacob Wagner I knew for years. He was closely associated with my uncle, Charles Osswald. One day my uncle told me that Mr. Wagner was a distant relative of mine. I had a lot of relatives in America and hadn't paid any attention.

When Mr. Wagner came to my house in 1936 I remembered that my uncle had said he was a relative of mine, and we started talking about this. According to his statements I knew then that he was a relative, although I could not remember my mother talking about him.

Mr. Wagner liked to talk about our relatives, and he would work in my flower garden in the back of my house. He planted flowers in the springtime and took care of them in the summer. Then I guess he must have become tired of coming over to our house, and there was a long time that I didn't see him when one day I received a letter from a man in Germany who signed his name, Cousin George. He stated in a letter than Mr. Wagner had told him about me how I was his relative and was so kind to him.

The man who he said was Cousin George said that for sometime Mr. Wagner had not written to him and wouldn't I please try to find Mr. Wagner and tell him to write. I had not seen Mr. Wagner for a long time, but I knew he lived someplace on Race Street near the market. I had never been to his house, but I remembered about the market being near his home.

I went to see him about him and inquired in the house at 1805 Race St. After a lot of trouble I found his apartment. I knocked on his door and no one answered. A Mrs. Colby, I think it was, came out and told me that Mr. Wagner was not at home. I left a note for him, saying that I had a letter for him from Germany.

Mr. Wagner came to see me and then came back again quite often like he did before. He always could come into my house when he wanted to. It was around this time that I found some old bankbooks in which some one had scribbled some figures to make it look like there was a lot of money in the bank.

He must have taken them for one day when I went to visit him he was not at home, and I stopped at a beer parlor on Elder Street.

He was telling some men there that I had taken his bankbook from his room. I never knew until then that Mr. Wagner had any money. I never cared about that. He was an old man, maybe a distant relative, and liked to talk with me.

He got angry, saying that I took his bankbook, and he went to the Fifth Third Bank[1] and showed a Mr. Schmidt[2] my old books with the scribbled in deposits. Mr. Schmidt told Mr. Wagner right away they were not good and that the amounts of money in them was forged.

1. Fifth Third Union Trust Company.
2. Arthur J. Schmitt, assistant vice president at Fifth Third Union Trust Company.

He told Mr. Wagner to bring the books back June 1, because the Monday was a holiday and that he would turn the books over to the police and maybe prosecute me. Mr. Wagner told me all about this, and I invited him to come to my house on Sunday, and I would give him a good dinner. I thought I could talk to him about taking those old books to Mr. Schmidt and starting some trouble for me.

Mr. Wagner did not come to my house that Sunday, and I started to get crazy with fear. All the thoughts about Mr. Palmer, what I had done when not in my normal mind, came back to me. I got scared that if the police would start questioning me maybe all this about Mr. Palmer would come out. I didn't want Mr. Wagner to start anything.

I went to see him Monday, the thirty-first, which was celebrated as Decoration day. I wanted to see him before he took those books to Mr. Schmidt at the bank June 1.

My thought just drove me out of my normal mind. Several times at my home I would catch myself doing little foolish things, my mind was so disturbed.

I don't know what put the things in my mind, but all of a sudden I found some poison in my hands. I put it in my pocketbook. Something told me not to let Mr. Wagner go to that bank and start to prosecute me. All I wanted was those bankbooks so Mr. Wagner wouldn't cause me any trouble.

I got to his house in the afternoon, I believe it was. Mr. Wagner was lying in bed. He told me that he was not feeling well. But he told me that he was going to take those books to Mr. Schmidt the next day. Then something cried out in me to stop him so that all my troubles wouldn't start again.

I don't know who guided my hand but I fixed him some orange juice and placed a half of a teaspoon of the powder poison, which I took from my purse, in the glass. Mr. Wagner drank it down. I stayed with Mr. Wagner until evening, and he did not seem to be any worse. When I went home, I couldn't sleep that night, thinking about Mr. Wagner.

Early the next day, Thursday, I went back to his room, and Mr. Wagner was very sick. I knew what I had done to him. Mr. Wagner promised to return the books to me, and then I called two doctors to try to save the life I had tried to take. Mr. Wagner got suddenly worse and on the advice of the doctor I sent him to the Good Samaritan Hospital.

I went with Mr. Wagner to the hospital, and I ordered the best room and the best attention that he could have so that he could get well. I didn't want to happen to Mr. Wagner what had happened to Mr. Palmer. I knew I couldn't stand a thing like that again and stay in my right mind. It was another mind that made me do these things. I didn't do them.

I told Mr. Wagner that I was doing everything that I could to make him well, getting him the best of everything at the hospital. He signed a $1000 check in pencil to pay expenses. I then signed his name to this check because the bank would not accept a check written in pencil.

I cannot describe how I felt when Mr. Wagner died and this had something to do with his death.

I do not show my feelings, my troubles in life starting when I had my baby had taught me to control my feelings, but when I went to Busse & Borgemann's, where Mr. Wagner was laid out, it was all I could do to keep from screaming. I felt as though I was bursting, knowing that I was responsible for this terrible thing and that everyone was looking at me and pointing their fingers at me.

Here was another one I had brought death to. I don't know what made me do it, all I can say is that my troubles were so big that it must have turned my mind.

I did not harm Mr. Wagner for his money. I never had such a thought. It was not until Mr. Wagner had died that I wrote the will. I placed it in his room in the afternoon that the man from the probate came to Mr. Wagner's room. The poison that they exhibited in the courtroom at my trial, I know nothing about at all. I never saw it before. The poison that I used is, for all that I know, still in my house. I found it first in the paint cupboard in the basement.

If I had never found that poison in the first place, I know that I would not be in all this trouble right now. If I had never found that poison at all, that something that turned my mind, I am sure, would not have happened. Finding this poison, I guess, made me do those things to

Mr. Palmer and Wagner. It changed my whole mind, it made it turn over and I never will know what made me give it to those men.

When I think of that poison even now, I feel a strange something come over me, something happens to my mind. I cannot say anything about those two other cases that came after: Mr. Gseallmann and that last one, Mr. Obendoerfer, except that they died of the same symptoms, and as I face my maker I only take full responsibility for what happened to them.

I do not try to excuse myself for my actions. They were not me at all.

I have made my peace with God, and someday He will explain to me what caused my mind to become so warped to do these things. It all seems like a terrible dream.

Life is moving so swiftly for me now. It is just like yesterday that I had my trial before that jury of all those women. I never thought that there was any women would do to another what those did to me on that jury. After all those lies about me laying down to those men. Those were lies.

There were times in that courtroom, the times that the newspapers wrote that I seemed worried that I was just about ready to cry out. I couldn't hardly keep my secret in me. It seemed that I would have to cry out, I wanted to cry out that they were trying another Anna Hahn and not this one sitting in the courtroom. But somehow I kept the secret.

Maybe it would have been different if I had only told my lawyers the truth. My lawyers fought so hard for me. But that it all over now, over the radio has come the news that the courts say I must die. I do not fear my end and my last concern is only for my boy. I hope that God will take care of him for I would not want anything to happen to him. I tried so hard to keep him from any harm, my boy who has given me the only pleasure in my life. I feel that God has shown me my wrongs in life and my only regret is that I have not the power to undo the trouble and heartaches that I have caused.

I have written this confession with the full knowledge that death is near, and I only ask one favor and that is that my son should not be judged for the wrongs his mother may have done.

[signed] Anna Marie Hahn.

EPILOGUE
"THE MOST HORRIBLE MOMENT"

Twenty years after Anna Marie's execution, Cincinnati's common pleas judge Charles S. Bell still had vivid memories of her trial and the mandatory death sentence he invoked. Here are his recollections, as told to Howard M. Greenwald of the Cincinnati Enquirer, *in 1959. Judge Bell died May 6, 1965, at the age of eighty-four.*

Many thousands of words have been written about the Anna Marie Hahn case of 1937, both before and after the verdict which made her the first woman in Ohio to die in the electric chair.

My role as presiding judge was not a pleasant one. Sentencing her to death, in fact, was the most horrible moment of my long judicial career. Even now, whenever I sentence anybody for anything, I think of that case. It remains far too vivid in my memory.

Mrs. Hahn, a woman in her thirties and mother of an eleven-year-old boy, was being tried for killing an elderly man by arsenic poisoning, presumably for his money. It was an exhausting experience. A jury of eleven women and one man listened attentively and patiently for about a month, sifting the evidence presented by the defense and ninety-six state witnesses in almost half-a-million words of testimony.

When the case finally went to the jury, few people in the courtroom had any doubt of Mrs. Hahn's tragic guilt. Evidence admissible under the statutes indicated that she had killed three more men and crippled another, all with arsenic.

Yet in spite of her obvious guilt, no one expected she would get the chair. Never before in the history of Hamilton County had a woman been convicted of first degree murder without a recommendation for mercy. It was everyone's belief that the jury—especially with eleven women on it—would never demand the death penalty.

I, too, doubted that Mrs. Hahn would be sent to the chair. So many little things can cause a jury to recommend mercy—a man's tie, a woman's hairdo, a manner of speech. It is no easy or everyday occurrence for twelve people to agree on a death penalty.

The jury filed back into the courtroom after three hours of deliberation. I believe I knew their decision even while it was being read to me. Tears streaked the cheeks of some of the women of the jury as the clerk read the verdict—first degree murder with no recommendation for mercy. More of the jury began to cry. Their action—in every respect a just verdict—was nevertheless a great shock to the court, the spectators, and to attorneys on both sides.

I set sentencing for three weeks later—weeks perhaps more terrible for me than for Mrs. Hahn, because throughout the entire trial and up until the very end she never believed she would pay the full penalty.

Always before when I had done my best in a trial, I had not been bothered by subsequent thoughts of it. But this one caused me great concern and no little loss of sleep. I had absolutely no choice—I had to sentence her to the chair.

It was the hardest job I ever had to do. Even on the day of the sentencing, Mrs. Hahn stood before me and maintained her innocence. I said what I had to say and not a word more. My throat was choking. When I pronounced sentence and asked that "God have mercy on your soul," I climbed off the bench and locked myself in my chambers. Then I cried like a two-year-old child.

There were many appeals to the case—to the Ohio Supreme Court, twice to the United States Supreme Court, and to Gov. Davey for clemency. But the trial was too sound, the evidence too conclusive, the verdict too right. Two days before the execution, Mrs. Hahn made a full and complete confession of her guilt.

On December 7, 1938, Anna Marie Hahn was electrocuted. It was the end of a chapter I wish to forget, but shall always remember.

AFTERWORD

> *"The female of the species is more dangerous
> than the male."*
>
> RUDYARD KIPLING
> *The Female of the Species*

A t the time of Anna Marie Hahn's arrest on August 10, 1937, Cleveland had its own serial killer on its hands. Nine victims, or parts of victims, had been discovered by then, and the local newspapers dutifully recorded each grisly detail as it surfaced. Although there were known to be at least a dozen "torso murders" in Cleveland between 1934 and 1938, the case remains unsolved.[1]

The Hahn case attracted wider attention for several reasons. There was an arrest and trial. The killer was a vivacious woman and a German immigrant at that. Fresh in the minds of many at the time was the name of another German immigrant, Bruno Richard Hauptmann, executed in 1936 for the 1932 kidnapping and death of the infant son of Charles Lindbergh. The Hauptmann case was front-page news around the world.

Save for perfunctory obituary notices, at the time no notice was taken of the deaths Anna Marie wrought, despite the close-knit Over-the-Rhine community around which all of her victims lived. She went undetected in death after death, and with each life snuffed out avoided the notice of authorities. Jacob Wagner's death was under investigation at the time of her arrest, but had it not been for the theft of the

---

1. For an excellent account of Cleveland's torso murders, see *In the Wake of the Butcher*, by James Jessen Badal (Kent, Ohio: Kent State Univ. Press, 2001).

diamond rings in Colorado Springs, police might never have been able to charge her in any deaths whatsoever. But when all the pieces of the puzzle were spread out on the table, the case lit up the interest of newspapers throughout the land.

The speed with which the Hahn case moved along kept it front-page news. There were very few gaps in the story between the time of her arrest in August and her conviction on November 6, 1937. Thirteen months later, on December 7, 1938, she was executed. Sixteen months from arrest to death by electrocution. Four hundred and eighty-five days.

"There is no one definition for a female serial killer," according to Robert K. Ressler, a criminologist and former FBI profiler who is widely credited with assigning the term "serial killer" to those who commit at least three murders at different locations, each one followed by a "cooling off" period. Dr. Katherine Ramsland, author of *The Human Predator* (New York: Berkley Books, 2005), defines serial killings as two or more in "distinctly separate incidents, with a psychological rest period between." Others see serial killings as periodic multiple murders of virtual strangers to the killer.

A few identify Mary Creighton, who went to the chair in 1936 for the murder of her lover's wife, as a serial killer, but most, including Ressler, do not. She was acquitted thirteen years earlier of two other murders.

It is remarkable how closely Anna Marie fits the profile of a female serial killer as defined in contemporary literature. For example, Dr. Deborah Schurman-Kauflin, author of *The New Predator: Women Who Kill*, notes, "Female serial killers murder their victims in plain view, for the entire world to see. But typically, no one believes that a woman could kill multiple victims, so the deaths are categorized as undetermined or unsolved. This is exactly why female multiple murderers can be considered more dangerous than male offenders: females can kill without anyone knowing what they are doing, and without anyone stopping them."[2]

Of Schurman-Kauflin's list of characteristics that make up the profile

2. Dr. Deborah Schurman-Kauflin, *The New Predator: Women Who Kill* (New York: Algora Publishing Company, 2000), 13.

of women who kill, regardless of whether serial killings are a factor, Anna Marie matched all seven attributes:

Married or divorced
Woman less than thirty years of age (or early thirties)
Unemployed
A mother
High school dropout
Economically unstable
Unable to cope with stress.[3]

Schurman-Kauflin's profile of female serial killers specifically also fits Anna Marie like a tailored suit:

Exhibit social competence
Worked at care-giving jobs
Planned the offenses
Controlled their mood during the crimes
Experienced a precipitating stress prior to the crimes
Showed interest in the news media after the crimes
Essentially hid the bodies.[4]

In Anna Marie's case, the bodies were hidden by cremation or burial. Anna Marie also was aware of the procedures of an autopsy and familiar with her weapons, namely arsenic and croton oil. It is unlikely that she "showed an interest in the news media," because, until she was arrested August 10, 1937, there were no reports of her crimes. Afterward, however, she both read newspapers and listened to the radio for news of what she had wrought. For a time, though, when prison officials thought she might be suicidal, they clipped out of the newspapers stories about her and denied her radio news broadcasts.

Schurman-Kauflin, who studied numerous female killers—but not Anna Marie—also found that such women befriend their victims and weigh "each person's weaknesses and how those weaknesses can be exploited. Once a victim trusts her, the female serial killer ensures that

3. Ibid., 151.
4. Ibid., 162.

the victim is vulnerable, and then she kills. She ensures that no one else is present and takes great pains to make sure that the body looks untouched."[5] Again, this was Anna Marie.

Michael D. Kelleher and C. L. Kelleher, the coauthors of *Murder Most Rare: The Female Serial Killer,* arrived at much the same conclusions. They noted the financial gain, which was what interested Anna Marie:

> The Profit or Crime (serial) killer is in the business of murder for an ancient and straightforward reason—to enhance her income. She is also organized, mature, meticulous, and manipulative. Although her numbers are not great among the ranks of female serial murderers, the Profit or Crime killer is a fearsome predator because of her intense motivation and highly dispassionate approach to murder. . . .
> It is difficult to imagine a more callous murderer than the lethal caretaker who claims her victims in the name of profit. This serial killer deliberately seeks out individuals who are often completely dependent on her for care and support. In her morbid obsession with profit, she will carefully plan her crimes and dispassionately slay individuals who have come to trust her completely.[6]

Anna Marie was the eleventh woman in the United States to die in the electric chair. The first was Martha M. Place, who killed her step-daughter in Brooklyn, New York. She was executed March 20, 1899, in Sing Sing Prison, Ossining, New York.

After Anna Marie, four years passed before the electrocution of another woman in the United States.

The State of Ohio abandoned death by electrocution in 2002. The last of 315 persons to die in Ohio's electric chair was Donald L. Reinbolt, who was executed March 15, 1963.

Philip J. Hahn retired from Western Union in 1969 and died September 23, 1989, in a quiet suburb of Cincinnati at the age of eighty-six. He never spoke publicly about Anna Marie after her death.

Oscar Hahn dropped out of sight immediately after the death of his mother. Although the Filser family in Bavaria suggested that he

5. Ibid., 163, 164.
6. Michael D. Kelleher and C. L. Kelleher, *Murder Most Rare: The Female Serial Killer* (Westport, Conn.: Praeger Publishers, 1998), 96–97.

return there, he reportedly was sent to live with a foster family in the Midwest and under an assumed name. Some believed he had been sent to the famous Boys Town in Iowa, but the school has no record of any thirteen-year-old, German-born boy from Cincinnati being admitted at the time. At the end of World War II, Oscar allegedly joined the U.S. Navy and was killed during the Korean War.

Judge Charles Steele Bell, who was elected to the Ohio Supreme Court in 1942, died at Good Samaritan Hospital on May 6, 1965. He was eighty-four.

Dudley Miller Outcalt became a Hamilton County Common Pleas judge shortly after the Hahn trial, but he left the bench in 1942 to serve as a colonel in the U.S. Army Air Force. On May 26, 1945, he was a passenger on a B-25 flight from Biloxi, Mississippi, to Washington, D.C., when the bomber crashed near the capital, killing all on board. He had celebrated his forty-eighth birthday on May 8.

Hiram Bolsinger Sr. died of a cerebral hemorrhage in front of the Norwood Baptist Church, Cincinnati, October 17, 1946. He was sixty-seven.

Joseph H. Hoodin, whose practice turned to corporate tax law, succumbed to a heart attack at his Cincinnati home on October 2, 1959. He was fifty-two.

George E. Heis, the "living victim," lived until he was seventy-eight. He died in bed at his home on August 12, 1953.

Detective Captain Patrick H. Hayes retired from the Cincinnati Police Department on March 1, 1953, after forty-five years on the force. He died of natural causes March 8, 1969, at the Cincinnati home of a daughter. He was eighty-four.

December 8, 1938: The court dismissed the grand-jury indictment that charged Anna Marie with the murder of Gsellman.

November 1, 1974: Judge Rupert Dean, presiding administrative judge, Hamilton County Municipal Court, dismissed the fugitive from justice and grand larceny charges filed against Anna Marie on behalf of the Colorado Springs police. The charges, the first against her, had been on the court's docket since August 14, 1937. It was the final legal action in the Hahn case.

APPENDIX:
BY ANNA MARIE'S HAND

The Victims	Relationship	Means/Date of Death	
*George G. Gsellman	friend	poisoned	July 6, 1937
Olive Louella Koehler	friend	poison suspected	August 16, 1937
Ernst Kohler	friend	poison suspected	May 6, 1933
Julia Kresckay	friend	poisoned	unknown
*Johan Georg Obendoerfer	friend	poisoned	August 1, 1937
Charles "Karl" Osswald	distant relative	poison suspected	August 14, 1935
*Albert J. Palmer	friend	poisoned	March 26, 1937
†Jacob Wagner	friend	poisoned	June 3, 1937
The Survivors			
Mary Arnold	friend	believed poisoned	
Stina Cable	stranger	believed poisoned	
Philip J. Hahn	husband	believed poisoned	
Margaret (Maggie) Hahn	mother-in-law	believed poisoned	
George E. Heis	friend	believed poisoned	

* Confessed to murder
† Confessed to and convicted of murder

BIBLIOGRAPHY

he arrest, trial, and execution of Anna Marie Hahn captured the fancy of the nation's press. For seventeen months, between August 1937 and December 1938, her story demanded front-page attention. In its day, it was *the* crime story that everyone wanted to read. Big-city newspapers dispatched their top reporters to the scene, and during the trial the "sob sisters"—female and male reporters who milked the story for every emotion—had a field day.

Following are the names of the reporters and the publications whose work was most rewarding in the research for this book.

NEWSPAPERS

Chicago Daily News. Robert J. Casey.
Chicago Daily Times. Karen Walsh and Rocco Padullo.
Chicago Herald and Examiner / Chicago Evening. Evelyn Oberman.
Chicago Sunday Tribune. Thornton Smith.
Chicago Tribune. Virginia Gardner.
Cincinnati Enquirer. Lee Allen, Joseph Garretson Jr., Herbert R. Mengert, Tom Mercer, and William W. Morris.
Cincinnati Post. Rollin Everett, Norine Freeman, Edward Halloran, Pat Kirwin, George Lecky, Walter Radtke, Charles Rentrop, Alfred Segal, Eugene Segal, Robert L. Stevens, and Walter Taylor.

Cincinnati Times-Star. George Elliston, Anthony P. Flamm, Charles Ludwig, Paul Mason, and Frank Rolandelli.

Clarksburg (West Virginia) *Telegram / Central Press.* Ellis Rawnsley.

Cleveland Plain Dealer. Ralph J. Donaldson, Regine Kurlander, and William F. McDermott.

Cleveland Press.

Colorado Springs Gazette.

Colorado Springs Gazette-Telegraph.

Columbus Citizen. Edward Bliss Jr., James T. Keenan, Mark Murphy, Charlotte Sherwood, and Arthur Robinson.

Columbus Dispatch. Lester C. Ealy, Dorothy Todd Foster, George Klenzle, and Kay Murphy.

New York Daily News. Mara Bovsun.

New York Herald Tribune. Geoffrey Parsons Jr.

New York Journal-American. James L. Kilgallen.

New York News. George Dixon.

New York Times.

New York World-Telegram.

Ohio State Journal (Columbus). Harold W. Carlisle, Sarah L. Dush, and Ben Hayes.

NEWS SERVICES

Associated Press. Wayne Adams, E. E. Easterly, Frank Avrin, and William T. Lewis.

International News Service. Gerald B. Healey.

Scripps-Howard Newspapers.

United Press. Ralph C. Teatsorth and Sam Brightman.

PERIODICALS

The American Weekly. Mignon G. Eberhart.

Cincinnati Magazine. Evelyn [Oberman] Lauder.

Columbus Dispatch Magazine. Phil E. Porter.

Official Detective Stories. J. Porter Henry Jr.

Time magazine.

BOOKS

Badal, James Jessen. *In the Wake of the Butcher.* Kent, Ohio: Kent State University Press, 2001.

Fogle, H. M. *The Palace of Death; or, The Ohio Penitentiary Annex.* Columbus, Ohio: self-published, 1908.

Fornshell, Marvin E. *The Historical and Illustrated Ohio Penitentiary.* Columbus, Ohio: self-published, 1908.

Galbreath, Charles B. *The History of Ohio.* Chicago: American Historical Society, 1925.

Hickey, Eric W. *Serial Murderers, Their Victims.* Belmont, Calif.: Wadsworth, 1997.

Perry, Dick. *Vas You Ever in Zincinnati?* Garden City, N.Y.: Doubleday, 1966.

Phelps, M. William. *Perfect Poison.* New York: Kensington, 2003.

Schurman-Kauflin, Deborah. *The New Predator: Women Who Kill.* New York: Algora, 2000.

Writer's Program of the Work Projects Administration in the State of Ohio. *Cincinnati: A Guide to the Queen City and Its Neighbors.* Cincinnati: Wiesen-Hart Press, 1943.

✳ INDEX